ALSO BY CHARLIE DICKINSON
The Cat at Light's End (stories)
The Wire Donkey
The Thieves of Shiny Things

LOSING LAIKA
a Soviet historical novel

Charlie Dickinson

Ch. Dickinson | Portland, Oregon USA | 2022

Copyright 2021 by Charlie Dickinson under a Creative Commons Attribution Non-Commercial No Derivatives license.

Some rights reserved. This book may be reproduced in print and digital formats when the author is acknowledged, the text of the book is unchanged, and copies are not used commercially. The language of the applicable license deed is available in full at http://www.creativecommons.org.

This novel is a work of fiction. Names, characters, places, and incidents are either the product of the author's imagination, or, if real, used fictitiously.

Published in the United States by Ch. Dickinson, Portland, Oregon
(http://www.charliedickinson.net)

Library of Congress Control Number: 2021903409
Publisher's Cataloguing-in-Publication
Dickinson, Charlie, 1945-
Losing Laika / Charlie Dickinson. — 1st ed. — Portland, Or.:
Ch. Dickinson, 2021.
356 p. 22 x 14 cm.

ISBN: 978-1-7366893-3-2

Summary: Petro Kondratovych Kravets arrives at a downed American U-2 spy plane on May Day 1960 to retrieve its camera. An experienced optics technician, his work defends the Motherland. Readers follow this Soviet Everyman, his family, and others through the Cold War with its international space race, Cuban missile crisis, Afghan War, and more up to—and past—the collapse of the Soviet Union.

1. Communism—Cold War—Fiction
2. Powers, Francis Gary. 1929-1977—Fiction
3. Soviet Union--History—1960-2010—Fiction. 4. Historical fiction.

Manufactured in the United States of America.

FIRST EDITION

For Nancia

Losing Laika

1
АВИАТОР
(THE AVIATOR)

Thick, telltale smoke climbed on the back of the wind, and a manifold of cords stayed the flare of a white parachute wheeling, jittering on terra firma.

Snick. The belt buckle straps out of the way. *Snick.* The chest buckle too.

He slipped his right arm out of the harness.

The chute yanked him around, his left shoulder on tether, his eyes transfixed by the clear sky beyond the black smoke and the orange flames a hundred yards away.

He had got out, and they would find him, but what happened?

He pulled the harness away from his left arm, and his body was released and its own again, but he couldn't stand. Sure, the chute worked. No broken bones, but he was waiting for the jelly legs.

The parachute, once freed, shot off, only to hug a pine across the way, its nylon draped like some popped balloon.

He stared at the bunch grass about his flight boots.

He had to figure out what happened.

2 Charlie Dickinson

Lifted off at o-six-two-six hours, Peshawar Air Station, just down the road from the Khyber Pass. First he had to get over the Hindu Kush. Then worry about those targets written out on the clipboard. Ten-hour flight plan, expected touchdown: Bodø, Norway.

Kept the ship on autopilot, its single engine droning along, seventy-thou altitude, slipping over the mountains into the Tadzhik Soviet Socialist Republic. Nothing but clouds. Not the best conditions for taking pictures. Skipped Stalinabad, hidden under the cloud shelf.

Then two hours out of Peshawar, the clouds broke up. What he saw affirmed he was on flight plan. He was ready. He'd reached the target at Tyuratam: the famous Cosmodrome where they launched those pesky sputniks. Yep, with the one-o-four wingspan ship in steady flight—near zero pitch—he flipped switches on the instrument panel, camera door opening and *blif, blif, blif*—the motorized-drive camera fired away, more and more intelligence on that sizey roll of film reserved for his run across the Russkie Empire.

The aviator hugged his head, hands palming his white helmet.

Then it was on to the next target on the clipboard: Sverdlovsk.

Seventy-thousand feet, thirteen-plus miles up, he was as invulnerable, supposedly, as though he'd been on the far side of the moon. But he didn't buy that, not one-hundred percent. He guessed the Russkies upgraded their radar installations all the time, though the Agency assured him they knew the risks in pressing Islamabad to continue these overflights.

Sure, they had rockets to lift the first sputnik into orbit three years ago—or deliver an H-bomb across the ocean. But tracking and firing a missile to bring down a craft at seventy-thousand feet? That supposedly, according to the Agency, was like a bullet striking another bullet in mid-air and the Russkies could not do that.

So how did it happen?

What got him? A SAM fired from the ground? Or an air-to-air from one of their fighters that max'd at fifty-thou? He shook his head: The possibilities—and they were the only ones—seemed, at best, remote.

It was coming back to him. What it was before he bailed.

Four hours into the flight, he was ready to take pictures over Sverdlovsk, its sprawling industry, when *blooooom* behind the ship. The sky fiery orange. The mighty arm of Thor tipping the right wing of the ship into the dive of Death. Jerked the stick back to the left. But the ship pitched like a stone skipping across water. Rudder probably taken out, altimeter spinning backward.

Pulling the EJECT lever wasn't an option. He'd lost control and been violently pushed way under the front edge of the canopy. No, any EJECT would be both legs severed at the knees. Had to be manual bailout. Somehow he unlocked, flipped up the canopy; it caught air, snapped off and sailed away. Then he levered himself back, then up, and climbed out, and dangling there, caught by the oxygen hoses, he must've broke free. For to his piss-in-pants relief, the parachute worked and he was floating.

Call it fate, the fuselage stalled beside him, then plummeted before him to the ground. As though something conjoined him to the ship. Only an aviator would understand: The ship wouldn't abandon him, would fall to the ground with him.

He pulled off the fishbowl helmet. Sneezed at the acrid smoke drifting his way. The matte-black pieces: Wing stub, fore-landing wheel, stabilizer tip, engine nacelle, all of it he'd find if he would get up and walk about. Wasn't this the best recon ship in the world scattered over this Russkie taiga? Was anything left to destroy?

4 Charlie Dickinson

He chuckled.

He was late for that smörgåsbord dinner at Bodø.

They shot him down.

They would find him.

He simply had to wait.

A few hundred yards away, a charred wing tank spilling fuel smoldered, releasing thick, black smoke. He laughed. Did they need a marker to find him? That fuel would burn for hours.

What had he done? He had nothing to tell the Russkies. He was a dumb flyboy, that was all.

He needed to get up, run, hide. But where to?

Run away from the wreckage? What good would that do? He'd starve. The poison would be quicker, easier.

No, he had to wait for his captors. They'd feed him. Save him. He laughed at how he'd be saved from a wrecked recon mission, nudging some grassy stubble on the ground with his boot.

Took a deep breath. The last time the Agency would get cocky about a mission like this.

Glanced at the chronometer on his wrist, Moscow Time.

They'd find him. Of that he was sure, as sure as he was of the smoking wreckage around him.

He had nothing to tell. Only name, rank, and serial number. Beyond that, he only had to admit those coordinates on the clipboard, what he memorized going through the flight plan.

Reached in his cargo pocket again, fingered the hollowed-out silver dollar with the toxin-coated needle for those hopeless situations. *If* this was the endgame.

It wasn't.

His ship was destroyed, and probably the flames were licking at what film he'd exposed. The only evidence of what he'd done.

The smoking wreckage about him saved him the trouble—as

he was trained to do—of setting it on fire and waiting for the fuel to explode.

He didn't have to destroy himself too. He only had to say nothing.

Glanced again at his chronometer: 11:50 Moscow Time. Before sundown, he'd be past due at Bodø. And soon even Ike would know he'd gone missing.

Took the dollar out, then flung the coin sideways to his left, as far as he could across the taiga meadow. He hung his head down, clutched his knees, and sat still.

Maybe he would never be trusted to fly a mission like this again. It didn't matter.

My life isn't over. I'm flying again. Somehow. Yeah, I'm flying again.

Away from the drifting smoke of the plane crash and the dazed aviator, a Mil Mi-4 helicopter lifted off the Ministry of Military Aeronautics installation at Sverdlovsk, rose two hundred meters above the tarmac, then dipped and headed toward the crash. The four men on-board expected a twenty-minute flight.

Commander Solovev piloted the helicopter and beside him sat Dr. Kosior, if medical aid was needed. The reason for the flight, however, was the two military police, Kalinin and Puzanov, in the rear seat. They were charged with taking the downed pilot into custody, where he would quickly be turned over to State Security agents and transported to Moscow. The Union of Soviet Socialist Republics took aerial spying over its territory seriously and would apply strict sanctions under its military justice code when it found out why an alien aircraft kept invading sovereign airspace, after the first radar spotting near the Aral Sea.

Opaquely black smoke climbed its own column in the

distance. The same heading where Commander Solovev knew a parachute sighting had been confirmed.

2
ПЕЛМЕНИ
(PELMENI)

Also making its way toward the crash site was a small convoy of old, rugged GAZ-63 trucks, four-wheel drives, rocking through the gullied road toward smoke from the downed plane.

The two men in the back seat of the first truck joined the convoy after flying down from OTS, the Optics Test Station of the Ministry of Military Aeronautics in Gorod. They understood a spy plane undeniably capable of military photography had been shot down.

Sleeved elbow out an open window and clad in gray overalls, Petró Kravets sat beside his colleague Ivan Shynkarchuk. Both were superb optics technicians and ready to remove the spy-plane camera. They'd been driving for more than an hour out into the wilds of the taiga. Petró wiped his brow. His pulse raced. This was an important assignment.

Steadily, the dirty GAZ-63 bumped and bounced along the road. "Has to be a spy plane," Ivan said.

Petró squeezed his right fist. "Yes, at twenty, twenty-five thousand meters, must be."

"American," Ivan said.

"Who else?"

Petró glanced at Ivan, whose face also seemed flush with anticipation. "Americans, they believe they fly over Mother Russia whenever they want." Petró turned and spit out the open window.

In the distance, obvious despite the mud-splattered windshield, the smoky confusion of an airplane crash lingered.

Earlier, a helicopter sat beside the wreckage, blades still spinning, its door lowered, a gurney taken out.

The dazed aviator offered no resistance when told to lie on the gurney. The two military police strapped him down anyway.

The gurney was hoisted back into the helicopter bay. *Whump, whump, whump.* The blades sped up, the craft lifted, briefly tipping its blades groundward.

The convoy of GAZ-63s kept rocking and wallowing, crash-bound.

"We'll remove the camera," Petró said. "I can't wait."

Ivan smiled at Petró. "The film might survive. If its magazine's away from the fire."

Petró kept squeezing his right fist. Consternation slipped across his face.

"Vanya," he said, using Ivan's familiar name, for they knew each other since they were youths assembling cameras at the FED commune in Kharkov, "can we take out the camera with our tools?"

"Oh, we'll try. We can always hacksaw, get the camera with the sheet metal out of the plane. We'll worry about taking things apart later." He laughed.

He and Ivan had no choice but to hacksaw the camera assembly off its mounting plates. They didn't have the right tools. Petró had never seen screw heads with a hexagonal recess. *What possessed Americans to use these?*

While they worked away, sawing out the camera assembly, getting ready to take it back to the plant, another helicopter arrived with the first of many specialists from the Ministry of Military Aeronautics, who would oversee picking up the remaining pieces of the wreckage and reassembling them in a hangar near Gorod. Everything would have to be taken out by truck. Petró gave the wreckage one last glance before he and Ivan had to leave.

Petró was late for dinner. He didn't have a way to let Olga know he'd be late, but she came to accept his occasionally erratic hours.

He climbed the cold stairwell of his block of flats on Chernozem Street. Theirs was on the third floor. He pushed open the front door. Past the dining table on the left, his easy chair on the right, Olga greeted him from the small kitchen area off the front room: "Working late tonight, no?"

He nodded.

At the dinner table, four-year-old Andrei intently drew on a piece of paper with his crayons and didn't look up.

He looked over Andrei's drawing.

She took her eye off the stove, wooden spoon in hand, then asked, "You guess what's for dinner?"

"No, but it smells good."

"Pelmeni. Your favorite, special for May Day. I rolled out the dough soon as I got home and mixed the filling. But you didn't come home at six, so I set it aside."

It was almost seven. Petró glowed. He was so lucky.

"I'll put together the dumplings right now and get the water boiling."

Clutching his black crayon, Andrei put final touches on a

crow flying over a tree.

"No problems at work?" Olga asked, once he left Andrei and stepped into the kitchen area, putting a hand on her shoulder and kissing her lightly on the cheek. She smiled, "Why did you work so late?"

He grinned. "You know how it is. Technical stuff, not discussed outside our work group."

"I wouldn't understand it anyway. I just want to know you're okay at work. No problems with your supervisor, that drunken sot!"

"Maks, hah. He's happy now. We're working on something important. This can only make him look great to the higher-ups."

"Ah, the water boils. Time for the dumplings, then in fifteen minutes, we eat."

Pelmeni was one of Petró's favorite dishes. A mix of ground roast chuck and a bit of onions wrapped inside dough balls. His tongue glided over his lower lip in anticipation of the butter and sour cream he would put on his pelmeni.

Soon, Olga brought over Petró's filled plate and a smaller one for Andrei, who had put away his crayons.

Petró was tired, but good-tired and hungry. His eyes went wide at the plate Olga handed him, even though the eight dumplings seemed crowded out by the side of cabbage on the plate. He dropped a spoonful of sour cream on the dumplings after buttering them.

The first bite melted in his mouth with the fondly regarded flavors of pelmeni the way Olga made them. He ate ravenously, like a starving wolf. Then chased the dumplings with the cabbage. Would have licked the plate, but Olga freed him from such habits when they first married.

"I'll say only one thing about work, Olya," he said using her familiar name.

"What's that?"

"All Russia might know before long, if this turns out to be what we suspect."

"Oh, good for you. I won't ask more. You enjoyed your dinner?"

Petró glanced at his empty plate. He realized he wanted more, but that was it.

3
МИГ-19
(MIG-19)

The next evening, Petró was again late for dinner. Mostly because of the talk about what he and Ivan would do next with the camera. Decisions came slowly. The higher-ups had to figure out the best way to go.

Another tasty dinner from Olga again left Petró peckish—might have been in his head, his new, important assignment making him hungrier than usual. Petró then took his tea and descended two flights of stairs to the social room on the first floor. Only a few residents had television in their flats. If someone like Petró wanted more than news on his radio, he'd crowd into the social room and watch a flickering black-and-white television, its twelve-inch screen housed in a great walnut cabinet. Usually, the television was tuned to Moscow Station 1, the official channel of TASS, the Telegraph Agency of the Soviet Union.

Petró stepped inside, past the door kept open by a wooden wedge, tea mug in hand, scanning the room for where to sit. On an overstuffed couch, Egor, wearing his blue-and-brown wool sweater with elbow holes where white shirt peeked through, turned to him, flashed a smile, then patted the empty space beside him.

Petró took up the offer, for in the room were at least a dozen men, occupying a few chairs, and the other overstuffed sofa, but most sat cross-legged like children on the floor, mesmerized by the television's sound and images.

What held the room's occupants rapt was a middle-aged newsreader and his shock of thick pompadour hair, who had raised his voice from the dry monotone Petró came to expect day after day. "Today, in Moscow, the Ministry of Military Aeronautics announced the successful destruction of a reconnaissance spy plane flying in Soviet airspace near Sverdlovsk. Details, at this time, are few."

Petró sipped his tea, studying some of the others in the room: Garry, Timur, Artyom, Kirill, sure they would pester him if they ever found out he'd been at the crash site of the spy plane.

"First indications are the plane came from a secret air base in Pakistan, operated by the Central Intelligence Agency of the United States of America. Positive proof will depend on more interrogation of the pilot, captured and taken into custody—"

"Oh, boy, oh, boy!" Egor exclaimed. "How does this American fly his plane over our country?"

"The Ministry of Military Aeronautics is pleased to announce the downing of this spy plane meant the foreign intrusion of Soviet airspace was successfully detected by several radar installations. Then the invader reconnaissance plane was easily shot down by a surface-to-air missile launched from an undisclosed location."

"What? Let this plane fly halfway across our country before they shoot it down? What defense is that? No wonder we lost so many lives when we fought the Germans." Egor slammed his fist down on the arm of the sofa. He was agitated. Enough so, Petró

Losing Laika 15

feared his sofa buddy might cause him to spill tea. Others murmured agreement with Egor, but nobody was as vocal as he.

"So it is with appreciation for their heroic efforts defending the Union of Soviet Socialist Republics," the newsreader added, "the Supreme Military Command of the Union of Soviet Socialist Republics today awarded the Order of the Red Banner medal to those military personnel who successfully intercepted the American spy plane. The Order of the Red Banner carries a distinguished history dating to the early days of the glorious Revolution of October 1917."

"Yeah, but where were our fighter planes, the MiG-19s, why didn't they intercept?" Lev, seated in front of the television, asked.

"Oh, you think this the first time Americans fly over us?" Egor asked. "First time they get their fingers caught, you ask me."

"We give thanks to this successful defense of our homeland and honor these medal recipients. Working our radar and missile defenses at undisclosed locations, these and other heroic defenders assure any foreign invader of our airspace will pay a heavy price." The thick-haired newsreader coughed and flipped the page.

Petró rubbed his nose, eyeing his fellow TV viewers. *Yes, what I know about this I can't tell these guys. All of it is classified, secret, and I will take it to my grave!*

"Elsewhere in the Republics today, the Ukrainian Ministry of Mines announced coal production for the three months of this year is seven percent more than the corresponding figure for 1959—"

"Now for the more interesting news." Egor laughed.

Petró kept sipping his tea, saying nothing. *I know too much about this.* But what he was hearing from Egor and others was to be expected. People would be shocked to know the Russian military defense, so vital given the heavy losses suffered in the Great Patriotic War, would allow an American spy plane to fly halfway across the Motherland. He smiled at Egor and the others for trying to guess what happened.

4
БРАУН ТОВАРИЩ
(BROWN COMRADE)

The next day, Petró was back at the Optics Test Station, a complex of one-story buildings on the outskirts of Gorod. An obvious military installation, cinder blocks walled the grounds. Strung atop the wall were three strands of barbed wire. Authorized entrance was by one guard station, manned around the clock, every day.

Inside OTS, workers thought hard, discussed intensively, and rushed about on different projects. All invariably classified for Limited Circulation. If a camera had a military purpose, someone probably worked on it there. Whether a miniature spy camera held in the hand, or something far larger, far more advanced, like a camera system designed for reconnaissance aircraft.

At lunch hour, Petró sat in the commissary opposite his work colleague Ivan. As always, inside the plant, they wore belted white work smocks over their street clothes.

"Maks talk to you today?" Ivan asked.

"Yeah, briefly. We're to leave the spy plane camera alone, keep it in Room 74." Petró halved a small new potato with his fork before stirring it in the gravy. "I think we keep working as usual, even though this spy plane thing has come along," he added.

"You're right." His friend took a bite of herring and chased it with a sip of water. Both men relished the meals served up at OTS. As a military installation, the food procurement was far better than what they customarily bought and prepared at home in their block flats. "This American camera's important. Only in war do we usually get stuff off the enemy like this," Ivan said.

"But this is war." Petró took another bite of potato, dripping with gravy. He then poked the air with his empty fork. "This is the Cold War."

"Yes, but no troops fighting—"

"No, different war. A war where missiles fly with atomic bombs—"

"And the spy planes can fly so high—" Ivan chuckled.

Having finished his potatoes, Petró savored his herring on the side plate. Swimming in oil, the bite of each melted on his tongue. Good Baltic Sea herring: fresh, firm when he would select a bite with his fork. The old canned herring Olya would buy in the market was edible, but broke apart and mashed into a soupy mess when he took his fork to it.

The daily ritual of lunch at the plant was a welcome break from work and especially their hard-nosed boss, Maksym Belenko, a stocky Ukrainian. Petró felt Maks should've given them slack, if not openly warmed up to his fellow Ukrainians, living among the Russians too. But no. He had bosses to suck up to and would put his manager control on display by yelling at Petró and Ivan as though they were still raw teens.

Ivan left and came back with a cup of coffee and a cup of tea for Petró. They always finished commissary meals that way.

Petró smiled at Ivan's thoughtfulness, though they always

treated each other well and took turns fetching hot drinks to top off their meal.

Yes, they were still, in some ways, like the teens they were when they met. Petró took a sip of hot tea. At the Kharkov plant where the first FED 35-mm rangefinder cameras were made. Copies of German Leicas assembled by hundreds of teenage communards.

Petró took another sip. Yes, maybe he and Ivan sometimes reverted to teenage enthusiasm. But that was good and the basis of a long friendship that took them well into adulthood.

But why is Maks so difficult?

Lunch finished, the two went back to work, where they had been busy cleaning and setting up hand tools on the disassembly tables, so they would be ready when they had the "go" for the new project: the spy plane camera.

Maks, dressed in an uncustomary brown uniform, waited in the work area. In his hand, a brown cap with a red star on its brim. Petró gave a second look. *What's Maks up to now? This military garb?*

"Kravets, Shynkarchuk, it's thirteen-ten," he said, glancing at his wristwatch. "In less than an hour, at fourteen hundred, we have an important visitor."

"Visiting us?" Ivan said, thumb to his chest.

"Yes, even you guys. The three of us will spend the rest of the day with the Chief Technologist from Optics Research at Moscow Institute of Technology. Dr. Natalya Dezhnyova. She's evaluating the spy plane camera."

Maksym Belenko crossed arms on his barrel chest. His torso seemed as unmovable as a blacksmith's anvil. "Dr. Dezhnyova decides how to disassemble the camera, okay?"

"Of course," Petró replied. "We know this camera's worth a lot.

We'll be careful." He said those words, knowing Maks was anxious to hear they would do whatever it took to make him look good in the eyes of the higher-ups, which was all he cared about anyway.

Hell, Petró mused, looking away from his humorless boss in uniform, *if some big-shot major or colonel in a brown uniform came up to him and had enough red stars on his epaulets and said, Maks, that camera must be destroyed at once, use a sledgehammer. His boss, no more able to think for himself than a herring lost at sea, would come back and yell: A million pieces, I want it smashed to rubble, now!*

"In the meantime," Maks said in the tone of voice he always had when he gave orders, "go over to Room 74. The camera assembly's there. I'll bring over Dr. Dezhnyova."

Petró nodded.

5
ЗВЕЗДЫ МЕРЦАФТ
(STAR TWINKLE)

While waiting, they passed the time with an airing of Petró's complaint of the day: "You know, our flat has toilets down the hall. Two for women, two for men." He shot Ivan a solicitous look.

"I know what you say now: One of the men's is broken."

"Well, it works, but every time you flush, water runs out the bottom. This disgusts me."

"Fix it, find out who fixes it," Ivan said.

"Nobody can. I asked the block manager to get out a plumber. He says, Sure. But you know how long that takes?" He laughed.

"My place is worse," Ivan said, rising to the poor-mouth challenge. "We still share a kitchen, a communal kitchen, people steal food—huh?"

Then Ivan's eyes wandered left, to the doorway. Petró's did too. She was there.

A tall blonde in her thirties. Face, fairest of skin, intense eyes, prominent cheekbones, a resolute mouth. Dr. Natalya Dezhnyova stood by shorter, squat Maks and looked down at their boss. That pleased Petró.

Unmistakably professional, she wore a black business suit and carried a tan briefcase. No sooner was she in the room than her eyes locked on the disassembly table behind them. She left Maks for the camera. Petró took the liberty of stepping over beside her to answer questions, ready to take notes on a clipboard.

"By the way, my name is Dezhnyova, but you may call me Natalya," she said, offering Petró her hand to shake. Her eyes studied him with the serious demeanor of one who had a doctorate from the prestigious Moscow Institute of Technology.

"Pleased to meet you. Petró Kondratovych Kravets. Likewise, call me Petró."

"And Doctor Dezhnyova," the neglected Maks called out, "please meet our other optics technician, Ivan Shynkarchuk."

Ivan raised his right hand. "May I be of service," he said, smiling.

"This camera's undoubtedly high-performance—what a spy plane has to have." She ran her long, delicate—Petró imagined piano-playing—finger across the black enamel surface of the assembly's metal housing. "Before we do anything, you must know what we want at the optics lab. The first priority is the lenses. Nothing must degrade or damage the lenses."

Petró and Ivan nodded.

Maks stood away from the trio, a look of irrelevance on his face, holding the brown comrade cap to his chest.

"We first separate the lens elements, so we can measure precisely the geometry of the design."

Again, agreeing nods from Petró and Ivan.

"So what'll we do now?" Petró asked.

"Our work goes in steps. I'll stay here at least a week. Tomorrow, we start removing the metal housing."

"Very good, tomorrow early it will be," Maks piped up, unable to contain feeling neglected by Natalya.

"I must telephone some reports to the lab, so I think tomorrow morning here at ten is best. We'll meet then." She gave Petró a warm look, intense and, in a way, trusting.

"Certainly," Petró said.

"We're so honored to have the Chief Technologist here," Maks interjected.

Natalya of the commanding high-cheekboned beauty shot Maks a flattery-gets-you-nowhere glance.

Maks persisted. "If we can do anything to make your stay more enjoyable, let me know,"

"Oh, don't fret about that. We'll make good use of our time," she answered.

"Ivan and I know how much your work means for the security of our country," Petró said. "We'll handle this camera like a newborn."

"Oh, thank you. But as for my work, what would I really like to do?" she asked, as though relaxed with the scope of the project set.

"Design lenses?" Ivan asked.

"No, that's the means to an end. Someday I'd like to—" She paused. "All my work in optics has been preparation to do one thing—"

"Which is?" Petró asked.

"Oh, I've always wanted, you know, to take the twinkle out of stars—" She chuckled.

As did the three men. Then she asked Maks to help her find the way back to her assigned temporary office, so she could make phone calls.

Petró and Ivan had to leave too. They had other work to do. But for some reason, Petró felt drawn back to the camera assembly. He brushed his fingertips across the jagged edges of the sheet-metal housing they crudely sawed away from plane fuselage.

He lifted his fingers away, a cautious smile stealing across his face. *No point shedding blood for this war booty!*

"Petrush, we've got to go to the workroom and look busy for Maks, don't you think?"

The voice of his co-worker snapped him away from more thoughts about how the metal assembly came to be there.

"Yes, you're right."

They left the room, knowing they'd be back the next day to work on the camera assembly.

Ivan walked swiftly, tails of his white smock aflutter, his tall, thin legs gliding over the linoleum floor of the dimly lit corridor toward a sunlight splash at the far exit-door window. Though he did, he didn't have to answer Ivan's question. They knew each other so well, often a nod, a hand gesture was enough.

Ivan stood at the exit door, held it open for Petró. Yes, Petró marvelled, such ready communication between the two came from a long friendship going back to their youth in the Ukraine. So many winter days, the two would be out practicing hockey on a frozen pond, their skates *shusssing, shusssing*, this way, that. They played one-on-one, hands gripping the hockey stick, the prize black puck shooting across the ice like escaped quicksilver; and, importantly, they watched each other's body, each other's arms, each other's face, each other's eyes for just a clue, just a clue of what they might do next.

Petró and Ivan got to know each other better than even their wives knew them. They shared a quick familiarity for any work they'd tackle. They were like four hands working in unison the next morning, as they lifted plate after plate away from the assembly, under the watchful eye of Dr. Natalya Dezhnyova. She stepped closer and peered at what was revealed.

"Hah, as I expected," she exclaimed. Lifting back the last of the surrounding plates, Ivan and Petró exposed the guts of the camera. "Two cameras in one! Stereoscopic, six-element lenses. They're huge. I read some intelligence we have about Dr. Edwin Land in Boston doing research on such a design.

"You know what's next," she continued.

"We take pictures of this?" Petró asked.

"Yes, photographs to document the assembly are essential," she replied. "I need to call my colleagues and bring them up to date. I can positively tell you, though, tomorrow you will heat the assemblies to take the lenses apart."

6
500 ЦЕЛСИЯ
(500 CELSIUS)

The next day, the three again met in Room 74 where Petró and Ivan had temporarily moved a special electrical oven. The two technicians donned white muslin caps for their hair, besides wearing their customary white work smocks.

Natalya, however, wore a white lab apron over her black suit and stood next to the electrical oven—large, a meter tall—on a steel worktable. The oven door ajar, she opened it wide, revealing thick, insulating walls.

"Yesterday, I called the reference library at the lab. They confirmed melting points for optical cements are between four-eighty and five-hundred Celsius—"

"This oven is capable of that, is it not?" Natalya asked.

"Certainly," Ivan said, stepping over to the oven. He pointed at the dials on the control panel. "This is a quality oven. You turn this dial to the temperature, and it stays there, unless the electricity goes off." He chuckled. "We've never had that problem."

"Okay, Comrades, we put the lens assemblies in there, we set the temperature--five hundred even, and we leave them overnight, okay?" Natalya said.

Petró's heart skipped. They'd walk away and let this extraordinary technology bake overnight? "You really want to leave them in so long?"

"Yes. What happens is the cement softens and flows imperceptibly downward. But you'll have to position the lens elements on edge. Then a bead of cement will form at the lower joining of the edges. I've done this before and believe it or not, when cooled, that bead can be cut and scraped away. The lenses separate cleanly."

"This I want to see," Ivan said.

"Oh, I'm sure you will," Natalya said. "And with the elements apart, I'll take them back to the lab and work on assessing their geometry, glass composition, other optical properties."

She turned, stepped over to the worktable with the assemblies. She held out her fingers, but did not touch the lenses. "What can go wrong? You might wonder that. Not too much we can do anything about. Any moisture on the lenses will be gone well before the target temperature is reached. No moisture can exist at that temperature."

"So what's the danger?" Petró asked, his heart seemingly in his throat.

"The danger is unavoidable, though remote," Natalya said. "This is optical quality glass, of the highest standard for purity, and yet an impurity might exist. We simply can't see any possible defect in these elements. A hidden defect doesn't affect operation of the camera. But high temperatures could bring the defect out. The lens might crack. For that, nothing can be done, except blame poor American technology." She chuckled, as did Petró and Ivan.

"You know, Comrades, in the capitalist system, where does the American military go for their weapons and equipment?" she asked rhetorically. "They go to the manufacturer with the lowest price. Hah! But I think these optics are from a reputable firm. I again checked research on this lens design—it's like Dr. Land in Boston, as I thought."

Petró took a deep breath. He knew what came next. He and Ivan would each take one of the two lens assemblies and put them in the oven, side by side, where they would sit like Siamese twins at some altar in Hell. The idea made him shudder. He would gladly leave Ivan with the honors, closing the door, dialling the temperature to five-hundred. Then they'd lock the room and hope for the best.

After breakfast, coffee, and tea in the commissary, Petró and Ivan stood outside Room 74 where the industrial-strength oven had baked through the night. Ten minutes early, they were ready to unlock the door *after* Dr. Natalya Dezhnyova arrived.

Petró wanted to be sure she stood beside them when the door was unlocked. If anything went wrong, better to have her as a witness he and Vanya were blameless.

"Is that her?" Ivan pointed down the hall. The blonde in a white lab coat, briefcase in hand, approached.

"Oh, yes. I hope we don't find exploded glass in the oven." He took a deep breath and gazed toward Dr. Dezhnyova.

"Comrades, top of the morning to you," Natalya said, drawing close.

Petró paused, then put the key in the lock and pulled back the door for Natalya and Ivan.

She wasted no steps going to the oven on the table. "Okay, now we turn this off."

Ivan dutifully dialled OFF.

She peered in the window of the oven, the view dim under double glass. "See for yourself, the melted cement hangs by a bead from the elements."

Petró squinted, but had to admit he didn't see a bead of cement. He was content, however, knowing if Natalya said the oven worked, it probably did. She had done this before.

"So it's just past nine hundred. We turned the oven off, and now you, Ivan," she said, "can open the door. Six hours is about right. We'll leave, lock the room, and then let things cool."

"And come back later?" Petró asked.

"Yes, at fifteen hundred, we'll meet here and see about separating the lenses. They should come apart easily."

When the three returned to Room 74, Natalya made a bee-line for the oven, its door ajar.

"Now, the big step is here. We separate the lens elements," she said.

Petró, unblinking, looked at Ivan, who also seemed content to let Natalya handle the lenses.

"Anything you want us to do?" Petró asked.

"Oh, just watch. I've done this many times." She opened the oven door wide and brought her right forefinger close to, but not touching, one of the lens assemblies.

"As I thought, it's been long enough. Cool to touch, but, of course, we never touch glass surfaces with our fingers."

"To handle lenses," Ivan interjected, "we always use microfiber cloths."

"Absolutely. I have some in the kit I left here earlier."

She went to a nearby worktable and unlatched a box. "All this is microfiber. Something for every possible situation."

She spread a towel-sized cloth on the table. "Now, these." She donned a pair of blue gloves. "Also microfiber," she said with a wink.

"Shouldn't we move the table closer to the oven?" Petró asked, his voice edged with concern.

"Yes, that would help," she said.

"Okay, Vanya," Petró said.

Ivan laughed, held out his arms, flexing his biceps. "Let's move this carcass."

Ivan grabbed the other end of the bulky worktable, and they carried it over to face the oven.

"Thank you, Comrades," she said, adjusting the gloves on her hands. "Now, I'll show you the separated elements, one by one."

Ivan and Petró stood the other side of the worktable and peered as Natalya put her gloved hands inside the oven and reached for the leftmost lens assembly.

Petró held his breath.

Natalya smiled as she slowly turned around and held a convex cylinder of glass, which she placed on the cloth covering the table. "There, one of six elements. Not a smidge of adhesive anywhere. Easy separation."

Ivan whistled as she pushed the round element sideways. She went back to her supply box. "I have pouches for each element," she said, selecting a black one, into which she gingerly inserted the glass element.

Soon, Natalya pocketed each of the six elements.

"They go back with you to Moscow?" Petró asked.

"Yes, testing and analysis. You two will probably disassemble the rest of the camera. The mechanicals like the shutter. First, though, we need to wait for more direction."

"We can help you pack these," Petró offered.

"No, that won't be necessary. They're in these protective pouches. I just need some packing, some newspaper, if I might trouble you."

"Oh, sure," Ivan said. "We have the old *Pravdas* in the cafe-

teria for the paper drive. I'll get some now."
"Excellent," Natalya said.

7
ДИСЦИПЛИНА, ТОВАРИЩИ!
(DISCIPLINE, COMRADES!)

"Dr. Dezhnyova thinks we're great," Ivan said, walking with Petró down Iskra Street, headed for the main thoroughfare, Narodniki Prospekt.

"Yeah, I wonder if Maks will agree."

"That's him. Unhappy. His only friend is you know—" Ivan held out a closed fist, tilting it to his lips. He laughed.

"Well, I think she's avoiding him." A bus on Narodniki lumbered through the intersection ahead. Ivan had to catch one home.

"She sized up Maks fast."

"Oh, you mean—" Petró flexed out his right thumb and took aim at the sidewalk.

"Yeah." Ivan chuckled.

They stood at the intersection of Iskra and Narodniki. Ivan had to wait on the next Number 15 bus.

"Tonight's football. You give that up, Petrush?"

"Mostly, but who's playing?"

"Dinamo."

"In Moscow?"

"Yeah, if anybody beats them, it's Spartak—"

"What time?"

He glanced at his wristwatch. "Seven-thirty, right after dinner, Channel Four—"

"I'm sure it'll be on our TV downstairs."

"Okay, maybe we talk about it tomorrow."

"Sure." Petró tugged the lapels of his wool overcoat in the autumn air and walked on.

At the Metro entrance, Petró skipped down the long flight of steps like the experienced commuter he was.

To the right, to the left, the tracks ran to nothing but an empty void of black. But here, on the platform, amid the straggly commuters, a brightly lit interior space made up for what it lacked in fresh air.

He scanned the white-tiled wall overhead that held an expanse of yellow billboard. For some reason, he gaped at the silhouette he'd seen so many times. The silhouetted man in green with raised hand, folded cap held aloft. Lenin. To the right, on the yellow background, the bold red letters: DISCIPLINE, COMRADES!

Petró's gaze rested on those two words in red. They had done it today. He and Ivan, working with Dr. Dezhnyova, had done something essential to the defense of the Motherland.

A warm glow calmed his back. Then approaching, the high-pitched hum of the train, but invisible in blackness far away to his right. He studied again the Voice for Everyman on the wall. Lenin.

The train screeched, then halted.

The windowed doors of the subway car slid open, and he pushed forward. Jostled by the other commuters, he brushed past the rubber flap of the door and saw a place to stand.

He grabbed a hanging loop to steady his ride. The train started forward, lurching, then picking up speed as the steel wheels rode the rails with an unearthly whine trapped inside the darkness.

Slowly tilting side-to-side, the interior-lit subway car plummeted on, and Petró's mind drifted off to memories. How he started working with cameras. *It's twenty years ago?* He gazed at a poster above his head, above the passenger seats, a smaller, easily read version of the one on the train platform. Yellow with red letters and the green silhouette of Uncle Lenin, cap in upraised hand. DISCIPLINE, COMRADES!

He believed those words even more back then. The year was 1940 in Kharkov, Ukraine. Petró would be ready for secondary school in a year and had to choose where to go. He was not studious and wanted to do something with his hands.

Earlier, in the thirties, a work commune for fatherless teens was started in memory of Feliks Edmundovich Dzerzhinsky, otherwise known as the founder of Cheka, which became NKVD, then the KGB, with an undisputed legacy of brutality in the name of State security.

But Dzerzhinsky's brilliant organizational mind saw beyond the State parasites, criminal deviants, and security risks. Petró knew he must have had a kinder side. The large numbers of street kids in cities were to touch Dzerzhinsky. They were orphans only because their fathers were killed fighting for the Motherland in the catastrophic Great War and Revolution which followed. He adamantly resisted the idea such street hooligans would be punished after the sacrifices of their lost fathers.

Before he died in 1926, Dzerzhinsky spoke and wrote on many occasions about how such youths easily fell into a culture of crime to survive. So he proposed a new education for such victims of war to follow Marxist scientific principles and give street kids a practical education: They would learn by running a manufacturing commune!

Thus, inspired by the respected, though often feared, founder of Cheka, the FED Work Commune in Kharkov was launched. Quickly it grew to several hundred communards, as they were called, and when Petró went there looking for a way to further his vocational education and do something with his hands, he mentioned his father recently was killed in the Winter War in Finland. He got an immediate assignment.

What might have seemed crazy to the rest of the world was that a factory full of fatherless teens, otherwise destined for a life of crime, would get an education and successfully manufacture Soviet copies of the vaunted Leica 35-mm camera from Germany.

The subway car tumbled on in darkness. But Petró's memory glowed, recalling how he met Ivan working on a long table assembling cameras from screws, levers, flanges, and other metal parts that sat, piled in trays about them.

He and Ivan sat on stools. Their hands and fingers, young and nimble, took to such precise work. The same could be said for how their keen eyes didn't tire during the day. Everyone in the room was young and seemed to like the demanding assembly. They knew they made history by building an affordable precision camera.

Ivan would often turn to Petró with a wisecrack like, "Why do you carry rocks in your pockets?"

Petró, having no idea, said, "I've work to do, tell me later."

Ivan persisted. "No, rocks in your pockets, why? Guess."

"Oh, no coins to spend, I need something in my pocket to not feel I have nothing."

"That's good, but the reason you have rocks in your pockets is so you'll stay on your stool and work and work. Not move until the whistle blows."

"That's no joke."

"I know it's not. We get a place to sleep, some food, some school. But no money. They might as well pay us rocks."

Unlike Ivan, Petró didn't complain about being a communard in the factory making Leica copies. He liked learning how the insides of a camera worked. He felt, with his eyes closed and by touch alone, he could take apart a camera shutter, then put it back together, hundreds of minute parts floating in his mind like a jigsaw puzzle he would always solve. He'd done so many times.

The screeching subway car halted. Petró looked out at the well-lit platform where people would leave and catch a crosstown subway at another level. Yes, that training was one reason he and Ivan were hired by MMA for the Optics Test Station in Gorod. Skillful hands that could take apart cameras blindfolded.

Petró took a deep breath and left the train. He looked up, as the train rolled on, leaving Proletarskii Stop, and studied yet another large green silhouette of Lenin. Yes, life had gone well. He was lucky. He had an important defense job and, as the day showed, worked with the likes of Dr. Natalya Dezhnyova from the Moscow Institute of Technology.

8

UNIVAC

A few weeks later in an OTS conference room, Petró, Ivan, and Maks again met with Dr. Natalya Dezhnyova. She was accompanied by a General Vadim Savvin, who, apparently stationed elsewhere in Moscow, was MMA.

Petró had no inkling why the general was there. Petró studied him, sitting beside Natalya, who wore her customary black business suit. His well-fed look filled out the military brown uniform, a few touches of red, here and there, representing the possible sacrifices, Petró guessed, he once was willing to make on behalf of the Motherland.

Then Petró shifted his gaze to a side wall, not wanting the newest visitor to take his curiosity as rude staring. He had no idea what Dr. Dezhnyova would say, but he was sure—with the general there—military brass back in Moscow must have been losing sleep about the American spy plane camera, in pieces, they had on their hands.

Whatever they were about to hear probably meant more work. Oh, Petró figured once they turned the lenses over to

Dr. Dezhnyova and she took them to Moscow, that was that. But, back again, here she was ready to tell them something.

"Comrades," Natalya began, "I first must tell you what an extraordinary camera we captured from the Americans. Another group at the optics lab successfully processed the film from the camera magazine." She glanced at a tablet of notes, then looked up, but as though she was sure her audience was hanging on every word.

Petró's eyes were wide with rapt attention for the brainy, blonde beauty. *If this is true, not only the camera, but the pictures taken by the American spy pilot—well, this is the best!*

"I cannot tell you what we've seen," she said, slipping a glance General Savvin's way, "but some prints show extraordinary resolution. Really extraordinary."

Petró sat up straighter. *Why, of course, the military targets, no need for me to know that!*

"We have preliminary work on resolution of the camera, about ten centimeters from an estimated twenty-one kilometers flying altitude. Of course, we're always working on such optical systems ourselves." She nodded at the general.

"So why do these stereoscopic lenses work so well? Several reasons, some too technical to discuss now. But I had chemical analysis done of the glass. Spectrometric results showed what I expected: The glass has been doped with the rare earth lanthanum and a thorium isotope. That can only add contrast to the optics. We do the same ourselves at the lab."

Petró eased back in his chair. *Oh, this is beyond me. This is why Natalya has a doctorate from Moscow Institute of Technology.*

"For geometry of the lens elements, an interesting departure from the usual astigmatic design so often used. We've done the needed measurements on the lenses, but obviously having geometric profiles doesn't give us the mathematical solution to the equations used to arrive at those geometries. We are working on our best approximation, and it takes time.

"I'll mention this is an exceptional six-element design. The math to decide curvatures for grinding the glass was probably helped by an advanced computing machine, such as the Sperry UNIVAC the Americans have."

Petró leaned forward at the mention of computers. He rubbed his left temple. Yes, he remembered, as a youth, back in the Kharkov work commune someone telling him how hard it was to design the lenses for the FED he and Ivan put together. The mathematics for grinding was so complex and had to be so accurate, he was told the lens designer might spend a day at a tabulating machine, solving difficult equations, then start again the next day if something had to be changed. Even then, Petró had no wish to design cameras if it meant such drudgery. He just wanted to put them together. But would an American computer make it that much easier? He bit his lower lip at the idea the Americans had such an advantage.

"So, yes, an extraordinary camera, and General Savvin and I want to thank the three of you for helping us. And now General Savvin has a few words."

Petró sat up straight. *This, surely, is the payoff for our meeting. The general will take Natalya's remarks and tell us what's next.*

Savvin toyed briefly with his military cap, resting on the table, brown, trimmed in gold and red. He cleared his throat. "Excellent work you all do. The Ministry of Military Aeronautics is proud of the Optics Test Station at Gorod and everyone here. I'm pleased to meet Comrades Kravets and Shynkarchuk, who will have an important assignment."

Petró gave the general a double take.

Savvin paused, again clearing his throat, before continuing in his basso profundo voice. "This was a serious breach of Soviet state security. This violated the most basic agreements among sovereign nations, and the Americans first denied this happened. They thought they could get away with it. Hah! But we have proof: the wrecked spy plane, the captured pilot. The world knows what a liar the American president is.

"When this reconnaissance plane entered our airspace, I am free to tell you, we knew. We knew when the spy plane flew over the Aral Sea. We picked it up with radar at several undisclosed locations. Easily."

He looked across the table, his eyes checking everyone for the unwavering attention his time with them deserved. "How the plane was brought down, I can't tell you. Perhaps someday, we'll talk freely. But things now are tense. We have the pilot in interrogation. We'll make him talk, and we have the pictures he took. And the camera. This is much better than a burnt-out wreck and a dead pilot." He smiled at his joke, then added, "But none of that is important to our discussion here."

"Comrade Kravets, Comrade Shynkarchuk, you two have even more service to perform for the Motherland—"

Petró smiled. *This is why he came. He tells us now.*

"Dr. Dezhnyova and I talked about this with your manager, Comrade Belenko, and for the next six months—at least—you will do nothing but create a replica of the American spy camera you disassembled."

Petró's eyes went wide; he gasped.

"Yes, a surprise perhaps, but essential to our security. We need a working copy of the captured camera. It's beyond repair. But you two, we decided, are the best to build a new one."

"Duplication of the lenses is KMZ in Moscow. They'll work on a crash program to get it right. The math is tough, so lenses will be a while. But we want you to take everything else you disassembled and figure out how to make a new camera. The parts obviously you must catalog and document with specifications—"

General Savvin said more, but Petró was in a daze. He could hardly believe the challenging project in his and Ivan's hands. *But for us then, is it not like when we built FEDs? When we were supposedly making copies of the German Leica camera?*

9
СТОЛИЧНАЯ
(STOLICHNAYA)

That afternoon, General Savvin and Dr. Dezhnyova met with Maksym Belenko. Such a camera had never been built in the Soviet Union, and who better to assemble this than the two superb technicians, who worked on cameras since their teenage years assembling FEDs?

Natalya thought so, even though Maks was not effusive about his optics technicians. The meeting was short, cursory, and the general dismissed Maks, saying he had security matters to go over with Dr. Dezhnyova.

Which was true. As the general explained to Natalya, assembling a high-performance camera was a military secret to be guarded. Possibly, the Soviets could improve on the camera, even though they had no current plans to build a similar reconnaissance plane in which to put it. But who knew what the Ministry of Military Aeronautics might authorize in the next five-year plan? The general winked at Natalya.

He stood up from his chair, then pulled back his jacket sleeve to show an aviator's chronometer on his brawny wrist. Built like a rugged Soviet tractor.

"Dr. Dezhnyova, it is seventeen hundred, fifteen. We may adjourn for the day. You return to Moscow tomorrow morning, correct?"

"Yes, Comrade, I take the nine-twenty Aeroflot to Moscow. You?"

"Oh, I fly out tonight, late. I'll have my driver take me to the airbase. It's a small military jet I sometimes use." He smiled a devilish grin.

"Yes, I see rank has privileges," Natalya offered, also getting up from her chair, tucking her papers inside the attaché case.

"Our responsibility for military command demands we move on a moment's notice," he replied with unapologetic self-importance. "If I decide I'd rather return to Moscow in the morning, not tonight ... One phone call, it's arranged. The pilot and the jet are at my disposal."

"I'll think about your situation when I fly back to Moscow," Natalya said.

"Oh, your work is important to the defense of our Motherland too. I insist I make up for your sacrifice—this torture of a morning flight back to Moscow—by our having dinner this evening. My treat. What do you say?" He held out his open palm, his shoulders pulled back in a military posture.

Surprised, Natalya watched him don his cap, brown with gold braid, a red star on the brim. Obviously, a man of influence. Here was an opportunity, she sensed, to make a connection much stronger. Someday, might she not call on him because surely he would remember dinner with her, idly chit-chatting about whatever struck their fancy? She thought it would be fun.

"Of course," she replied.

An hour or so later, General Vadim Savvin—still in military regalia—and Dr. Natalya Dezhnyova were seated in a booth at the Black Sea Restaurant, having consumed fare appropriate to the general's discriminating tastes: appetizers of caviar and smoked salmon torte, followed by a glass each of exquisite German Müller-Thurgau wine, then some pirozhki, a main course of chicken kotlety with a side of braised cucumbers, and a dessert of cranberry kissel with currant squares.

Natalya, even with her position at the prestigious Optics Laboratory, couldn't remember when she ate so opulently, as apparently the General did every night, given how knowledgeably he ordered.

To suggest more serious conversation, possibly, the general asked that a bottle of the finest grade Stolichnaya vodka in a silver bucket of ice be brought to the table. He poured shots and edged closer to Natalya in the half-circle of the cozy booth seat.

She felt, however, the general might get too relaxed after the day's meetings at the plant. This was not how she expected to wind up her visit to Gorod.

"To our future collaboration on this important project for the Motherland." He held up his second glass of vodka to clink hers.

"Yes," she said, hoping if he kept talking, he would slow down.

She slid sideways several centimeters, enough so he wouldn't be leaning on her. Yes, she slid sideways so she could face him more directly, look him straight in the eye.

"Another glass?" he said, downing his vodka like a dropped anvil.

"Why not?" she said, not willing to forfeit a future payoff from this military officer with obvious influence.

He poured a shot in each glass. A sly smile snuck across his face.

He didn't bother with a toast. He simply downed the drink and offered up a lingering look that begged to rest on her face.

She was flattered, but stymied by the attention. She knew he must want to postpone his flight until morning. Teasingly, she slid a few centimeters closer, raising her glass to sip the vodka. "General Savvin, tell me why it's important to build this replica of the spy camera." Her eyes implored him: She knew someone in his station had answers.

"Oh, Comrade Dezhnyova," he said with slurred words, the effects of the Stolichnaya showing in his eyes that looked for refuge in hers. "Our sputniks in orbit must have high-performance lenses in the cameras. That's the future. That's what we want."

She gasped, having only heard speculation about such ambitious plans back in Moscow. Spy-quality pictures from outer space? Sure, people speculated, but these words from a general confirmed. The spy sputnik was on its way.

"Will this happen soon?" she asked, eyeing the general who moved closer to her, as though he thought she was showing an interest in him.

"Oh, that's not our project, so I can't say except—"

She gave him a wide-eyed look, as if this man of military importance might drop another revelatory plum in her lap, if his hand didn't get there first.

"We won't bother—" he said with a dismissive sweep of the back of his hand, "with flimsy spy planes like Americans. We are the Union of Soviet Socialist Republics. We put sputniks in orbit around earth, around the moon. But we'll do better, no blurry images. Only the highest quality images for intelligence. This I say with certainty." He smiled, but Natalya was not sure if his facial expression meant to convey something else.

She slid away from the friendly general, sat up straighter. "Oh, is that true? You don't think the Americans will do the same, especially after their spy plane was shot down?"

"But, of course," he said, evidently realizing a new gap of several centimeters between them needed to be closed.

"A spy satellite for them too?"

"Sure, but we are the Union of Soviet Socialist Republics. We'll have survey sputniks in place before the Americans. Superior Soviet technology!" He raised his glass of Stoli and downed it, quickly pouring another one. Natalya waved his offer away, still nursing her drink.

"Well, I hope what we make the optics technicians do here—reconstruct the American camera—is not pointless," she said, suddenly realizing the general also admitted somewhere else, some group was building a far better camera, one to work in the reaches of outer space.

"Oh, the work of—who is it, Petró? That other guy?"

"Ivan."

"Yeah, the work's important. We need America's camera to make our design better." His voice faded off as he dreamily stared into his glass of vodka and scooted sideways on the booth seat until Natalya felt his fleshy leg tight against hers.

She knew it was time for her au revoir.

Like any experienced single woman, Natalya Dezhnyova knew how to time an exit. She reached down, took the general's free left hand and squeezed it, then set down her half-empty glass of vodka and abruptly slid out of the booth and stood. "I'm so sorry to leave you now, but I must get my beauty sleep," she said, not waiting for a reply.

10
СПУТНИК ДЕТСКИЙ ЛЕПЕТ
(SPUTNIK BABY TALK)

As he would do at the close of so many workdays, Petró slipped past the open subway door and began ascending stairs to Narodniki Prospekt above, where he could stroll, enjoying cool twilight, back to Olga, son Andrei, and dinner at home. The sky at stairs-end had a first flickering of stars. The word Спутник, Sputnik, popped in his head.

It's already three years ago? Those days of October 1957 when the world looked to the Union of Soviet Socialist Republics, knowing Russian technology reigned supreme in the world. The Americans were shocked. Their ex-Nazi rocket boys failed to deliver. So the Americans lost out to the unstoppable might of the Russian R-7 rocket.

Sputnik, little wanderer, was up there, going round and round, free of gravity, orbiting earth below, and every night for weeks, at least once after dinner if not more, Petró would study the wall clock and say, "In ten minutes, Sputnik's above us."

He had climbed from the subway stop into the open air and a dusting of snow to his block a good fifteen minutes away.

Andrei, at the time a year old, still in diapers, didn't understand how this orb, with the four jutting antennae could circle the earth. But what he did understand was Sputnik made sounds. It beeped.

In her house dress and apron, Olga, who would be filling the sink to wash dishes after taking Andrei from his high chair and sitting him on the rug in front of the big wooden radio cabinet, would say more than once, "I can't believe I'm alive for this."

"Petya, will little Sputnik ever fall back to earth?"

"I'm not sure. But I read in *Pravda* it will probably stay up a few more months. Only if its orbit is much higher will it never fall."

Diapered Andrei at his side, Petró would be kneeling next to the radio with its pie-shaped, fabric-covered speaker, turning the dial slowly to where he affixed a bit of the black electrician's tape off a roll he brought home from work. And there—on the taped spot—predictably, Sputnik would talk the baby talk even Andrei understood:

Beep. Beep. Beep. ... Beep. Beep. Beep. ... Beep. Beep. Beep. ... Beep. Beep. Beep. ... Beep. Beep. Beep.

Petró would pat little Andrei's towhead. Sputnik was a triumph of Soviet brainpower!

His son looked up at the radio. His ears obviously heard wonder in the *beeping*. How could he ever know the out-of-this-world source of those calls from the Little Wanderer above? A flush of pride filled Petró's face as he admired his young son's curious eyes and ears. *What a future he has. The Soviet Union, now the most technologically advanced country on earth.*

For weeks, Petró had Sputnik mania like everybody. At home, at work, and on the street. Petró could not get enough of this Russian achievement. He read everything he could find in *Pravda* and journals. He listened to the radio nightly. He took time to go downstairs and watch the TV broadcasts there. He couldn't help but swell openly with pride.

Unbelievably, two years later, Petró and everyone in the Motherland enjoyed another equally amazing space feat. The brilliant rocket scientist Korolev pulled off something that left no doubt who was winning the space race. On October 4, the second anniversary of Sputnik-1, Korolev launched the much more advanced Lunik-3 satellite for moon orbit and radio-transmitted back pictures of the dark side of the moon! For the first time in history, anybody in the world could see the side of the moon it kept turned away from earth. Yes, Soviet technology triumphed again.

Those years, 1957 and 1959, were good ones to be Russian. First in space, first to photograph the hidden side of the moon, Russia showed the world a technological command to go with being the largest country on earth; its resources were immeasurably large, and the future should never have looked brighter for communal progress. The tug of the present, however, gave Petró the sight of his block, seven stories rising in marked similarity to its neighbors, looming ahead.

He sighed, his steps slowed.

But now was 1960, and nothing changed. The Americans went into space, too, and then this: They send a spy plane over the Motherland. *They're aggressors and take pictures of military installations.*

When does this Cold War end?

All he knew was that if he and Ivan did their job well and gave Comrade Dezhnyova the replica of the spy camera she needed, their efforts might help keep the American menace at bay. Security for the Motherland. *What other goal is more supreme?*

II
КРОЛИК УХА
(RABBIT EARS)

That night, after dinner, Petró left for the social room to watch TV news. If he were less tired from the day's work, he might have, instead, tackled that novel Ivan lent him by the American author Jack London.

Seeing the usual gang there, Petró walked in and stood by a side wall. He didn't feel like the floor was for him, and the chairs were filled up.

The black-and-white picture was big enough to watch from four meters away, but tonight the screen turned snowy: bad reception. Someone said a vacuum tube was dying inside: How long would it take to get one of those?

Skinny Fedor got up and twisted the rabbit ears of the aerial on the TV cabinet. "Better?"

"Yeah, you piled the snow to the side. Leave it!"

Fedor shrugged and sat down.

Petró didn't care if the picture went bad, as long as he heard sound and got the news. Sure, TV pictures were nice, but when the newsreader droned on, as he was then, reading a report that the

Ministry of Hydroelectric Power in Uzbekistan reported a four percent rise in production for the year, his eyes weren't about to be glued to stock film of a waterfall flooding the round TV screen.

Suddenly, however, the tone of the newsreader changed and became animated, not intrinsically dull.

"Several weeks ago, we were able to report our air defense forces shot down an American reconnaissance plane in Soviet airspace—"

Petró's ears pricked up. *What can he say? This is so hush-hush.*

"We didn't report much before," the newsreader continued, "but tonight after extensive interrogation by investigators in Moscow, we can report on the pilot of the American spy plane."

A picture of a round face, topped with closely cropped hair, tight eyes, and a frown, flashed onto the screen. Petró studied the picture, blurred by snow, as though everything he was working on came down to that image in the middle of the TV. *What, from such heights, did he photograph? Where would he land? The Motherland, so much to fly over.*

"Here is the pilot. His name is Francis Gary Powers. His birthplace is Burdine, Kentucky, in the United States of America, and he is thirty-one years old. He is employed as a civilian pilot for the United States Central Intelligence Agency—"

From his seat on the floor, Fedor turned around to face the rest of those watching. "This pilot's in our trap. Hah." He pulled his index finger across his throat.

"No," someone else said. "The authorities get information from this guy, better to keep him alive."

Petró took the comments as amusing, not free to tell what he knew about the downed plane, his trip to the crash site and later, taking apart the camera. But that was classified work. Some in the room knew where he worked, but nobody, what he did.

He kept gazing at the screen image; it could have been an icon. The head shot of spy pilot Francis Gary Powers.

What were the Americans saying about this? Would he ever read that in *Pravda*? He hoped so, for surely here superior Soviet military technology threw the Americans and their spy plane into chaos. Their spy pilot might pay the full price, if not be crucified outright.

"Today," the newsreader continued, "the pilot made a formal apology to the Soviet people from our studio in Moscow—" The TV picture cut to the young pilot, again a round face with dark, cropped hair, standing with both hands on a lectern, one holding a piece of paper. Powers blinked at the bright studio lights, then bowed his head and began reading while a Russian translator gave a voice-over of his English.

"I, Francis Gary Powers, a civilian pilot employed by the United States Central Intelligence Agency, come before the Russian people. I have an apology to make—" he said in a wooden voice, his head unmoving, as though he would not leave the words written out before him for even the briefest glance elsewhere.

Petró, guessing about Soviet interrogators, figured Powers must have had plenty of help composing his statement to the Russian people.

"On May 1, 1960, I left the U.S. military base at Peshawar, Pakistan, and flew over the Hindu Kush of Afghanistan, and then into Soviet airspace, approaching Sverdlovsk from the south—"

Powers moved the paper slightly with his right hand. His left hand gripped the top of the lectern tightly, and Petró could see, as the camera zoomed in, the fingers bunched up.

"You see that?" Fedor yelled. "Look at the guy's hand there, he's starting to give the cameraman the finger. Hah! What balls that

American has." He laughed.

Petró stared. What was Fedor talking about? Sure the middle finger was longer, but had the pilot pulled back the middle digit's two neighbors? No, he was so nervous, he had too much to worry about.

Powers took his left hand off the lectern, awkwardly sticking it in his side pocket and kept reading.

Petró took a deep breath. *This is tense enough without that nervous American pilot accidentally flipping us off!*

"I apologize to the Russian people for violating their national boundaries with this reconnaissance mission. The pictures I took, I am told, are in the possession of the Ministry of Military Aeronautics, and I plan to cooperate fully with their investigation. Thank you."

With those words, the film clip ended. The newsreader came back on-screen.

Petró looked around him. He knew what the American had done was terrible, flying over the Motherland. But Russia got a break when they took the pilot into captivity. His neighbors, though, in the TV room didn't know how bad it was for the pilot. They thought this Francis Gary Powers didn't care about his capture and could gesture obscenely to TV cameras! Petró wouldn't dare tell what he knew, what he'd learned about the captured film from that camera. He knew he had to be even more careful about keeping his mouth shut: He and Ivan would be working on a project to fix this breach in Soviet defenses.

12
КАРЕЛИЯ
(KARELIA)

The months rolled over into a new year, the American aviator sat in Vladimir Central Prison, 250 kilometers east of Moscow, and as winter tapered off, the Kravets family had a national holiday to celebrate: February 23, Red Army Day. A day when families across the Soviet Empire made their way out to cemeteries, especially ones like the War Heroes Cemetery in Gorod, and paid respect to those who sacrificed themselves to meet the challenge of defending the largest country on earth.

The morning of the holiday Olga awoke early, before Petró and little Andrei, both fast asleep. Once outside, in the dark, Olga made her way up a sidewalk flecked with overnight snow, plodding in her leather winter boots, a heavy coat over her house dress and sweater, and the usual babushka scarf tied about her hair whenever she left the flat. She was on her way to the flower seller, who set up a stall near the bus stop at the intersection of Chernozem and Narodniki. Later in the day, the woman would sell out of flowers and before that have impossibly long lines waiting to buy.

Irina, the flower seller, lived in a nearby block and told Olga she would be putting out flowers at five. So there, at five, was Olga.

Plenty of chrysanthemums that time of year.

With keen anticipation, Olga's eyes took in the bouquets Irina was making, tying off stems with lengths of string, then jabbing each bunch in a large jar of water.

"Oh, I'll get the best selection," Olga said in greeting.

"Good flowers, yes, and the sun brings a happy day," Irina said.

That was true. Olga knew few things were sadder than going to the cemetery to lay flowers on a grave in stormy weather. Today would be a clear day. Good for remembrance. She rubbed her nose. *Petró's papa, my uncles.*

"How much, three bunches chrysanthemums?"

"Eighty kopecks."

"So much?"

"I'm sorry. Prices keep going up. I must eat."

Olga made a show of reaching about in her dress pocket, even though she knew she had only fifty kopecks.

"What about one bunch and two little ones, fifty kopecks? That's all I have."

Irina kept busy, tying off stems.

"No. These bunches each have nine flowers. I'll give you two bunches for fifty kopecks because you're here first. A better price than three for eighty."

Olga rubbed her nose again, hesitating. *Yes, two for fifty is better.*

She took the fifty-kopeck note from her dress pocket, quickly held it out. Just as quickly, Irina retrieved two bunches of chrysanthemums from the water jar and took the fifty-kopeck note.

Olga clutched the flower bunches and turned on the snowy path back to her block and a breakfast to prepare for Petró and Andrei. Both would be up soon.

A few hours later, the Kravets family, having had a hearty Red Army Holiday breakfast of sour cream blinchiki crepes with sugar, got off the No. 85 bus at the War Heroes Cemetery, set in the vast Saltykov Park Preserve.

The diesel bus then ground away, completing the turnaround and city-bound, left. The cemetery was the end of the line. Petró hesitated, observing the dozen or so others who got off too. Olga held little Andrei's hand, who was big enough to stand on his own.

Dressed for the occasion, Petró wore, under his great overcoat, his brown suit, white shirt, and red tie, and held the chrysanthemums, which Olga re-tied as three bunches.

After some argument back in the flat about Petró's papa deserving a full-sized bunch, the two uncles sharing the other, Petró insisted all three deserved equal flowers: Each gave his life for the Motherland.

But Petró's father was the first to be visited. They had a walk up the hill to the plot beside the towering bare-leafed oak tree, skeletal in its wintry majesty. Petró peered ahead, thinking it favorable to be buried next to such a notable tree among uncounted granite slabs in this War Heroes Cemetery.

Andrei walked slowly, in the tug of Olga's hand. The sadness in her face was unmistakable as she took in the panorama of stone stumps dotting the grounds. YURII FILIPPOVICH SUSLOV 1918-1940. VYACHESLAV MIKHAILOVICH PEGOV 1922-1939. ANDREI ANTONOVICH ZHILIN 1915-1940. One after another, she read names of the fallen as they walked up the slope. So many died in that Winter War with Finland, the dead quickly overwhelmed the War Heroes Cemeteries in Leningrad and Moscow. Petró was reminded again, surveying the countless gravestones, why the boxes of his father and uncles were instead sent east to the newly expanded War Heroes Cemetery here at Gorod. Petró strode briskly as if late for an appointment with the papa with whom he would never again exchange words. But who, he knew, was there ahead at the oak tree to visit, if only in spirit.

Olga smiled when Petró stopped, turned about, then waited for her and slow Andrei. "Perhaps Andrei should carry the chrysanthemums to place on the grave—" he said, seeing his son's reluctance to walk across a landscape of tombstones. "He's here to honor the grandpapa he never saw."

"Yes, you're right." She let go Andrei's hand. The son stopped, unsure what to do. His eyes darted about, evidently seeing nothing to amuse him. "Why are we here?" he bawled out.

"Andrei, not now." Petró knelt down. Held out one bunch of flowers to Andrei's fist, tightly clenched in panic. "Here. Open the hand."

Andrei would have none of it. Didn't want to hold the flowers. Turned and started to walk back down the hill. "Come on, Andrei, we just have a little longer to go."

Soon, they trudged on.

With the oak tree's skeletal presence towering above, Petró stood with Olga and Andrei at the tombstone of his papa.

Petró had come to the same grave this Red Army Holiday every February for fifteen years. Chrysanthemums in his hand, he was at a loss for words. One day he might know the words, but those words never came to mind. Possibly that was the point: He would never forget his papa because he never could say in mere words the truth of the loss he felt.

His papa was more than characters on flat stone: KONDRAT VLADMIROVYCH KRAVETS 1908-1940.

He knelt on the ground and rubbed the fingers of his free hand across the incised letters—the K, the O, the N, the D—and he felt a faintness, a lassitude in his mind, as though in that moment he was forgetting his wife Olga, his small son Andrei, both beside him, and becoming cold where ...

The white snow under the scudded, gray skies was knee-deep. But he slogged on, as he must, for he was on patrol, heavy Army boots encasing his tired feet, two sets of wool socks, still dry. The Finnish snipers were out there. He squinted at the endless birch trees of this Karelian wasteland. He'd yet to see so much as a shed. Who could live here? they joked on the train from Leningrad. Only the dumb Finns would try. Was that why Mother Russia let them have this land back? After more than a century of being a Russian duchy, didn't the Motherland decide the Finns were ungovernable, not worth the bother? No civilized countryman would put up with such a wasteland.

The fur ear flaps of his Army *shapka*, red star on its brim, didn't keep him from hearing the slightest movement, the most delicate of snow crunches. Sound travelled flawlessly in still air. His breath visible when he exhaled, any sniper out there would surely exhale ice fog too. He kept looking, saw nothing but scabby birch trees.

His company sent five scouts out on patrol for the day from camp. They'd bivouacked three days, had yet to see any sign of the Finns. Unless they saw somebody soon, they would pull up camp and march westward into the Karelian forest another twenty kilometers or so and hunt again for the dumb Finns lurking about, toting their Moisin-Nagant rifles, nothing, however, like a Soviet Army issue Kalashnikov.

He'd slung his across his back, the cold metal of its stock too much to keep carrying in two hands on patrol. His gloves moreover, weren't warm. Seeing anybody on this third day of patrol would be better than endless days in this bitter, white wasteland called Karelia.

Yes, nothing but countless birch trees. Skinny, bare-branched trunks, splotched in gray and darker gray against the deathly silence of gray skies and snow.

Kraaaaaccccckkkkk.

Then a wetness at his chest. The falling backward in the deep snow. A cold wet bed held him. Icy snow on his beard. Gray sky overhead. *What is this?*

The ear throbbing slowed. The wet pool on his chest, below his thick wool coat, the hard length of the Kalashnikov pressing on his back. Had to move, couldn't move. *The sky overhead. The Soviet Army defends the Motherland. Soviet Revolution 1917. Starting school. Uncle Lenin. The New Social Order. A civilization of ideals for every man. Yes. Son Petró left behind for this Winter War in Karelia. Coming here, was it months ago? Was snow falling then? No memory when they left the train from Leningrad.*

His head listed to one side. As though a neck ligament released its hold.

The breath intake quit.

The ear throbbing stopped.

The jaw sagged.

The heart chamber refused to pump.

Eyelids wide open. Eyes stone still, glimpsing forever.

Nearby, footsteps crunching snow.

Blue, yellow flag patch on the shoulder.

Kneeling, knowing the shot was sure, through the heart.

The raised hand waved and summoned others among the birch trees.

Kneeling Petró traced his fingertip over the R, the A, then

pressed his thumb on the T.

He raised his fingers to his lips, kissed them lightly.

His father's name: KONDRAT.

The name that was his patronymic. KONDRATOVYCH.

How his father had left, and he, Petró, the son, had only a picture of Papa in his Soviet Army uniform—yes, when he left by train for Leningrad—to recall. But, oh, the return.

He took a deep breath. Oh, the return.

The wooden box, this very spot. He was thirteen, but he would not forget any of it. Everything. The earth was opened. The red and yellow flag draped over the pine box, and he and Mama stood there in the cold when the flag was pulled away, and the box, slung on ropes, lowered into the deep beside the dirt piled high.

He cried. But he knew like so many boys his age, he would grow up having lost a father. He was his mama's boy, the man in the house before he got older and left home. Yes, to start his family, marry Olga, and have his young son here, Andrei. No war for him, no war for Andrei. Life was better, even though his mama, not too many years later, died of what Petró knew was a broken spirit.

Oh, the Finns, they were such blockheads they fought for the Germans. They joined the losing side rather than be occupied as their peace-loving Nordic brothers: the Danes, the Swedes, the Norwegians. What did they get? Despised to this day by other Scandinavians and the Russians. He would never forgive his father's death at the hands of one of those worthless Finns.

He ignored Andrei beside him, who kicked the ground aimlessly.

Petró took the chrysanthemums and placed them in one of the flower holders, available from a large wooden box at the cemetery entrance. A cone-shaped tin receptacle with an attached rod he jabbed in the ground. The white flowers looked nice there, the only bright spot on the dark leaf-strewn ground around the dark marble slab.

"I want to go home, I want to play," Andrei wailed.

Again, Petró ignored his son and stood to his feet. Tears welling, he turned to Olga, who smiled sweetly. He rubbed the top of Andrei's hair. "That's it for this year. I visited Papa, okay?"

He felt a glow of satisfaction in his chest. Somehow, this year, he sensed more of his papa's spirit with him. Something he could take back to work when he and Ivan tackled the important defense project. Something in its own way to keep Mother Russia from having to fight yet another war to defend its people and its lands.

Petró again looked up the hill. They had to find Olga's Uncle Anatolii and Uncle Leonid. "Let's go, Andrei," he said to his recalcitrant son.

13
КОММУНАЛЬНЫЕ ЧЕЛОВЕК
(COMMUNAL MAN)

That evening, Petró was alone in the flat, Olga having taken little Andrei to visit another mom with a young son on the second floor. The strong feelings of having been to his papa's grave lingered. Wasn't it the wordless tug of long-lost years?

But he had work tomorrow. He and Ivan had to give their absolute best if they were to replicate the spy camera well enough to satisfy Dr. Dezhnyova in Moscow. Surely, boss Maks would see a new opportunity to drive them like plow mules. He would be relentless. Petró was unsure how much of the weeks ahead he would enjoy.

Yes, the visit to the War Heroes Cemetery wouldn't let him go.

Petró had only memory of a papa—before that return from Finland in a pine box—he never knew well enough. So as little Andrei grew, he did too—becoming the father for Andrei his papa wasn't given enough time to be for him. Perhaps that was why the memory tugged so. His life was to make up for the father he'd lost.

Petró wanted to relax. But anxious thoughts about work the

next day and the wistful memory from this Red Army Holiday wouldn't leave him alone as he drank tea and listened to the news broadcast from the cabinet radio opposite his bolstered easy chair.

"That's the roundup of world news from Radio Moscow, so as your host, Sergei Kolyashenko, I bid you good evening. Until next time." Throaty march music boomed out the radio speaker, and Petró sipped more of his black tea, no sugar, no cream. Just straight Georgian he got at reasonable cost in bulk from someone he knew in grocery distribution.

Then the march music arrested mid-measure. A woman's voice calmly announced: "Tonight, our program honors Red Army Holiday with a special treat for you, our listeners. A rare recording of Comrade Lenin speaking to the Soviet Army troops October 7, 1922, at the fifth anniversary of the Revolution. Listen with me, please, as we hear those inspiring words from Vladimir Lenin, available to us tonight four decades later through our superb Soviet recording technology."

Petró leaned forward. The march music resumed mid-measure. Then a fadeout, as the scratchy recording began: "Comrades, we engage in a historic struggle for all mankind. Not just for Russians, not just Ukrainians, not just Belorussians, not just Georgians, but for workers everywhere across our great country, the Union of Soviet Socialist Republics, and more and more countries throughout the world—Europe, Asia, the Americas—as the universal Communist ideal takes hold of workers' imaginations everywhere.

"Our future is ours to take!"

Petró gulped more tea, then set the mug on the rickety side table. The words of Comrade Lenin were so vital, he could forget about relaxing. He stood to his feet. As though joining the troops facing Comrade Lenin at the podium.

He stepped across the carpet to the wall opposite the radio cabinet's booming speaker. Comrade Lenin, his voice still strong decades later, even though his remains lay entombed in Red Square under glass. *No, Uncle Lenin is back, across the room.* Petró knew rank upon rank of willing soldiers in brown uniforms with red trim swelled the crowd between him and their Revolutionary hero—Comrade Vladimir Lenin—the radio speaker giving voice and bringing to life that same entombed corpse transported to Petró's flat and now standing atop the wooden cabinet of the radio!

"What is our workers' movement? I ask you. Is it not an expression of what is best for all of us, so our cooperative efforts might build a modern society that benefits everyone, not just property owners, who do no productive work and have no sweat on their brow, but only hands open to grasp rent money? Is it not from the sweat of all our brows that the collective reward of work joyously undertaken is then for all of us?"

Petró stood up straighter, as if the words of Comrade Lenin were lifting him. Taking away the burdens of memory and the holiday. Yes, his father, though young, might have heard the same words rebroadcast only a few years later, when he heard his first radio. The words were timeless, for they spoke to what the Revolution would always be about.

He saluted with the sureness of a shackle lock closing on belief. Every man about him, ready to give life and limb for the Motherland, also brought hand flat against forehead in that instant Comrade Lenin raised his hands to acknowledge the liberators of the proletariat assembled before him. Each man committed to always follow the Marxist-Leninist way of the communal man.

"Comrades, as you shoulder your rifles, as you go about your missions, remember you defend the Motherland against those who deny the march of history proves those who live by the sweat of their brow no longer need be slaves to property owners. Never. This is our Revolution of 1917, these are the days of glory and the days of pride for what we now do for civilization everywhere and for a future sure to be ours!"

Now they would march into the streets of the city. Doing so, they would affirm the truth of their leader's words. The Motherland was theirs to protect, the ideals of the Marxist Revolution were theirs to serve, the respect of countrymen everywhere was theirs to share. They would advance across the globe, pushing back and defeating the capitalists, led by America, everywhere.

Tears came to Petró's eyes. The sacrifice of his papa defending the Motherland. That was for the collective effort Lenin said would bring a better future. Mistakes of mankind misguided for so long were never easy to overcome. But property owners, who made slaves of hard-working laborers and put yokes of oppression on their necks, were sure to be defeated, at last. The American imperialists will be no more.

He paced the floor, the timeless words of Lenin with him.

Yes, this is it! Tomorrow Ivan and I will work hard on the camera replica Dr. Dezhnyova wants. Boss Maks would get caught up in their enthusiasm too. He knew it. *This camera is important for defense of the Motherland. The same cause for which Papa gave his life. Americans must not invade our airspace again.*

Petró wiped his tears with the back of his shirt sleeve, not yet ready to sit down or make more tea.

"Comrades, the Revolution of 1917 means one thing: Our future is ours to take!"

14
БОМБОУБЕЖИЩЕ
(BOMB SHELTER)

The next morning, Petró's steps joined those of others, echoing down a linoleum-surfaced hallway. A few fluorescent lights gave the walls a pallid glow, like walking through a tunnel to his work area. But first he'd stop at the commissary for hot tea, something he needed mornings after putting up with the crowds on Metro.

The commissary room was bright, bringing zest to the start of the day. He stepped up to the cafeteria-style counter and waited his turn. Fellow workers tended to order a light breakfast, paying only a few kopecks. His tea, however, was free. That and coffee, work benefits.

"One tea," he said to the scarf-clad young woman at the cash register. No money to change hands, so she got a porcelain cup, opened the spigot of the tea urn, then offered up a steaming cup.

"Thanks," he said. Her eyes left his and went to the next in line.

Petró stood at the condiments table and noticed where Ivan sat with others. He'd join them. He liked his tea black. Never added milk, but sometimes, like today, a lemon slice was a special extra. His tea cup in hand, he made his way over.

Ivan looked up. "Good morning, Petrush."

Then *Blaarrrrrrre. Blaarrrrrrre. Blaarrrrrrre.* From the hallway loudspeakers.

The tea cup dropped. Spilled tea everywhere. Porcelain breaking, inaudible in the din.

Then, a long, whining air siren from outside.

The blaring hallway speakers. The air siren on the roof. "This is an emergency, this is an emergency," a man's voice echoed from loudspeakers—in the hallway, throughout the commissary. Breathless words.

Petró had to keep his bearings and stay calm. No time for the tea spilled on the floor. They had to leave. Ivan, everyone, walked out into the dim hallway.

At once, from the commissary, from the nearby workrooms, a throng of chattering colleagues—many in white coats over street clothes—made their way through the hallway to where the blue-shield civil defense sign pointed to an open door and stairs that descended to an underground basement. The evacuation room was specially built below a reinforced concrete ceiling, four-meters thick, and supposedly strong enough to take bombardment short of a direct nuclear explosion. One such room was under each building in the Gorod OTS complex.

Petró squeezed in, slipped over against a wall, making room for latecomers. Much like his morning subway ride, endurable only because it was—he wanted to believe—temporary. Except he, Ivan, and the others, fifty or more, had no choice but to wait for loudspeaker instructions.

"I was eager to start work this morning," Petró said, who'd eased over next to Ivan. "Now this."

Ivan shrugged.

"More drills lately, don't you think?"

"Oh, our leaders, they worry—" Ivan replied cryptically.

"Possibly for good reason," Petró said.

They exchanged knowing smiles. Few of those around them knew what the two worked on in Room 74.

Petró and Ivan stopped talking. The minutes crept along, more so because it was a dark, stale basement. Someone said, "The Americans are coming." Then chuckles. Another voice said, "We shoot them down like their spy plane. They should know better." More chuckles.

Even if it was only a drill, Petró knew one day they might be caught by surprise. Then it would be everyone-out-for-themselves chaos. Still they were a defense plant, a potential target.

Then the same male voice from a small loudspeaker on the wall, but calmer, quieter: "Comrades, this has been a practice alert. A practice alert for civil defense evacuation drills. Repeat, this has been a practice alert. If this was a true emergency, you would now hear where to dial on the radio in your evacuation shelter for more instructions. This was a test of our civil defense preparedness drill procedures. Please review with your colleagues the steps you took today to evacuate. Evaluate how you might do better in an emergency that might happen at any time. Your life and that of others around you depends on disciplined execution of these drills. The defense of the Motherland is at stake. Again, this was only an evacuation drill. Please return to your usual workplaces and continue your assigned tasks. Thank you."

They began leaving the basement shelter. Petró noted the dried-food rations stacked against one wall by the hanging air-filter pipes. *How long would fifty people in this room last eating that?* Petró shuddered, thinking that. If he and the others around him even had time to eat. OTS was a prime military target, and one American ICBM surely had their address on it.

Petró pressed his fingertips to his brow and followed the others out. *This civil defense drill was okay, if the missile missed its target. Otherwise, we would be blown to bits.*

The spilled tea still lay on the linoleum, and with a bit of asking, Petró found a mop to clean things up. Then he went for another cup of tea and once again joined Ivan and the others for some chatter.

When they finally got to their work area, Petró and Ivan started drawing up a list of the parts that would have to be manufactured in the months ahead. The lenses were to be supplied from Moscow, Dr. Dezhnyova's optics lab and KMZ taking care of those.

"But this shutter," Petró said, "this is heavy-duty, works with such large lenses."

They studied the mechanism in Petró's hands. They couldn't reuse it in a replica camera. That was not how the work was to be done. The MMA might want more than one camera. Manufacture of all the camera had to go forward and be documented, so other copies could be made.

"Oh, now the tough part, we need notes about how we take this apart," Ivan said.

The rest of the day went quickly. Petró and Ivan looked at each other. They didn't finish taking apart the shutter: too many intricate parts. But the shutter curtain was not unlike the one in the Fedka back in Kharkov. Petró smiled at discovering this, but how were shutter speeds to be set for such a large shutter? This he and Vanya had to learn.

He couldn't wait. They had the Motherland to defend.

15

РОСТ ТРУБЫ
(RISING PIPES)

That evening, on the crowded Metro ride home, Petró, as usual, stood clutching a strap loop. The train *screeeech'd* to a stop and *whoosh*, the doors opened, passengers left, and others entered. The newcomers pushed in, jostling those aboard, trying to find room. Head down, watching his planted feet, Petró glanced up and saw beside him a familiar face, one he'd known for years: Svetlana Zhzhyonova.

Even with the scarf on her head, there was no mistaking those searching eyes he, for one, knew held in check a potentially unbridled passion. They'd been lovers once. He was single, only nineteen. Now, however, she was married to Viktor, a card-issued member of the Communist Party in the Gorod Oblast whose job as public health inspector for restaurants and grocers kept him in touch with many people.

Viktor had pull, *blat*. Petró and others saw him as important. He knew bureau apparatchiks; he knew how to move the levers; he made things happen.

"Petya," Svetlana said, addressing him by his familiar name, for it had been that way with them. "A pleasure we ride the subway together," she said, her eyes raking him over, as though she, years later, would never forget.

He glanced away, knowing some of Svetlana's posturing as a woman was just Svetlana: when in that mood, addicted to the thrill of the sexual chase. But he was married. If she wanted tease, okay, but there could be no more. He was willing to indulge her fantasy only as debt owed for the past they shared.

Again, he looked her in the eye. "Odd I don't see you more often. I ride this train back and forth to work. You?"

"No, I don't usually ride this train. I had an errand downtown." The subway car swayed, shuddered; but the steady, gray eyes of Svetlana hung on his, like summoning embraces from the past, because she knew he'd known the promise beneath her taut, violet sweater.

"So how has Svetlana been?"

She shrugged.

"Well, how's Viktor?"

"Oh, Viktor, don't mention Viktor—"

"His important job, he busy?"

"I don't know, he's off in Moscow. All week." She gave him a look that might make pancakes. "I'm by myself."

"Oh," he said.

"Bored stiff. You—" She quickly looked away, releasing the lock of her eyes on his.

An electric thrill shot up his spine, and he gaped, his tongue tasting something in the stuffy air he never expected to be there. Her hand, her delicate hand, pressed against the small of his back, as if she were drunk and needed Petró to keep her standing.

"Sveta," he said, despite himself, using her familiar name, "I value the friendship of you and Viktor."

She didn't reply at first, just kept leaning on him in the rocking subway.

"Oh, yes, Viktor, everyone likes Viktor. He makes arrangements. He knows who does what, what they want. I call him Comrade Arranger." She laughed nervously, then said, "But I'm bored."

Again, she pressed her hand into his back, as if ready to usher him into her flat for a drink.

"You know, what Rykovich once wrote, that famous poem of his—"

She looked at him with an intensity that was much more than curiosity.

"He said—" Petró paused. "I forget the exact words, about the pleasure of the moment and then the pain that won't go away. Such a true thought. How many foolishly make such a trade for enduring pain? We're different, no?"

"But, Petya, it's no moment for me. It's a long time. I'm fed up."

"Any marriage has challenges—"

"But I'm married to this cold Party hack. At first, I thought he was what I had with you. But no, now he's as cold as good old Gorod winter nights. I feel the passion in me dies one day at a time. It's torture, don't you understand?"

Petró looked at Svetlana with soft eyes, for he felt she was trapped in a loveless marriage. But what they had and threw away was gone. They were each married, for better, for worse.

He nodded his head slowly, mostly to acknowledge his sorrow about her suffering.

"You remember how it was, the two of us?" she asked.

A minute or so later, Svetlana got off at her stop, and Petró remembered.

He had arrived in Gorod a year before at the ripe old age of eighteen, having left the Ukraine, ready to start his military service assignment as a security guard doing graveyard shifts at the same military complex where he worked to this day.

Single and knowing almost nobody, Petró regularly went to a dance hall on Saturday nights. He was there to meet girls. Sometimes it worked out: He'd meet someone. But usually, it didn't. In any case, there was vodka to drink. Saturdays soon became drinking night.

After he'd been going to the dance hall on Brigada Street for months, the picky finger of luck surprised him, tapping his shoulder.

Her name was Svetlana Ardankina.

Tall—maybe even a centimeter taller than he—she had about her a fluidity he found hypnotic. Some womanly grace of movement and a superb dancer of the Argentinean tango. He always felt in heaven when holding her. Her hair, cut short, didn't cover the nape of a neck he found worthy of contemplation. And after they met at the hall for the second time, he asked to walk her home. They had drank far too much, but he sensed, behind her wooziness, she liked him.

They meandered back to the front steps of her block, where she lived with the folks, and standing there below the feeble street light, his inhibitions, relaxed as they were, left him bold enough to kiss her lips. She didn't resist. But she also didn't respond.

"It's late," she said matter-of-factly. "My parents must be asleep. Everyone else is."

Still, *that* October night wasn't that cold out, and she didn't seem in a rush to leave him. Petró wanted to talk more, so he pressed on.

"I wish I could buy you something, do something besides just walk you home, but military service, it doesn't pay well. I don't have a kopeck to my name. Let me show you."

She blushed at his honesty and appeared willing to listen a while longer.

He pulled out his wallet and opened it.

Her jaw dropped, and her eyes darted about like small fishes.

For there in the fold of his wallet, where he would have liked to have a fistful of rubles, was something he'd forgotten. What he'd bought months ago, when he began going to the dance hall to meet girls: a lambskin condom. Pristine with its original sprinkling of powder inside. Untested.

"Oh, what you want you want for free," she said, a bit of a tease in her voice. "Here, kiss me again."

He snapped his wallet closed, dropped it in his coat pocket, took his tall dance partner in his arms and went for those thick sensuous lips like the morning sun need never rise again.

Breathless, she stood back from him, looked him up and down. "I've never done this."

"Me neither," he replied, the truth or a lie, it didn't matter; he wanted her to feel that they might have a mutuality of adventurous spirit.

"But I don't know. Someone with experience might be easier for me," she said.

He didn't answer, simply pulled her close again and kissed. The kiss was like falling off a cliff. Only the need to breathe would stop them, so suffocating was their passion in the moment.

She pulled away. "I know a place inside."

"What?" *Is this a dream?* Petró's eyes went shock-open.

"Yes, the boiler room in the basement, this building. Empty at night. Noisy, but empty."

"But isn't the boiler room locked?"

"Yes, but I know where the superintendent hides the key. Come with me."

She needed to say no more. Petró followed lanky Svetlana down the hallway, down the stairwell, down to where she took a key off the top of a fire extinguisher mounted on the wall. She unlocked the door, opening it quietly, and waved him to enter. Then let the door close to, click. She pulled the light cord. Before them, the inferno of a coal-fired furnace heated the steam boiler, and endless pipes branched across the ceiling, bound for the five floors overhead. But off to the side, by the wall, a cot. It even had a pillow and blankets. Evidently, the superintendent put it there to nap on the job.

In the dim light, Svetlana held up the key. "His only one. With the door closed, nobody gets in." She smiled. He was taken with how her high cheekbones were in such harmony with the strong line of her jaw.

She drew him close to kiss again.

He was breathless when she stepped back and slipped off her coat, letting it drop to the floor. Kicked off her shoes. Then she sat on the edge of the cot and began taking off the rest of her clothes.

Petró had to catch up.

When she finally unhooked her brassiere, and exquisite breasts slipped forward from her soft shoulders, Petró felt an unstoppable stiffening in his loins. He was as hard as a steel pipe. He couldn't think anymore about what was next.

Away from the small cot, the furnace ceaselessly turned hard black lumps of coal into fire, boiling water for steam and Petró was ready to explode like a boiler.

16
ВЫТЕКАЮЩЕЙ ТУАПЕТЕ
(LEAKY TOILET)

The youthful affair with Svetlana ran its course. Petró accepted the inevitable: She was looking for a secure future, something better than what everybody else had with dreary waits in line to buy food. No soldier boy, no Petró for her!

So Svetlana's pragmatic ways with men—the same initiative she showed seducing Petró—led her to also abandon him after six months for a guy with connections, one who would be her meal ticket and guarantee a future not complicated by waiting in queues: Viktor Zhzhyonov. Viktor was a card-issued member of the Party and had *blat*: He was plugged-in, and so he and Svetlana didn't need to live—suffer—like everyone else.

When she left, she said she was too young to get serious, to be tied down. She wanted to have more friends. He wasn't surprised, though, when she married Viktor, not even a year later.

Still the memory of leggy Svetlana walking away haunted Petró until he met Olga.

Olga was different. She didn't have Svetlana's lithe sexiness. No, she was more the young woman with a good heart, whose word would always be golden. Petró knew this had to be the woman who would go the distance with him. They became engaged two years later. But before he was ready for marriage, Petró wanted to know where he'd get a work assignment once he finished his national service. Only after he was assigned to the Optics Test Station, secure work for national defense, did he and Olga set a date.

Surprisingly, the wedding took place in the same dance hall where Petró met Svetlana. Olga's parents' idea was to rent the place and have the ceremony and registration done by a local magistrate, Grigory Nomolov, known for his effusive pronouncement of wedding vows.

So that Sunday afternoon, years ago, at two in the afternoon, Petró stood in his best brown suit, white shirt, and black tie in the outer lobby of the dance hall, sitting on a long, low bench with his best man, Ivan, ready to stand up for the march music and walk the aisle between the rows and rows of fold-up chairs set out for the occasion.

More than fifty came—relatives, friends, co-workers—many motivated, Petró thought, by the prospect of ample good food afterwards.

Minutes later, Petró stood, his back to the crowd, facing Magistrate Nomolov. The music resumed, and he turned to see his bride, Olga Pavelova, walking toward him, wearing a showy, white gown, whose likes must have been rented by the day.

The solemn steps of Olga brought her closer, slow, slow steps—even though the joyous music urged her to quicken—as steady as sand grains falling in an hourglass. That was how it was done as marriage was for keeps.

At last, she stood beside him, the two facing the magistrate, ready to hear the words they knew well from other weddings, except this time the vows were theirs. "Marriage is a permanent contract under Soviet law and not one to be entered impulsively or lightly. So I would like you, Petró, and you, Olga, to listen to my words, keeping in mind the decisions you each make are for your lifetime."

Petró gazed over at Olga, who in turn had eyes only for him. A softness when their eyes met, as if the cosmos deemed in that moment and for eternity they'd be together.

Before long, what the magistrate was to say, what they were to say, was said. Petró bent close and kissed Olga long on the lips. She blushed, as she would, feeling strong emotion.

Olga then turned to face the crowd, and her bridesmaid handed her a scarf. Olga took the scarf and placed it over her hair, tying the ends below her chin. She then reached out and took Petró's hand. The blue scarf on her head—a Russian folk tradition—signified from that moment on, as long as Petró lived, she was his woman and his alone. She'd live a long life and become a proper babushka. She smiled as only a woman who had got her man could.

Moments later, they were walking down the aisle, ready to share their happiness with everyone. In an adjoining room, they would cut the wedding cake and partake of bounteous food, whose likes nobody would see again except on another such occasion. That Olga's parents were able to get such extraordinary fare and drink was because of Petró's willingness to call on Viktor Zhzhyonov, who sat in the crowd with his wife, Svetlana.

He left the Metro, the indulgence in memories, and trudged the last steps to his flat and looked up the side of his seven-story block housing, admiring the new mural that rose overhead. A fair-haired man, seemingly fifty-feet tall, dressed in overalls, stood with a scythe in one hand, a sheaf of wheat stalks in the other; his wife, shorter, a scarf about her hair, beside him with a young infant clutched in her arms. THE FUTURE FOR RUSSIA, the caption read.

Petró smiled. *Yes, that could be me, Olga, and little Andrei, but it isn't. Young Russian couples don't live on farms anymore.*

People left that hard life for cities like Gorod. There was no turning back. A tractor did the work of a dozen oxen, or the work of a dozen times a dozen men with a hoe. The future this mural so proudly proclaimed was gone. The future for Russia was, well, what he was doing. But that up there was art for art's sake. He shrugged and went in the building.

After a satisfying dinner—one of Olga's best—fish with cheese and mushrooms, Petró settled into his easy chair by the big Popov wooden console radio, a mug of Georgian tea in hand. The radio had shortwave and AM reception, but invariably was tuned to Radio Moscow, the strongest signal on the dial. Petró, as he got older, became a news junkie. After a nice dinner, he liked to have his news and tea. Moreover, tonight he was not going to join the guys in the TV room downstairs. That meeting with Svetlana—all the memories dredged up—threw him off-kilter. He wanted to find his old equilibrium and stay in the same room with Olga, exchanging smiles.

Son Andrei had already finished eating what he felt like eating and sat in the corner of the room, surrounded by a scattering of toy soldiers. Every now and then, he'd toss one of the soldiers in the air and make an explosive noise. Petró took a sip of tea. *Does he know land mines toss real soldiers in the air?*

Possibly his son was innocent about land mines and simply wanted to scatter his toy soldiers, so he could pick them up later.

Petró clicked on the radio's VOLUME knob and waited a few seconds. He saw the vacuum tubes through the vented side of the console warm up, get orange-hot. Then he could fine-tune the other knob to bring in Radio Moscow loud and clear.

Losing Laika   85

"The Ministry of Mineral Resources reported today iron production in the Belgorod region for the last six months is up four percent from last year, making the aggregate tonnage the best in history. The total of six point three thousand metric tons earned the Governor of the Belensky Mines a trip to Moscow this week for a ceremony in which he received the Hero of the Socialist Labor and the Order of Lenin medals for an outstanding contribution to Soviet economic progress."

The newsreader ruffled papers before the microphone. Petró sipped more tea, wondered how anybody doing classified work for the military like he and Ivan could ever be recognized publicly, if what they did was hush-hush, even in their own families. They were working on a spy camera, not mining iron. He didn't care. What juicy beef steaks would those medals buy anyway?

"Also in Moscow," the newsreader continued, "Soviet Premier Nikita Khrushchev suggested in an interview with a *New York Times* correspondent that the American spy plane pilot, Francis Gary Powers, captured and imprisoned last year, might not serve his full ten-year sentence."

The tea mug in Petró's right hand quivered. He could've spilled but didn't.

"Premier Khrushchev said the U-2 spy plane pilot, Powers, has been interrogated by Soviet intelligence and offers little value if he serves the rest of the prison sentence. This hint of leniency for Francis Gary Powers by Premier Khrushchev was well-received by Americans and interpreted as another sign of the Kremlin's willingness to improve relations with America and its new president, John Fitzgerald Kennedy, who took office in January of this year. Until more develops on this matter of international relations, Francis Gary Powers will remain in Vladimir Central Prison, 250 kilometers east of Moscow."

Petró sat up straighter. Something connected to his work was in the news. He looked over at Olga, who knew nothing about where he went last May Day.

Yes, her face showed no interest in the newsreader's words.

He again sipped his tea with contentment. But he couldn't wait to ask Ivan tomorrow what he thought about the U-2 pilot Powers possibly getting out early and going back to America.

"We also have a report, just in, the Russian national hockey team has defeated Finland, three to one, in the European championships held this week in Stockholm. So the hockey team can expect a big welcome when they arrive at Domodedovo Airport on Thursday. That's the news from Radio Moscow and once again, your host, Pavel Kulakov, wishes you good evening."

After drinking all that tea, Petró needed to relieve himself. He had to use the toilet down the hall. A communal toilet, stalls for men, stalls for women next door, and an overused shower was not the most convenient arrangement, but Petró consoled himself: At least it was indoors. In the countryside, the poor souls made do with an outhouse. In the snow, that was no fun.

"I'll be back soon," he said as he stepped into the hallway and closed the door.

Brightly lit, the bathroom had a floor of white hexagonal tiles, which also rose halfway up the walls. But the grimy tiles asked for a wash of bleach solution every month, every week. Petró didn't know what it would take, if clean tiles were the goal.

One of the men's stalls was occupied, so Petró went to the other.

A mop leaned against the wall. Water, faintly tinted, puddled about the base of the toilet. Petró felt like gagging: This was the leaker and recently used.

He studied the water, spread and positioned his feet just so—as if he were dancing with a fat woman—unbuttoned his trousers, then commenced his business. His stream was strong and into the bucket. But as for the leaky base, what was to be done? All the world's complaints to the superintendent of Public Housing No. 17 in Gorod were pointless. The toilet repair was scheduled.

The question was, What year would the toilet be fixed?

He stared at the toilet bowl, the yellowness, and braced himself, as he bent forward and flushed, knowing what would happen next. Sure, the flush swirled in the bowl, but slowly the lake at the base grew larger, making it worse for the next guy who took a leak or—if he was the guy the gypsy said would have a week of unrivalled bad luck—who wanted to sit down and take a crap.

The complaints about the toilet started six months earlier. Some men, seeing the good one occupied, were not like Petró. They would not use the leaker. They'd wait or even go next door and use the women's toilet. Others, more easily embarrassed, went to another floor.

Something had to be done, but he had no authority. He stepped outside the stall, fastening the last button on his trousers flap and saw his neighbor Egor, who had finished too. Egor paused to hold up to the light his flask bottle of vodka and gauge what was left.

"The toilet gets worse, and they'll never fix it," Petró complained to the familiar face from the TV room.

"I don't bother with that one," Egor said, uncapping his bottle of vodka and taking a swig. He held out the bottle to Petró, who accepted and took a small taste, but only out of courtesy.

"You know what they told me when I complained?"

"No, what?"

"They said it's scheduled. If acceptable stalls are occupied, I must go to another floor. They said this!"

"This is what we get living in State housing. This would never happen if we lived privately like a Party member. They get their toilets fixed like that." He clicked his fingers, took another swig of vodka, then held out the bottle to Petró, who again obliged.

Egor, a burly man, his hair dark, tousled, gave Petró a searching look with his coal eyes, as if he were a boxer, sizing up an opening for another punch. But they were friends, or at least hallmates.

"You know, we could fix that toilet ourselves." A sly grin crossed his lips, through which passed another sip. He held out the bottle.

"We don't fix toilets," Petró said. "Pipes, water. Plumbers do that. We do it wrong, we might flood this place." He gasped, then took another obliging sip.

"True, what you say is true, Comrade. But if the State cannot offer plumbing services, we workers might have to take matters into our own hands."

"What do you mean?"

"All we do is turn off the water, disconnect everything, and pull up the toilet. We replace the seal underneath."

"How do you know this?" Petró stared at Egor, having no idea how this now resolute neighbor, so given to tippling vodka and floating through the evening aglow, knew this.

"Oh, last week, I was out front talking to a fellow who lives on the first floor—"

"Yeah?"

"Fedor, he's a plumber." Egor took another sip, held out the bottle again. "He knows how to fix it!"

"Will he do that?"

"No, he can't. He said if they found out he did, he'd lose his job. He can't work anywhere else."

"So if we try to fix it, what good is he?"

"He can get the beeswax seal. Bring it home from work."

"And watch us fix the toilet?"

"No, he only gets us started."

They finished the last of the vodka, standing there on the dingy white tile floor. "We should fix it soon," Petró said, suddenly enthused he might not have to skirt a urine-tinged puddle anymore.

17
ИСПРАВЛЕНИЕ ПЧЕЛИНЫМ ВОСКОМ
(BEESWAX FIX)

The next evening at the problem toilet, Petró and Egor met with skinny Fedor, the plumber. He said he only gave advice: Turn off the water valve. Disconnect the pipe. Take out the water in the toilet. Then remove the two threaded nuts holding the toilet down. Lift it up, and set it aside. Replace the beeswax seal. Then put everything back together.

The way Fedor described it, the job would take less than an hour. But as Fedor cautioned: "Pray hard when you finish. Nothing must leak." He laughed and promised to bring home a seal for them.

The next Sunday afternoon, Petró and Egor were back in the men's bathroom of the third floor, ready to tackle the job. They had on shirts and pants one patch away from being discards. They even put an OUT OF ORDER sign on the stall door of the leaker. Egor had brought home a few wrenches from work to make the job easier. He set down the tools, so he and Petró could talk their way through the steps. Once under way, there would be no turning back if things went wrong, What plumber would fix it? Not Fedor.

Petró studied once more the beeswax seal, wrapped in brown paper stamped GOROD PLUMBING AND ELECTRICAL REPAIR STATION. In his hands, the seal was certifiably stolen property. But they had a job to do.

With a big, ham-sized sponge and a bucket, they set about taking the water out of the toilet. Egor turned off the water-supply valve by the wall. Kneeling, he managed to avoid the leaks on the floor because they'd laid out newspapers to soak up water. "Okay, water supply is off. Now we do this." He pushed down the flush lever, and water emptied out of the tank. Egor set the top cover off to the side. A little water remained on the bottom.

Egor pushed the sponge into the tank, then squeezed it in the bucket Petró held.

"Now the ugly part," he said, eyeing the toilet bowl. Encrusted with years of mineral deposits, much doubtless from vodka-drinking visitors, the bowl had a wonderful reddish-green hue of decay. But it was full of water.

Egor sponged out the water. Petró took the water bucket to the next toilet to dump. Soon the bowl was empty.

Slowly, slowly, Egor set to turning the two encrusted, wastewater-corroded nuts holding the toilet fast to the floor.

"Damn, I hope this works."

Soon, the two threaded bolts, each side of the toilet were free of the securing nuts. The toilet was ready to lift. They each grabbed half and with a *huff* brought the toilet forward and put it on the floor in front of the stall.

Before them, on the floor, was the stark reality of what a toilet means. A gaping hole in the floor, where the soil pipe came up and joined a flange plate capped by the problem seal. The remaining beeswax seal was beyond hope, broken, and misshapen. No wonder the toilet leaked.

Petró unwrapped the new seal. A big flat doughnut of wax, it felt soft. Egor set to scraping away the old one with the end of a screwdriver.

"Here, put this with the paper wrapper," he said, handing over the pieces and scrapings of the dead seal.

"Give me the new one."

Egor centered the new beeswax doughnut over the soil pipe and the floor flange.

"Okay, we'll drop the toilet on these two bolts, and it better seal up tight." Egor said.

"Yes, every toilet in Russia probably has a beeswax seal like this," Petró said. "They're all alike. Standardized fittings are how our country manufactures." Petró remembered standardization as the Soviet way from his days putting together FEDs in Kharkov. He knew of what he spoke.

Next, they lifted the toilet and holding it directly above the twin bolts, began lowering, slowly, until they couldn't see the mounting bolts under the toilet bowl sides.

"This is not something to do by touch," Egor said, not wanting to ruin the delicate wax seal by placing the toilet wrong.

They raised the toilet and set it aside.

"I know what we'll do," Egor said. "Just a minute."

He returned, a brick in each hand, bricks used in the laundry room for doorstops. "Borrowing."

He put one in front and one behind where the toilet was to sit. "There, now we again lower."

The toilet then sat on the two bricks, but just above the floor bolts. A bit tippy. Both men kneeled and could see a slight push to the right and the toilet holes and bolts would line up as though they were made for each other.

"Ready to take out the bricks?" Petró asked. "I'll hold, you pull them."

Petró strained, holding up the toilet. Egor edged out the two bricks, then stood up to help Petró. "Okay, lower," Egor said.

They did, and Egor replaced and tightened the nuts on the bolts.

"Now, as Fedor says, We pray hard." He laughed, reconnecting the water pipe to the toilet and turning on the valve.

The tank began filling with water. Nothing leaked.

A smile danced across Egor's face.

"I think we might have a chance," Petró said.

The water finally shut off; the tank was full. Egor put on the cover.

They peered at the discolored toilet bowl, again filled with water.

"The test," Egor said.

With a flourish of his hand, he pushed the flush lever.

The water ran out, and soon the tank refilled.

They studied the side of the toilet.

Nothing. Dry.

"I think it's done," Egor said.

Egor kept smiling, then produced a flask of vodka from the coat he'd left by the wall.

In days to follow, Petró took great pride, as his colleague Ivan heard, in having fixed a toilet at his flat. It wasn't as though the governing procedures for plumbing repairs had been thwarted. No, around him, everyday, he would see others who went about fixing broken refrigerators, broken stoves, not to mention what he and Egor did with a toilet. Like them, others could not wait, or, more probably, afford to pay for a repairman to fix what went wrong.

But one of the hallmarks of Russian manufacturing, with which Petró lived, was that everything was designed to be as durable as the machinery of first manufacture: farm tractors. Refrigerators could not break for lack of an obscure, unfixable, unobtainable part. No, they were built to be fixed, re-fixed, and then re-fixed.

With some of this sense of how, in the Soviet tractor tradition, things must be made, Petró and Ivan went about recreating the captured spy camera from the American high-flying plane.

They struggled.

"Look at this," Ivan would say, holding up a tab of plastic he guessed either a spacer, an insulator, or nothing. "Why such plastic crap? This does nothing. And still we need to make it?"

"Yes, this camera is full of stupid plastic parts," Petró would reply. "The Americans use cheap materials. Only the lenses are first-rate. The rest is crap. You know in their capitalist system, Natalya says only the company that has the lowest price gets the order."

"Yeah, and it shows," Ivan would say. "Most of what's in here isn't the quality of our cameras. You see parts already rusting? Cheap American junk. No wonder that plane got shot down." He would shake his head.

And so Petró and Ivan spent the rest of the year replicating the American spy plane camera. Many problems had to do with finding who could make the seemingly insignificant parts—usually plastic and disposable in appearance—that over and over caused Ivan to say, "We would never make it like this."

And yet they did, almost a full year after Francis Gary Powers parachuted out of his spy plane.

18
НОЧЬ КОСМОНАВТА
(NIGHT OF THE COSMONAUT)

A spring night in April of 1961 was one Petró would never forget. After that day, Petró and every other citizen of Gorod knew the world in which they lived changed. Earlier that day, the brave Soviet cosmonaut Yuri Gagarin sat atop a towering Petrograd rocket in his tiny capsule and rode a thunderous burst of flames toward the heavens above, hurtling him into black space, where his lonely cabin detached, then tumbled around the earth six times before he safely returned. All as planned. Yuri was the first man in space.

Chernozem Street, in front of their housing block, was aswarm with celebrants: men, women, children, many waving red and yellow Soviet flags. This was a moment for the Motherland. Petró, Olga, and little Andrei, clutching his mama, were out there on the street, milling about, talking with their neighbors, knowing the moment was years in the making.

For Petró, this was *the* triumph of Soviet technology and proved finally the superiority of Soviet socialist science. Nobody could doubt the Soviet rocket scientists were not the best in the world.

"Here, Comrade," his neighbor and fellow toilet-lifter said, holding out his liter of Rodnik, Moscow's best. Egor wavered on his legs, but it mattered little, for the smile on his lips was the payoff for the hard life he had and could endure.

Petró took a sip. The vodka was the finest. Egor's choice entirely suited the occasion. "Egor," he said, taking his arm off his dear Olya, her face a mix of joy and apprehension about the happy chaos enveloping her. "After today, nobody can ever doubt the might of the Union of Soviet Socialist Republics. First in space, first in rocketry, and first in—" he hesitated to say more, knowing what he knew from working at OTS was restricted and secret, "and, yes, proving to those Americans our country's best!"

Egor took another long swig from his bottle.

Then spontaneously, the hundreds who gathered in the street began singing a song in memory of the many Russian soldiers who died in past wars defending the Motherland:

"Motherland hears, Motherland knows,
Where in the clouds her son is flying,
Full of friendly caresses and tender love—"

Petró joined with Egor, belting out the words with an intensity that no other day would so prove the truth of the song: Motherland's son was flying beyond where the clouds reached, into the heart of the cosmos.

"With her eyes of red Moscow Kremlin stars,
Kremlin towers' stars,
She watches you—"

No band, no orchestra, just hundreds of voices, singing as though no sound, other than human voices, could express the emotion in that moment. Petró looked down and saw little Andrei, standing free of his mama's hand, looking heavenward. *Oh, sweet Andrei wants Cosmonaut Yuri to still be up there, waving down at*

us from his space cabin. Oh, if it could be so.
Petró took a deep breath, singing again:
"Motherland hears, Motherland knows,
How her son wins his hard-fought victory,
He never gives in!
By all your destiny you secure,
You defend
The great cause of peace."

The singing went on, then paused after someone with a loudspeaker down the street made an announcement that kept the party going for hours more: "Everyone, listen. We just heard from Radio Moscow that Cosmonaut Gagarin, who's safely back with us, will speak to the Russian people soon. Preparations are under way now. Listen!"

And so Radio Moscow was hooked up to the loudspeaker, adding to the celebratory singing a recap of nonstop details about Yuri's return from his trip into the heavens, after circumnavigating the world as the new outer-space Magellan. The explorer who defied gravity, who had no need for a ship on the waters.

Beside him, Andrei kept staring agape at the darkness above. *What is he looking at?*

Petró kneeled, as if he might see through four-year-old eyes.

Andrei stopped squinting heavenward; his eyes, large and dreamy, turned to Petró.

"Papa," he said insistently.

"What is it, Andreika?"

"I looked a long time, Papa. There's no man up there."

"No, Andreika, Cosmonaut Gagarin is back here. He'll speak on the radio soon—"

Andrei looked puzzled.

"Just wait."

Andrei's dreamy eyes convinced Petró this was a wondrous night for all the Soviet Union, especially Andrei. Would Petró tell his young son his eyes couldn't see that far? No, the night of the cosmonaut wasn't the night to tell Andrei he saw things wrong.

He patted Andrei's towhead and stood up.

Even with the blare of Radio Moscow's breathless announcer in the background, the party and singing would not stop. Nor would the vodka.

Egor held out his empty bottle. He smiled, as miraculously his other hand found a full one. "Where do you get this?" Petró asked. It was fine vodka. "Oh, Viktor. The Party wants us to celebrate and has opened up the vodka stores. That's what he says."

Petró knew Svetlana's husband, Viktor Zhzhyonov, was a schemer and probably knew a way to appropriate the vodka from central stores without getting caught. But so what? This was the night to celebrate.

"Russia's best," Egor said, his words slurred.

"Yes, we've shown the world the future, our technology, our science," Petró said, repeating words he'd heard a hundred times listening to Radio Moscow, but now the words were true. Cosmonaut Yuri proved the stock phrases Petró heard from Radio Moscow had, at last, true meaning.

"America must catch up," Egor said.

"America will never catch up," Petró quickly replied, taking another long swig of Egor's vodka. *But America's aggression will never go away.* That sobering idea was prompted by all the work on lenses for spy satellites yet to be done at OTS.

"*Motherland hears, Motherland knows*
What her son finds along the way ... "

The spontaneous singing, the street drinking, the blaring loudspeaker with Radio Moscow—it all continued late into that

April night, and Petró knew everything was different.

19
МАЛЫЙ ПАКЕТ
(SMALL PACKET)

Once Cosmonaut Yuri Gagarin successfully orbited earth, the Ministry of Military Aeronautics had ambitions for outer space missions seemingly as lofty as the heavens above. Which was good for Petró: He and Ivan worked on the cameras that were to go into orbit.

Moreover, Petró and Ivan were, once again, to be personally briefed by Dr. Natalya Dezhnyova and General Savvin. Or so Petró understood. He sat at a table in the otherwise unoccupied meeting room with Ivan and their boss, Maksym Belenko, ready to hear news about their work.

A squeal came from the gray, metal door, inset with a small wire-mesh window. Petró wasn't positive who opened the door, then he was. For in walked sleek, black-suited Natalya. Not only brainy, but easy on the eyes. Beside her lissom figure and swift steps plodded the shorter General Savvin, a red-starred brown cap on his head, which he took off and set down on the table across from them. He and Natalya took seats.

"We're here for a simple reason," Savvin began in his gruff

voice. "The MMA leadership council met recently, and we gave a five-year plan for orbiting reconnaissance sputniks, and, Comrade Belenko, your team of Ivan Shynkarchuk and Petró Kravets is included.

"No one knows about this plan except a select few in MMA and the big shots at the top in Moscow." He smiled with a goofy look, meaning ol' Nikita himself. "As of eighteen-thirty yesterday, we have successfully launched into orbit our first Zenit 2 reconnaissance satellite, and we expect to retrieve pictures from the capsule when it drops out of orbit in a few days—"

He paused, looked his audience over. "Yes, it's true our brave Cosmonaut Gagarin, a year ago, showed the world the Motherland leads America in space exploration. Yet nobody talks about America orbiting spy satellites after we shot down their U-2." He smiled. "But as of yesterday, we, too, have our reconnaissance satellite up there. More are on the way."

He then turned to Natalya. "Perhaps you can explain the technical details. But before you do, I want to stress one thing. The whole world will soon know what the public is to call the Kosmos 4—not the Zenit 2—satellite. We can't hide a satellite. Everyone can look up and see it move across the sky. But nobody, except those in this room and the design team, knows this satellite's real purpose. Security clearances must stay in place. Okay, Dr. Dezhnyova, please—"

"Thank you, General. Today is a happy day. The launch of Zenit 2 with its five excellent cameras—four 1000-millimeter lenses, one 200-millimeter lens—culminates the work of Comrades Kravets and Shynkarchuk. We now have an orbiting satellite, but even that's changing."

"What do you mean?" Ivan asked.

"Very simple, Comrade Shynkarchuk. In a few years, we won't

wait until the satellite returns to earth, then develop film. The satellites will go up for permanent orbit, and we'll use telemetry to return the scanned images by radio signals. But your job, as you did so well with this satellite, is still assembly of cameras. They, of course, will always make imaging possible."

"If I may interject, Doctor," General Savvin said. "I agree, the camera and its lens are everything. Without the best possible camera, we can have fancy telemetry but just see garbage. These two men across from me I must commend as they are two of the best optics technicians in the Soviet Union, trained as young men in the FED commune—"

Natalya shot Savvin a withering look as if he was getting carried away and missing the point of the meeting.

"Ahem, I don't mean to say anything more than the telemetry, the rockets are nothing if we don't put together the best lenses in space to look down on us. Thanks to you two, we do. On this, we must agree."

The general looked back at Natalya and gave her the broadest of smiles.

"Yes, as the general will outline later, the five-year Zenit satellite program calls for a number of launches. Many are needed because of the constraints of the orbit path and the different surveys we want to conduct," she said, using the euphemism of "surveys" for the unavoidably obvious plans of espionage. Petró smiled.

"This afternoon, I'll meet with Comrades Kravets and Shynkarchuk and go over the thinking about the latest designs you'll work with for some time. Okay?"

Petró and Ivan were buoyant after they walked away from work that evening.

"We did it!" Ivan said, hunkered over against the cold, fur flaps of his old military-issue *shapka* hugging his brow and ears. He had on a heavy gray wool coat and a scarf wrapped about his neck. Scattered snow from the last storm covered the sidewalk.

"Yes," Petró, dressed the same, replied in a whisper, not because it was *that* cold, but because he and Ivan worked on confidential projects. Nobody must overhear them.

"The camera sputnik's up there," Petró said. He pointed to the darkening sky and the planet Venus making her early appearance in the clear night, "We put it there, its eyes assembled with these hands." Petró held up his gloved hands and, in one, a small packet.

"You think we'll get better pay?" Ivan asked, always the pragmatist. He glanced around to see if anybody was nearby. Nobody was. They had reached Narodniki Prospekt. Petró had farther to walk for his subway.

"Of course not," Petró hissed. "The military always has new money for up there, but nothing for us, we who walk down here. Ha. Ha."

"But things cost more now, and we met our goal."

"What did Marx say? 'From each according to his abilities, to each according to his needs.'" Petró smiled, *How could anybody argue with Marx?*

"Yes, but who's more equal than others?"

"No, the only way we'll get more pay is if our job changes classification."

"Okay. So we make our job more important to change it."

"Maks, the sourpuss, won't help."

"He's no help, I agree."

"Oh, I leave you here, there's your bus stop," Petró said, pointing to a sidewalk shelter on the other side of the boulevard.

"Yes, Comrade," Ivan said. "Oh, before I forget, what're you taking home?" he said, pointing to Petró's small packet.

"Oh, *this*? I'll tell only you. I borrowed some tools from work, little project at home I'll get to when I'm not so tired."

"For your sake, I hope nobody saw you leave with that—" Ivan chuckled.

"Well, I could say it was a mistake."

They slapped each other on the back and parted, Petró continuing along Narodniki to his East-West line subway stop.

20
ПЛАТОН КИНО
(PLATO CINEMA)

Petró decided they all would go to the movies. Andrei could sit through a movie at a Sunday matinée. So that became a family outing.

The three took the Metro downtown and walked up wide Decembrists Prospekt to the Plato Cinema, a swooping monument to Russian Futurist architecture, its columns soaring three stories high. Petró stood at the glass booth and bought two tickets. Andrei was free.

Petró handed blue-scarved Olga a ticket. She held Andrei's hand, his eyes agog and sparkling under the marquee lights. This was not like being in their flat. This was luxury for the masses, opulence as might have been enjoyed by the tsars during their heyday. But the Revolution changed that and returned a few such luxuries to the people, to the workers.

At the entrance, a red-serge-suited theater attendant tore the tickets in half, putting stubs in the slot of a stylish silver canister by his side.

What the lobby held for them was something that always

surprised Petró. A world different from where he worked and where he lived. The great space rose overhead to a second-floor mezzanine above the far wall. The length of the lobby sported twinkling chandelier after chandelier, and at the far end, velvet-topped, stuffed benches for Olga and Andrei to sit while Petró went to buy popcorn.

Petró handed one of the three small bags to Andrei.

"Don't spill it," Olga told her son.

Andrei walked unsteadily at first, his eyes locked on the bag of popcorn he held tight to his chest.

Petró thought Andrei would be okay once they got seated. An usher with a flashlight helped them find seats.

They settled in. Soon, the lights went dim; the curtains pulled apart, and a flickering took over the big screen.

The theater was only half full, which was not surprising for the cold October afternoon. Petró liked the movies less crowded. His son was less likely to get separated from them.

He took a handful of popcorn, the salty crunchiness pleasing to his tongue. A black-and-white newsreel came on. WEEK IN REVIEW. Always the newsreel. Then the cartoon Andrei would like, then the main feature. Today, *Trans-Siberian Lovers*.

Andrei kicked his feet about, free of the floor, jamming popcorn in his mouth, his eyes gleefully darting about in the flickering light from the spinning spoke and descending numbers on the screen as the newsreel started.

Olga reached over to stop Andrei kicking.

"In news this week, tensions continue to mount in Havana, Cuba," the newsreader intoned. On the screen, pictures of downtown Havana, Spanish Colonial buildings, arcades and stucco, streets lined with palm trees. But the palm tree fronds whipped about in a stiff wind as the camera panned sideways for a shot of the Caribbean Ocean and waves breaking on the shore.

"In 1959, Cuban revolutionaries led by Dr. Fidel Castro and Che Guevara overthrew the corrupt dictatorship of Fulgencio Batista and founded a socialist Republic of Cuba. And yet one-hundred forty-five kilometers away lies the United States of America, where intelligence proves many nuclear missiles from Florida would be launched against our socialist comrades by a mere push of a button, when the command to destroy Cuba is given."

Petró glanced at Olga beside him, her blue scarf wrapped about her hair. She seemed less concerned with the dire world news than keeping an eye on little Andrei, who not surprisingly had finished more than half his popcorn, eating handful after handful with gusto, unlike Petró, who was caught up in the news about Cuba.

"Our socialist comrades in Cuba called on Moscow last month. Dr. Castro led a delegation to ask for help defending the people's fledgling revolution against the imperialist Americans.

"Earlier in July, the United States organized an invasion at Cuba's Bay of Pigs, and it failed. Kremlin experts weren't surprised the Americans and their Batista lackeys couldn't take Cuba in man-to-man fighting. They suggest Americans might now try to take Cuba by dropping atomic bombs on our brave socialist brothers and sisters."

Petró gasped at the audacity of the Americans attacking a small country, such as Cuba. *Why does a great country, America, fear a socialist country—no, just an island?*

The cameras showed another shot of open ocean and an aircraft carrier, flying the Soviet flag, pushing through waves. On its deck were four tubular missiles. "Accordingly, the Politburo, led by Prime Minister Nikita Khrushchev, authorized the dispatch of short-range missiles to defend the Republic of Cuba.

"Dr. Fidel Castro recently addressed the Cuban people in a radio broadcast, emphasizing these missiles were needed to counter the imperialist designs of the powerful neighbor to the north, the United States of America, which has openly welcomed and given refuge to the dogs of the failed Fulgencio Batista dictatorship. The Americans have powerful nuclear-tipped missiles trained on Cuba, which is utterly defenseless against such an attack."

Petró squirmed in his seat, stunned by what he was hearing. *Nuclear missiles aimed at a defenseless country? Is America so shameless? This is just like the arrogance of flying that U-2 over us a few years ago.*

"Dr. Castro added that by appealing to his socialist comrades in the Union of Soviet Socialist Republics a solution was found. The first shipment of Soviet missiles arrives soon in Cuba. They might be followed by more as military experts evaluate the threat imposed by American imperialist designs on the fledgling revolution in Cuba.

"In other news this week—"

21

ДОБЫЧА ВИНТ
(DROPPED SCREW)

Monday night, after Petró got home and had dinner, once Andrei was doing homework, and after he had tea in his easy chair and read *Pravda*, he was ready for his new project. He stood up.

He unfolded the copy of *Pravda* and laid it down to protect the dinner table. Then he set out the tools, the ones he borrowed from work, the ones Ivan saw him take. Mostly micro-screwdrivers, Phillips and slot heads. He rolled up his shirt sleeves. Disassembly was what he had in mind.

He took out, in its worn leather case, his most prized possession, the Fedka. Petró would never part with it.

Sure, the Fedka in his hands was a supposed copy of the more famous German Leica. But made to durable Soviet standards. Much more affordable, much easier to fix than the Leica.

Alas, the camera was showing its age, something Petró noticed the last time he took pictures. He, Olga, and Andrei had vacationed for a week, staying in a mountain cabin out in the Urals to the east. The pictures from that trip showed light leakage.

Something he had to fix.

He'd look at the cloth-curtain shutter. A hole or tear would leak light. This would be an easy fix, even though he had not assembled a FED in more than twenty years. He had put together so many, he probably could make one in his sleep.

What he needed, though, were the right tools. The camera had delicate mechanisms. He picked up a Phillips, the second-smallest, and turned the camera over, after removing the lens from its barrel mounting.

Biting his lower lip, Petró slipped the screwdriver onto the cross-slotted screw and nudged a counterclockwise turn. The screw would not budge. "Shit," he said.

"Petya, not in front of Andrei," Olga said from the kitchen sink, where she washed dishes. "This language he mustn't hear at his age."

Petró glanced behind him. Andrei had a devilish grin, but kept his eyes glued to the pages of the book he read.

Petró bit his tongue. Why was it, when he was doing something that needed concentration, Olga would watch over him like a clucking chicken? He again tried coaxing the screw loose. Nothing.

He didn't know what else to do. Of all the FEDs he'd assembled he never had one where a screw failed to budge. He stopped. Looked over at Olga, her hands vigorously moving the wet rag back and forth on a dish, which she then put on a stack of other dishes to be rinsed.

He knew what to do: He would unscrew the matching one on the other side of the camera back plate. Again, he pushed the screwdriver tip on the cross-slotted screw and twisted counterclockwise gently. His hands felt joy as the screw turned. Yes. His face beamed. He kept easing a rotation to set it free. The screw slipped off the camera plate as he pulled away the screwdriver, then—before he could move a finger—the minute screw jumped across the table, bouncing, rolling, and then inaudibly went off the edge and into the rug to hide.

"Goddammit," Petró said despite himself. "I'll never find it now."

"I told you. The language. If you don't stop, you must not work near Andrei and me." Olga scowled. Petró knew by her voice she would not back down.

He went to the floor beside the table. Hunched over on his knees. "I have to find this, please be quiet." He knew as soon as he said those three words, Olga would be furious.

She turned off the rinse water. Heavy steps past him. He didn't look up.

"Andrei, come with me. We're leaving now."

Petró looked up. *What is she doing?*

"We go to the television room now. Leave you to your silly screw. I hope you find it."

"But, Mama, I need to finish reading."

"No, your papa must be alone now. To think about his language."

The two slipped out the front door, which closed sharply.

"What have I done?" he asked of no one.

When he worked in Kharkov, taking apart, putting together the most intricate and demanding assemblies, he never, never had problems like this. A wife at his back telling him his language was foul. What went wrong?

Was he crazy, trying to work on the Fedka at home? Maybe he was. He had no privacy, no peace, no quiet. He needed a work area separate from the family, where he could close the door and concentrate. But that? Never.

He had to find the screw.

22
СЧЕТЧИК ГЕЙГЕРА
(GEIGER COUNTER)

The next day, Petró was leaving work, matching strides with long-legged Ivan down the corridor leading to their customary exit, when they saw a queue of departing workers before the airlock lobby at the front doors.

"What's this?" Petró asked out loud.

"More security," a fellow in front said. "New thing. Who knows?"

The woman security guard, wearing a brown uniform, but no cap, stood by a table with a sign, STOP FOR SECURITY CLEARANCE. In her hand she held a wand, connected by a cord to an electrical meter on the table. A worker was being wanded up and down.

Petró took a deep breath. *Why this?* But he had to comply. Reasons might or might not come later.

The woman guard adjusted a knob on the meter, flashed a bored look, then turned and summoned the next in line.

A few more, then it was Petró's turn. His hands up, the guard bent over slightly, moving the metal wand up and down each pant leg. She glanced at the meter. Then studied its dial. The needle moved. She waved the wand across the front of his coat. Again, she stared at the meter dial. Then she brought the wand to his coat pocket.

"Comrade, this is a problem. Your coat pocket has tools from this plant. Why?"

He turned to face her again, lowering his hands, puzzled, but reaching to his right coat pocket. *She has X-ray eyes? How does she see inside my pocket?*

He took out the magnetic pickup, with its collapsible tubular handle, the one he and Ivan used if a metal part fell into an out-of-the-way place.

"This? Yes, I must have left it here."

"You always wear this heavy winter coat at work?"

He hesitated, looking to Ivan, as if stalling for a reason. "No, only when I walk between buildings," he said excitedly, his hands turned up, fingers spread wide.

"You, a technician, must know the importance of returning tools where they belong."

Petró nodded, sure his reason hadn't been good enough.

"Don't do this again. These tools have been dosed with low radiation. This Geiger counter lets us know when they leave the plant. Remember that."

She took the magnetic pickup from him, placed it on the table.

"Your name, please."

He showed his ID card. She took a pen and wrote on a paper tablet his full name. Then made a notation beside it. She looked at her wristwatch and wrote the time too.

She tore the sheet from the tablet and taped it to the surrendered tool, the closed lips on her face one straight line.

She waved him away. "Next," she said.

A week went by. Petró asked Maks—who he was sure had learned about Petró trying to borrow a magnetic pickup—what he knew about radiation to mark tools. Was it harmful?

"I don't know about the radiation, except plant managers must have ways to unobtrusively stop theft."

"Unobtrusively?" Petró exclaimed. His face reddened, reliving the embarrassment. "I was singled out in front of my co-workers!"

"So? You weren't charged with theft. I understand they said not to take tools again."

"Still, it was embarrassing."

"My report said it might have been an accident."

Maks's response to Petró being caught was unsatisfactory. Maks had little, obviously, to say about why radiation was used to mark the tools. Petró hoped it was no more harmful than the radiation used to mark the fancy military chronographs with blue numbers that glowed in the dark. But why the sneaky tactics? As Petró went about working with his tools, he started to imagine some were tagged, and some weren't. After all, who could go around and have the patience or thoroughness to mark hundreds, probably thousands, of tools stowed away in cabinets everywhere in the plant complex?

But when Petró got called in for an *informational interview* later that day, he began to understand that the security at MMA Gorod Optics Test Station was relentless.

The room was cramped: four meters by four meters. A bald incandescent light lit the white-walled space. Petró sat on a hard metal fold-up chair. He looked down to his lap, cinched the belt of his white work smock with a few desultory tugs. Opposite him, across a large steel-topped desk, two Soviet officers he didn't recognize. Maks sent him to Room 171 on short notice, as though the informational interview was hastily arranged.

The stout, bearded fellow on the right had a folder in front of him. On the left sat a clean-shaven fellow, also stout.

"Kondratovych Kravets. You were born in the Ukraine. Exactly where?" the fellow on the right asked.

"A small village, Celo, the outskirts of Kharkov, no more than a half hour by train." He wanted them to explain why he was being asked these questions, but he knew a typical tactic of security was to keep asking questions, wear the person down, and get a confession. He was on guard.

"You were born at home?"

"Yes, my understanding, what I heard years later. Yes."

The fellow on the left made notes.

"You were at the worker commune in Kharkov and assembled FED cameras. Good. Good. But right before that, in January 1940, your father Kondrat Vladmirovych Kravets was killed on military duty in Karelia. Correct?"

The pine box at the cemetery on that cold February afternoon flashed in his mind's eye. "Yes," he said, trying to manage a brave face. "That's true."

The leftmost fellow kept making notes, did not look up.

"Okay, after the war, you came here for military service, then in 1949, a job also here at OTS. You've worked in the classification of Optics Technician for twelve years. True?"

"Yes, of course."

"You were married in 1951 to Olga Pavelova, true?"

"Yes, a matter of public record, I married Olga Pavelova." Petró glanced away briefly, wondering what they didn't know about him.

The leftmost fellow kept his head down and made notes.

"Your work here is important and needed. The reviews from Comrade Belenko, your supervisor, testify to this. The current series of Zenit satellites have camera lens assemblies you put together. Is that not true?"

Petró flashed a smile, then caught himself, for he was, after all, under suspicion. "Yes, I make a small contribution, but others do more."

The leftmost fellow kept taking notes.

"So, Comrade Kravets, your file shows in 1960 you and your co-worker travelled to the site of the American reconnaissance plane crash and retrieved the camera assembly. The notes say that. You then assisted the later investigation headed by Dr. Natalya Dezhnyova from Moscow. An important assignment for defense of the Motherland."

The interrogator paused. "So everything in this file shows you, Petró Kondratovych Kravets, to be an outstanding worker at MMA Gorod Optics Test Station except for one incident a week ago. We'll talk about that now."

Petró felt as if his stomach had collapsed. Everything was in jeopardy. He had words to watch like the cat at a mouse hole.

"The Office of Plant Security operates a new program of random inspection of employees to stop theft of State property and materials. On last Thursday," the interrogator said, looking at his notes, "shortly before five-thirty in the evening a security officer examined you with a Geiger counter. You had in your coat pocket a hand tool from here. True?"

Petró's face felt flush with indignity. "A magnetic pickup I forgot."

"The security officer notes say you claimed the tool was taken accidentally. We won't determine if you removed this tool with intent right now."

Right now? Petró's face screwed up in puzzlement. *What does this mean? Do they hook me, reel me in later?*

"What we'd like to know, as long as we're reviewing your information file, is if you had any use for this tool away from work? Please answer that."

His interrogator stared at him with intensity, apparently searching for crumbling in Petró's explanation. Petró fidgeted on the chair, aware of the trap ahead. "It was in my coat pocket accidentally. I've said this already." He bit his lower lip. "I must have put it into my pocket when I went between buildings." Petró could feel the ground slipping out from under his explanation. What could he do, if he didn't tell the truth?

"One doesn't go between buildings after work. Is that not true?"

"Well, perhaps I did earlier, thirty minutes before my scheduled departure. I think that day I did." Petró sat straighter, a perk of confidence coming over him about his well-conceived comeback.

"You have good answers, Comrade Kravets. Let me try asking you a different question. It's important to us that you try to answer as honestly as you can. Will you do that?"

"Yes, I will."

The interrogator again fixed his eyes on Petró's. "Sometimes, as we know, we do things without being fully conscious of what we are doing. This hand tool is specialized. You know that. You would not use it for something like chopping ice to put in your icebox—"

Petró smiled. *How did he know they still had iceboxes in Public Housing No. 17? They weren't scheduled to get refrigerators for five years. At least!*

"So the question is simple. Take as long as you like to think about it and answer truthfully. The question, Is there anything in your flat for which you might use this small hand tool? Anything? Please answer."

Petró's chest heaved up and down. He was going to have to tell the truth because the way these security guys operated, if they didn't like his answer, they would come straightaway to his flat and

Losing Laika 123

turn everything upside down looking for an answer. What choice did he have other than to tell the truth? "I have a big cabinet radio," he began, weighing his words, speaking slowly. "But the radio, I only need to take off the back with my own screwdriver and take out the vacuum tubes to replace them. No, it's not the radio."

Petró glanced around the room, then at the bare light bulb overhead. "As you mentioned earlier, I was at the work commune in Kharkov and assembled FED cameras. Yes, that experience led me to work here, and I have fond memories, putting together one camera after another. Even with my papa lost in the war, I still found happiness in my work at the commune, day after day—" He paused, smiled weakly at his interrogator, the note-taker, too, then as if asking permission to continue, glanced away, and said, "Even today, I have strong memories of those days because in my flat I have the Fedka camera I got, as did other communards who worked there. We each got a Fedka as a bonus for that year, 1940."

Petró's eyes glistened, tears beginning to well, for the strong memory, the inviolable bond with the past. "So, yes, Comrades, I have in my flat a Fedka, a reminder of some happiness in that year I lost my dad and a reminder of the work that brought me here. Sometimes, I work on it, adjusting things. I have special screwdrivers. But I am older and must be extra careful. If a tiny screw falls on the rug, it's so hard to find."

"Your work here, your father's sacrifice for the Motherland, it is appreciated, Comrade Kravets. We don't have any more questions of you today. The matter of the hand tool I will take care of in my report. It is my opinion, after talking with you, that, yes, you went between buildings, took the collapsible magnetic pickup in your coat pocket and forgot about it. That happens. You might have been interrupted when you went to the other building. But it also would waste our time to try and decide exactly what happened. The important thing is your work here and your father's sacrifice for the Motherland. Thank you for your cooperation during this inquiry."

With those words, Petró was dismissed and returned to his workplace. In a way, he had told the truth, and his interrogator knew the truth of why the pickup was pocketed. It was okay. This one time.

23
ФАРЫ
(HEADLIGHTS)

Petró pondered what getting caught at work was about. A personal lesson, sure, but he had also run up against a distinct trait of Soviet society: The few at the top, the power elite, had to know everything. Or given the license from 1917 of the Revolution, a society based on scientific method and rational Marxist principles worked best by collecting data and keeping tabs on everyone. Not that Pyotr the Great and the rest of the tsarist lineage hadn't written the book about making sure every peasant's business was their business too.

So from his earliest memories, the need of those in power to know everything was something Petró accepted as a less-than-pleasant fact of life, something to gulp down. But in defense of his tool "loan," it was also true people would walk off work with "toting pay." How else would they get things amid chronic shortages and endless queues? Petró's offense—borrowing a work tool—was small potatoes, and yet the way he was grilled about his past and why he had the magnetic pickup—he could've ended up sweeping sidewalks, or so he felt in the hot seat.

A disastrous proposition to be sure. His family would suffer heavily if he lost his assigned work. Olga's work in the bakery was not enough to get them by.

Like everyone around him, anywhere—work and home—Petró kept alive a mild case of paranoia, the defense mechanism he, like any other Soviet comrade not a Party apparatchik, was seemingly issued at birth.

This paranoia meant he could talk about certain things only with people he trusted. Ivan at work, his best friend from childhood, okay. But most of the people he came into contact, not okay. Anyone wearing a Soviet Army uniform, never.

Petró thought after surviving the Great Patriotic War, everyone would live in a society where trust might grow among neighbors and co-workers. And probably more trust, potentially, was there.

But people heard stories of those turned in by their neighbors. No one knew who the secret police informers were: That was how KGB tactics succeeded. An informer might be anybody. And so like something unseen, but invisibly there, like radiation tags on hand tools—Petró smiled at that—the tactic of instilling paranoia among the general populace worked its black magic. Once burned, twice shy.

People lost trust in each other.

Watching Andrei grow as a young boy, Petró wondered how much the collective paranoia from the adult world would affect his son. Or infect him.

Before long, he got his answer. Andrei was seven, seemingly keeping up with schoolwork, but also enjoying the art lessons at school. He went from crayons to drawing with colored pastels.

Andrei drew mostly at home, but nonetheless always took his drawing tablet back and forth to school in his bookbag. Petró guessed his son liked showing his teacher what he'd done.

As usual, one evening Andrei was at home, sitting on the floor, back against the wall, hunched over the drawing board on his lap, when Petró asked, "What are you working on now?"

Andrei looked up, keeping the yellow pastel chalk firmly in hand. "Oh, this special. This is a picture of me!"

"Really!" Petró said, kneeling by his son, who turned the drawing around to face his dad.

On the paper, Andrei had patiently shaded in a black night sky, covering the upper half. In the sky, a few yellow dot stars. Petró gazed intently, though, at the boy in the foreground, walking toward the viewer. "How do I know it's you? I can't see your face."

Hunched over, coat collar pulled up against his neck, face unseen, just blond hair atop the head, and two hands clutching the coat collar tightly against his neck.

Petró gasped. *If this is a self-portrait, my little Andrei is walking at night, alone, snowflakes falling everywhere, a cold, cold night.*

Andrei trudged on his snowy path toward the viewer.

Above and behind him, the dark night and a few stars. But also two headlights beaming off Andrei's left shoulder. Automobile headlights, each white-yellow hot, swirling with Van Gogh-mad intensity, and aimed at Andrei's back. A car behind him in the pitch-black darkness, yes, one that might stop, question the poor, small hunched-over boy in the foreground: his Andreika!

A tightness gripped Petró's throat, then a wash of sadness. Even little Andrei knows paranoia.

Why were those automobile headlights, if not the secret police, watching a boy trudge alone through the darkness on a snowy night? *Are the KGB bullies so ruthless they intimidate a seven-year-old boy?*

He forced a smile. Andrei seemed to hang on every word

when Petró said something about his artwork.

"You have much talent, Son. Such expressiveness in your composition and the story you tell. You're walking home from school?"

"I don't know where I walk in this picture. It's just how I feel when it snows, and I walk alone."

"Well, you should keep this. I'd like to have it." Petró beamed, for he knew his son might do well as an artist.

Perhaps he could use this talent when he grew up. He wasn't sure how Andrei would find an occupation that used his talents. Painting murals on the side of concrete housing blocks? Possibly. But more likely, working in a manufacturing plant, doing the technical illustrations for a manual about vacuum cleaner parts, or some similar, practical assignment of his artistic talents.

Andrei detached the sheet with the drawing from his tablet and offered it to Petró.

"Oh, first you must sign it with your signature. You are the artist!"

And so he did, writing *Андреи* in big letters beside his likeness in the picture.

Petró took the drawing. As light as a fallen leaf. A faint smile of pride about his son's talent and endurance lit Petró's face.

He again studied the headlights. *How do the Chinese say, A picture is worth a thousand words?*

24
ЧЕТЫРЕ ГЛАЗА
(FOUR EYES)

A few years later and in no rush, bookbag slung over his shoulder, Andrei walked the remaining hundred meters to the front door of Public School No. 27 tucked inside an old, gray stone building and where he'd be stuck for the rest of the day. The eight-thirty tardy bell had yet to ring.

From his left, from his right, others arrived with similar loitering gaits like school-shy Andrei. Except one, farther away on his right, walking briskly, the stride Andrei knew instantly as Nikolay, whom he'd known from first grade, when the two took to trading sandwiches from the lunches they brought to school.

Andrei looked again. Something was different. *What is it? A haircut?* He looked again. The glasses. *When has he ever worn glasses?*

"Kolya," Andrei called out. "Why the four eyes?"

Nikolay gave Andrei an embarrassed look, as if hoping to sneak into school unrecognized until ready to admit, yes, he was wearing glasses for the first time and, yes, he was getting used to them.

"You never wore glasses before," Andrei said, drawing closer to his fourth-grade chum.

"No. But I had trouble seeing the blackboard. Teacher Frolov told my mom to take me to the eye clinic." With both hands, he uneasily adjusted the way his round wire-frames sat on the bridge of his nose. He smiled. Andrei wondered if he had strained his eyes reading too many books.

Then the school bell rang. A look of panic crossed up Andrei's face. He shot a glance to the school door. The others had gone inside. Just he and Nikolay were left outside.

"Oh, I want to hear more—" Andrei said.

The two scrambled up the steps.

At the lunch recess, Nikolay did have more to say about the glasses. He was nearsighted. Couldn't see well far away. The ophthalmologist said he needed a strong prescription, and in six months they'd check if his eyes improved. The doctor said sometimes glasses help the eyes get stronger.

"But I'm afraid I can't play football," Nikolay said.

"Why?"

"The doctor said I may play football with these," Nikolay tapped his glasses, "only if I wear protective goggles too."

"So why don't you?"

"Too much trouble. Besides I've never been a starter on the team. Never."

"Maybe that's because you didn't have glasses," Andrei shot back.

"Oh, I'm sure you're right, but my eyes have been bad for so long, I don't know how I'll catch up."

"Still you might give goggles a try."

Nikolay shrugged.

Although Nikolay got used to wearing glasses, when the ophthalmologist checked his eyes again, they hadn't improved. Nikolay saw that as one more reason, besides the goggles, to not even think about playing team sports. He told Andrei that something like chess was better for his eyes.

25
ДЕРЕВЯННЫЕ ВИНТОВКИ
(WOODEN RIFLES)

Petró didn't know what came to stunt the artistic spirit that drew the haunting picture of little Andrei walking in the snowfall, followed by two headlight beams. Perhaps the challenge of living with a dose of paranoia in his tender years surrendered to the greater demand of wanting to belong, to be accepted by other boys and girls his age. Nine-year-old Andrei was old enough for the local Communist Party club for children, the Young Pioneers. They met after school. Because the club was sanctioned by the highest powers in the land, belonging carried many privileges, such as field trips during school hours to special events.

Andrei was in Young Pioneers for only a few months, when he took part in his first parade on May Day. No school for Andrei and Petró was off work. Parades were essential to the holiday.

That day, Andrei spent much time getting ready to go to the club, where he'd join other Young Pioneers, then march in the parade. Olga handed him a khaki long-sleeved shirt she had ironed crisp the night before. Then a red tie to complete the picture, as he stood with black pants and shiny black shoes.

"There. You're ready to march," Olga said.

Andrei beamed, then looked over to Petró, who'd walk with him to the clubhouse.

They walked briskly and had only a few kilometers to go. "You're really liking the Young Pioneers," Petró said.

"Sure, we do fun stuff every week at our meetings." Andrei looked up, beaming.

"What do you mean?"

"It's not like school, that remembering stuff."

Petró saw Andrei's report cards and wasn't surprised to hear that. "So you don't enjoy school, but Young Pioneers after school is better?"

"Yeah, it's not just sitting at your desk. We do things. We work together."

"Like this parade," Petró said, seeing the stadium ahead.

"Yeah, and guess what?"

"I don't know, what?"

"Next week, we go collect scrap metal. That'll be fun."

Petró was pleased Andrei enjoyed the club activities. Getting along with other kids his age was where friendships were built, ones that might last a lifetime. He thought back to how he and Ivan became friends. Andrei was much younger, but even so, these club activities could only help him in later years as he became an adult.

The clubhouse where the Young Pioneers met was packed: fifty or so boys and girls. Everyone wore tan shirts and red ties. And as Petró left Andrei to get Olga, he saw his son fit right in, like peas still in the pod. A possible member of the Communist Party in the making. His artistic sensitivity probably irrelevant.

That Saturday afternoon, the parade assembled in Nevsky Stadium, ready to march out onto Narodniki Prospekt, where Petró and Olga and thousands flocked on the curbs for the spectacle.

The first float emerged, much as a butterfly unfolds from its cocoon, through the stadium archway. A large hammer and sickle of red roses. The out-sized, flower-studded structure tremored. The truck hidden beneath the floral wrap, except for its wheels, hesitated, then revved up.

Behind the float, an inevitable crack platoon of marching soldiers, all heads facing right as they high-stepped past Petró, who was wondering how long he and Olga had to wait to see Andrei and his Young Pioneers, obvious amateurs compared to these professionals, some of whom might have understandably felt they had marched in one too many parades.

Then, mounted on a truck-drawn trailer, a missile. Petró quickly recognized the newer version of the surface-to-air missile that brought down the American spy plane years ago. This model was much more capable. Petró took great pride in his satellite optics work at OTS, and understandably some of that pride was reflected in how he kept up with advances in Soviet military defenses.

Then a brass band.

A company of Navy sailors in sparkling white and blue.

Another float.

Another band.

Then—Petró stared hard, turned to Olga. "Is it possible? Look at them—"

He couldn't believe his eyes. After the disciplined military marchers—everyone a professional—a roaming group of kids, the leader out front holding up a banner with the words *Young Pioneers*. Petró marvelled: *Can it be?*

For there, among the fifty or so errant marchers—how was anyone in step with anybody?—there in the middle, halfway back, was the face he recognized.

Andrei. Dressed in tan shirt, red tie, and mounted on his right shoulder, a wooden rifle. Each Young Pioneer bore one on their shoulder.

"Yea, Andreika!" Petró yelled despite himself. Cheers went up, perhaps out of pity, because the Young Pioneers were so disorganized.

"Andreika!" he called again.

Andrei, however, showed discipline and looked straight ahead. Not turning to face the voice calling him. Even if, amid the shouting, he heard his papa. Petró saw his son was trying hard to march properly, not looking right or left, but only keeping up with the leader holding the banner, even though Andrei and everyone else was out of step.

For Petró it was the briefest of passing moments: Young Andrei carrying a wooden rifle on his shoulder, eyes fixed determinedly ahead, walking fast to keep up. Then the moment left like a child's ball rolling away. Petró gazed hard at the backs of the Young Pioneers, all astray, and caught a glimpse of Andrei's shoulder, the wooden rifle tip. Then they were gone. The next marching group saw to that, blocking out a last look.

For a few years, Petró had been taking Andrei to Kosmos Gorod hockey games. Andrei loved them.

On one such night, having taken their seats, Kuzlov Ice Stadium was packed. Kosmos was playing Diesel Sverdlovsk.

He looked over at Andrei sitting on the aisle seat. "You see everything?"

"Yeah, I like being high up."

Petró liked the seats down lower, closer to the action. But this open-aisle seat he wanted for Andrei. During past games, Andrei, now ten, would miss too much when everyone stood up. Only an aisle seat would do.

"Here," Petró said. He held open a small bag of peanuts they'd bought from a street vendor outside the stadium. "You've your water bottle. Drink that when you're thirsty." They always sold snacks downstairs in the lobby, but they cost more, and Petró wanted to save his rubles. The ticket prices were already steep enough.

The blue-and-white Zamboni on the ice headed for a side exit—even the Party guys above agreed, the one good thing to come from America—its driver looking intently out from his perch seat aboard the whirring machine, apparently satisfied he'd given it a good once-over. He shut down the engine, and immediately, as Gorod hockey fans always did, the stadium erupted in a thunderous demand of stomping feet to get the game under way.

Soon enough, though, there they were: the six starters for each team, the referee ready to drop the black puck into a face-off of raised sticks held by the centers for each team: Kosmos in hometown red, Diesel in visitor black.

Game under way.

Slissss, slissss, slissss, slap. Back and forth, the Kosmos forwards passed the puck, but not yet over the blue line. Petró had played enough hockey to know what they were doing. They were trying to find which Diesel defender was weaker, which to play off to set up a scoring try. So the play, in those first minutes, was tentative.

Andrei studied the action intently, his fists under his chin.

Slissss, slissss, slisss, slap.

Petró bumped Andrei with his elbow, offering him more peanuts. His son took a handful, stopped hunching over, cracking the shells, popping the peanuts in his mouth one at a time. Petró knew Andrei enjoyed the game, even though it was scoreless, and the first period was closing.

A starter pistol shot rang out. The first period was over.

"More," Andrei said, looking at the bag of peanuts in Petró's hand.

"Here," Petró said. "So far, the play's tentative. Those Diesel defenders, they're like Siamese twins, so balanced, they don't get out of place no matter what. I think Gorod'll have a tough time scoring—"

Andrei tossed a peanut shell at his feet.

"Not one good shot," Petró added. "We took that wide shot. Their goalie didn't even need to reach for *that*."

The minutes ticked away. Then the centers once again faced off, ready to dig their sticks into the ice and get the puck out to a teammate. The referee dropped the puck.

The puck sailed down to the Kosmos end. Two Kosmos defenders were on the puck, popping it back and forth, trying to keep it away from the Diesel forwards, who hounded them like flies on a slice of honeydew melon.

Then, out of his side vision, a flash of hockey stick got Petró's attention. At the Diesel end, a Kosmos forward had taken a barrelhouse swing at a Diesel defender, who now, in black uniform, lay on the ice, blood covering his nose. "Oh, oh, that was a bad foul. Shame on you, Yakovlev," he said of the Kosmos forward, who nonchalantly skated in a circle to the side of the fallen Diesel defender.

Whistles everywhere. The referees stopped the game.

Petró reached over, grabbed Andrei's shoulder. "You see that?"

"No, what?"

"Bad foul. If the referee says it's intentional, ten minutes in the penalty box."

The Diesel defender stood up, the team doctor having cleaned off his nose, satisfied the bleeding had stopped. He was going to stay in the game.

The Kosmos forward skated stubbornly for the exit to sit for ten of the remaining eighteen minutes in the second period. Down a player, how could Gorod avoid a score on them?

"Any more peanuts?" Andrei asked.

Petró showed him the empty paper bag.

Andrei took a drink of water and stared at the two centers facing off for the puck drop.

Slissss, slissss, slissss, slap, slap, slap. If Kosmos was down a man, they didn't play that way. Petró saw immediately the penalty seemed to energize the home boys. They weren't about to waste themselves trying to defend their goal, short a man. No, they picked up the tempo and aggressively went on offense.

Petró slapped his forehead. *Wide shots, but they're moving!*

Then Grishin, the Kosmos center, hammered a shot, taking the puck away from an oncoming Diesel forward, crossing up hockey sticks, but still a solid slap of a shot, the puck ricocheting off the side wall and forward, skipping halfway down the rink and then—Petró held his breath—the most watched flying object in the arena seemed to pause, floating in air toward the squatting Diesel goalie, who with both arms held out his stick, when from who knows where appeared the only Kosmos forward left in the game during the penalty, Bubnov, who swatted the puck with everything he had, catching the black disk right there in thin air, a meter above the ice. Petró was beside himself, reaching over and slapping Andrei, already standing, on the back, and, yes, the hard puck sailed like a missile for the goal netting, past the outstretched right arm of the Diesel goalie, who had no chance, his hockey stick low and useless. The bulky goalie moved too late.

1-0.

The scoreboard kept flashing over and over. Kosmos Gorod had scored.

Everyone stood, cheering, stomping their feet, clapping.

"And a man down. What an amazing shot!" Petró shouted at Andrei.

"I saw it, I saw it!" Andrei yelled back. "This time I saw the shot."

Petró was happy for Andrei. The puck was in the right place for a score, but a mid-air swing like that? Incredible.

The rest of the second period went scoreless. Even with Yakovlev back in the lineup, it was a stalemate on the ice, apparently the miraculous score left everyone spent for more heroics.

Alas, the third period, like the first was also scoreless, and so the game ended. Home team defeating the visitors one to nil.

As they left the stadium, Andrei turned to Petró. "Papa, where's that guy selling peanuts."

Petró looked around, as if indulging his son, "Oh, he must've sold out, he's gone. He'll be back next game."

"Let's buy those again. Those peanuts, so fresh and good. Best I ever had."

Petró smiled. He wondered if Andrei would have said that if Kosmos lost the game.

26

САХАРАЯ ЛУНА
(SUGAR MOON)

A few more May Days slipped by, and Petró happily saw Andrei growing into a young man of whom he could be proud. At work, Petró kept getting busier. The reconnaissance satellites the MMA scheduled for orbit, circling earth, radio-transmitting images of military targets in foreign lands, were increasingly too many to count. On cold nights—when the air was clear and still—Petró would look skyward and always—so he believed—see one of his crafted progeny zipping overhead, looping the heavenly circuit, arcing a brief passage, and minutes later, it would wink out in the darkness, and then, as if he were about to wave good-bye, another would flare into view.

One after another. He would peer. *My, what we've done to the heavens! Too many up there. So many dead, too. They've stopped working, and they won't come back.*

Petró knew, however, much of what he saw was not Russian, but American.

And so the space race would continue, Russian sputniks not to be crowded out by the American eyes-in-the-skies.

On a Monday morning—like all the warm July mornings that year—Petró had to get to work and so walked quickly to the Metro station. But before he got there, he saw something odd, something he had never seen.

Ahead, a crowd, maybe three dozen or more, filled the sidewalk. By the State liquor store, but nobody was going into buy vodka. Anyway, at that hour, they couldn't. The place wasn't open. No, they huddled and fidgeted about on the sidewalk, like sparrows toeing after dropped bits of bread. He didn't know why. He picked up his steps.

He next heard the excited voice of a newsreader: "This is a live broadcast. I repeat, this is a live broadcast. The American space mission commander is about to set foot on the moon!"

Petró gasped. *My ears, do they hear okay?*

He stood as close as he could—everyone was so packed—to the portable TV he knew was there, outdoors, on the sidewalk.

Petró couldn't see the picture. Could only hear the sound.

He had to see something. Anything.

He didn't care. Went to his knees, stuck his head between a woman's thigh and what must have been her daughter. The woman glanced down and smiled. He smiled back.

The grainy black-and-white screen sat on a folding table, a long electrical extension cord trailing back into the State liquor store. Petró's eyes went wide, full of awe.

Is that ... is that the moon?

Like a bowl of sparkling white sugar, full of dimply glints and bumped highlights and beyond the small curvy horizon, deep blackness. A pang of nausea arrested Petró's wonder. The American team had gone so far to land on the moon. Would they make it back to the same solid ground on which he stood?

Americans, sure, they already send out crews to circle the

Losing Laika   143

moon and they come back okay. Did this twice. And we send our two turtles around the moon and they returned. But orbit is not like landing. Will their spacecraft launch off the moon? Nobody's going rescue them there.

Petró stared uncomprehending at the TV. *These stakes are so high. Trying too soon to be the first on the moon—will pride trip them up?*

November of 1957, fortieth anniversary of Bolshevik Revolution. Yes, too much pride doomed that poor mutt. Poor little Laika. Space suit, floppy ears, she wasn't ready to be first in space. That second sputnik was rushed because ol' Nikita wanted something else to boast about. He shook his head, stared at the screen.

But the legs of a spacesuit went down the steps of the ladder to the sugary surface of the moon.

Fat spacesuit legs, big boots.

The left boot stepped on the sugar moon. The moon dust was like flour and flew up.

Petró held his breath. *This is true!*

"That's one step for man, one giant step for mankind."

Petró didn't understand much of the garbled English, but he knew what he saw.

Hoooraaaaay! one fellow yelled.

"What if they don't make it back?" Petró yelled up to those standing over him.

A chill spread over his back. Yes, he played a part in the space program for the Motherland, but he did not expect this day. Man on the moon. Everybody watched it happen. But was it too soon? Would there be a successful return? Petró stared at the screen, as if his eyes and those of billions earth-bound might draw the space voyagers back home.

Commander Neil Armstrong, reflective bubble-shield helmet and spacesuit, bunny-hopped around, kicking up weightless dust like spilt flour.

Again, the newsreader spoke: "We are watching, I repeat, the live broadcast of the American space team's landing on the moon, this twenty-first day of July, 1969. The spacecraft circled, as we reported earlier, the moon for twenty-seven hours before today's landing on the lunar surface. The Soviet Space Institute has on its own confirmed the achievement of this American space team. Some skeptics call this a movie-set stunt. It is not. Our scientists verified the authenticity of what you are seeing. I repeat, the Americans have successfully landed on the moon. All of us in the Motherland join billions elsewhere to wish these American space explorers a safe return home and a deserved welcome back to earth."

Petró's eyes stayed with the skipping hops of Commander Armstrong, then looked beyond to the black void recumbent on the horizon. He fought back another pang of nausea. *Yes, what if they don't make it back? What if like Laika, they suffer, suffocate? That brave dog swept off the streets of Moscow and sacrificed in outer space.* He shook his head. *Maybe the Americans will make it back. Maybe unlike us, they prepare properly. The moon orbits. They might get back okay. They did it twice before. If they get back, yes, we're behind. Really behind. All we've done is send two turtles around the moon.* His eyes stayed on the TV screen.

The minutes were for lingering, as if everyone wanted to keep the grainy black-and-white images. They never would see such an event again. Petró was sure daily life everywhere in Gorod had stopped after news got out this was on TV.

Here he was, on the sidewalk, before the State liquor store across from Metro and seemingly, like everyone else, waiting for the breathless newsreader to say, That's it, go back to normal life. But for Petró that would not happen. He was watching his country's chances in space about to die there on TV, on that snowy white surface of the moon.

"We expect Premier Nikita Khrushchev to join other world leaders in congratulating American President Richard Milhous Nixon on this splendid achievement in space exploration. As was widely reported, the goal of reaching the moon by Americans was given by the late American President John Fitzgerald Kennedy in 1962. Americans would set foot on the moon before the decade was out, he said. Sadly, only a year later, in 1963, President Kennedy was assassinated.

"So today Americans have realized the ambitious goal of the late President Kennedy. This is an achievement of which they are justifiably proud, despite the violent political protests that have swept through the country after President Kennedy first set the goal. The invasion of Vietnam by Americans has pitted the young against the old in continuing violent clashes. American cities burn in race riots. And political assassination not only claimed President Kennedy, but last year his brother, running for president, Robert Fitzgerald Kennedy too. And also last year the political assassination of the prominent American Negro leader, Reverend Martin Luther King Jr. So, today is a moment of joy and achievement for what has been a largely tragic decade for Americans. On that note, let us wish the American space team a safe return. This is Sergei Ablonov reporting live from Moscow. Thank you."

27
РЕКРУТСКАЯ ПОВИННОСТЬ
(RECRUIT OBLIGATION)

Years later, in Andrei's last year of high school, Petró couldn't help but notice his son's uneasiness about the upcoming comprehensive exams for university admission. Andrei's adult future would be determined by how well he did, and the exams weren't ones for which he could prepare. No specific topics, the teacher said, just everything he had learned in school until then.

Andrei had never been fond of school, so with trepidation he entered the auditorium of Senior School No. 15 one Saturday for a four-hour set of tests.

Three months later, Andrei came home from school to find Petró alone in the flat, Olga still at the bakery.

Petró looked up from his *Pravda*. "You got something in the mail. Over there on the table. The University Test Bureau—what's that?"

Andrei snatched up the envelope and tore it open, as though he wanted the decision about his future, one way or the other.

He unfolded the letter, and Petró saw disappointment spread over his face.

"What's the matter?" Petró asked.

"Oh, these are exam results for university. Others have been getting them and talking about where they're planning to go."

"So how'd you do?"

"That's the problem. This grade is not enough to get in anywhere. I needed a seventy." He palmed his forehead. "I only got a sixty-three."

Petró stepped over to Andrei, put his arm on his son's shoulder. "Well, you can do other things besides go to university—"

"But my friends are. You know Nikolay got a ninety-two. He has plenty of choices; he can pick where he goes."

"Oh, you'll make new friends. Trust me."

"But I have no idea what I'll do."

Petró patted Andrei on the shoulder. "Think about it. What else can you do?"

Andrei gave him a quizzical look, as though Petró was about to suggest what he might consider.

"Look at me," Petró said. "I never went to university. You don't always know where you're going. You have to try things."

Andrei smiled, as though he realized if anybody should have gone to university, it was his papa. Working at the Optics Test Station on space satellites. Why he worked with physicists from the Moscow Institute of Technology!

"You're right. I've got to think about this." Then a look of panic came over him. "But what if the others ask my score?"

"Say the score must be lost in the mail. In a week or so, they won't even ask."

"Oh, but Nikolay will, even months from now."

"Tell him the truth, but say it's okay, you're thinking of something else."

A few days later, Andrei was fortunate to have a counselor at high school go over the exam score and discuss how it affected his future plans. What the counselor mentioned that stood out to Andrei was how he might first get his mandatory military service out of the way.

"Going to university only postpones that, as you know," counselor Bagdolov said in a serious tone that left no doubt in Andrei's mind his counselor had dutifully served his two-year obligation to the Motherland.

The counselor then suggested Andrei think about a military career as a way to get more specialized training, which he might use later in life. Moreover, if he tried for a career as an officer, he surely would avoid the more humdrum assignments given ordinary recruits.

The only question was, Could Andrei enter the service of his choice: the Soviet Air Force?

Evidently, his years in the Young Pioneers, followed by the Marxist Cadets paid off. He had the talk the military interviewers wanted to hear down pat. He knew how to talk about working for the team, supporting the goals set by the group leader, and knowing each cadet had to have an assigned task.

Plus Andrei never wore glasses and had exceptionally keen eyesight. He was accepted for basic training in the Soviet Air Force. He'd start in Vladivostok, Siberia.

Andrei, in his letters to Olga and Petró, wrote that even though his rank was a lowly airman, he didn't want to stand around a plane, moving drip pans, or sit at a desk completing lists of company stores. He wanted to fly.

So he kept applying for pilot training. He dreamed of flying a fighter plane. A MiG-25. The fastest plane, he understood, in the world. But what did it take to become a fighter pilot? Only the Air

Force officers knew, and they didn't share what they were after—other than good eyesight—with anybody. The interviews seemed obtuse, but probing:

"Do you have a good memory?"

"What frightens you?"

"Do you awake easily in the morning?"

"How is your best friend like you?"

"When did you learn to walk?"

Finally, Andrei called with the news: He was headed for pilot training at a base near Leningrad. He was about to leave, but he'd be sure to stop in Gorod for a hurried visit.

"So how long have you known?" Petró asked Andrei, just arrived with duffel bag in tow. He stood tall, dressed in his black-striped Air Force whites, and then with the athletic grace of one in topnotch physical shape, he took a seat on the same sofa where Petró remembered his son sat in diapers. Not that many years ago. So it seemed.

"Got the word a week ago. Helicopter training starts in ten days. They want me over to Leningrad now." He flashed a smile, as though he was not only following orders, but his dream too.

"Helicopters?"

"Yeah, I'm gonna be a helicopter pilot, jockey the whirlybirds. That's where the openings are."

"We have a lot more of those than fighter planes—"

"Fighter planes, yeah, that's what I wanted to fly. But the more I learn about helicopters, the more I think they would be fun—"

"But they're dangerous, no?" Olga asked.

"Oh, Mama. Did you know if a helicopter's engine quits, you can land it, no power at all. You keep it upright, and it floats down just like a little maple seed, spinning its blades to slow the descent.

That's a trick I'll have to learn. I heard it from a helicopter pilot."

"You can't do that in a fighter plane," interjected Petró.

Her face flush from kitchen labor, Olga slowly raised her hand and pointed to the oven in the kitchen area. "Just for your good news, I make prianiki honey biscuits."

Andrei knew those biscuits. The aroma was what hit him when he first walked in the door. Memories of his mama's baking reached back to his earliest years.

"Yes, we'll enjoy your prianiki with some hot tea. Perfect way to celebrate," Petró said. "So how long is helicopter school?"

"Oh, classroom, flight hours—it'll take a while. I won't be a full-fledged pilot for more than a year. So much to learn. Not only controls of the helicopter, but classroom work like weather, how to read terrain. See, helicopters don't need runways. So it's stuff besides simply putting in flight hours with a teacher beside you in the cabin."

The tea kettle whistled. Petró went over and poured the hot water in the teapot. He'd let it steep.

"Here, these I know you'll enjoy. They came out well," Olga said, setting the prianiki down on the table.

Andrei's gaze fastened on the glossy biscuits, his eyes wide with hunger, but he'd resist until he had some nice hot tea to savor between each bite.

"So you'll get some time off at Leningrad, visit us?" Olga asked.

"Well, it's not Siberia and that impossible distance, so I'll be back here a few times next year. Of that, I'm almost sure."

"Very good," Petró said, pulling out the side chair where Andrei customarily sat for so many years. "Now the tea must be done," he added. He went over to get the teapot, ready to serve everyone.

Later, Petró saw Andrei off at the train station downtown.

He waved at Andrei sitting in a coach car beside a steamy window and knew what he was giving up. His son, the familiar face at home after work, the companion for Sunday afternoons in the park, the opponent when playing indoor games like blackjack after dinner on the rug in the flat. That familiar face, now, however, smiled so broadly behind the railway car window and seemed so confident, so sure he had no time to waste: He was following his dream to fly at last.

Petró wiped a tear at the corner of his eye and turned about.

The train lurched. Outbound from Sokolov Station, the train rolled away, steadily, steel wheels on steel rails.

28
ИТАЛЬЯНСКАЯ ОБУВЬ
(ITALIAN SHOES)

Andrei kept his word and a few months later, in October, came to visit his parents. A hurried visit—three days—but the stay meant much to Petró. As though the years spent fathering Andrei paid off in his son's independence: a flight officer in helicopter training.

But Andrei didn't want to talk about flying helicopters, talk Petró was ready to enjoy. No, his son only wanted to talk about girls, and especially one.

"What's her name?" Olga asked.

"Yelena." Andrei's face lit up with effusiveness.

Petró smiled for he, too, once knew those early weeks of love at twenty.

"Maybe I'll bring her by next time I'm here."

"You do that," Petró said, but wondering, if at age twenty, Andrei would have the same girlfriend in a few months. He would wait. He would see.

A few months went by, and again Andrei visited, but with girlfriend in tow.

Petró did a double take. Yelena was a fashion plate. A dish. Petró mused: *Perhaps there's something to being a Soviet officer-in-training and the ladies!*

"Yelena Gorbunova, my parents—" Andrei said, beaming at the prize catch by his shoulder.

Andrei helped Yelena take off her overcoat, draping it over the back of the sofa beside them.

She was dressed in a sleek, black silk pant suit, the sort Petró glimpsed in Western magazines; and Andrei thought after dinner all four of them could take in the local Gorod Officer's Club, for which he was entitled to bring guests. But that could wait. Olga had golubtsy baking in the oven.

Most striking were Yelena's shoes. Black patent leather pumps. Olga knew no such shoes were made in the Motherland. They had to be from France or Italy. *How does she get them?* The high heels, unlike the practical, durable shoes Soviet women wore, even for a night out on the town.

"Your shoes, so stylish, where did you find those?" Olga asked, unabashedly inquisitive.

"Oh, these, I'm glad you like them. They're Italian. Black market. I got an address for a shoe importer, sells shoes like these out of his flat. Every time I save up some money, I go by and see what he has." She gave Olga a grin, as though as a young woman she could afford such indulgences for vanity, which Olga—more the babushka—had long abandoned.

"Oh, it's nice you find stylish Western shoes near you. I see nothing like that here, but then Leningrad is more worldly. You people travel more—" Olga added, stepping back into the kitchen area.

"Yes, my shoe importer really administers bauxite contracts to the Germans, Italians, French, the Benelux countries, and this shoe business, just something on the side—"

"Oh, so many people have two jobs," Petró laughed. "One official, one black market."

"What?" Yelena said. "He just carries shoes in his suitcases." She laughed.

"He must have big suitcases—" Petró added.

"Travels all the time, so his flat fills up with shoes."

Petró had to admit Andrei's taste in women was adventurous. Where was his son's resolve to find a woman who would be a good homemaker, a mother to his children? Yelena seemed more the playgirl type, wanting to ape fashions of the West. She was probably more like the rest of the younger generation. They didn't fully understand the sacrifices their elders made to defend the Motherland and the noble social experiment of worker equality. The Marxist ideal state traded for a pair of Italian shoes! Petró knew life must mean more than that.

Petró rubbed his brow. *Yeah. The Americans. Man on the moon. Our younger generation gives up. No more sacrifice. They want things. They want Western things.* He smiled Yelena's way.

They finally sat down at the dinner table, Andrei and Yelena opposite each other, Petró and Olga too. They started in on the golubtsy.

Petró smacked his lips: Olga always made the stuffed cabbage dish with exceptional skill. He shot a glance at Yelena, wondering how good a cook she was. Andrei would have to understand to live a long life with any woman, she had to be a good cook. The way to a man's contentment was through his stomach, three times a day!

"Here's a toast." Petró raised his glass of water. "To happy times for Andrei and Yelena in Leningrad." Glasses clinked. "And, of course, to Andrei's successful completion of his aviation studies." More glass clinks.

"I'd like to make a toast," Yelena said. "Here's to Petró and Olga for raising such a fine young man. I'm lucky."

Petró felt his face redden with pride at what this new woman suddenly touched on in an endearing way. *Has she set her sights on our Andrei?* He wasn't sure, but felt he would be seeing more of Yelena Gorbunova. Which was okay with him. He felt despite her ways with Western fashion, she did have a good heart. That, more than anything, was what counted.

29
СВАДЕБНЫЙ ТОРТ
(WEDDING CAKE)

After the cold winter months, spring arrived. Petró wished he had seen more of Andrei. Wished when graduation day arrived for his son to get pilot wings pinned to his chest—Andrei, ready in that moment to take command of his own *ship*, an Mi-24 helicopter, equipped with fierce Kalashnikov combat-ready gunnery—he and Olga hadn't missed it, but they couldn't get away to Leningrad.

Andrei's other graduation into adulthood, however, was one Petró could not miss: Andrei and Yelena would marry in Gorod. Although her parents were in Leningrad, the couple decided to wed in Gorod because Andrei's new assignment took him to a base not far from the city. All of which made Olga and Petró, if not Yelena's parents, happy: They could see their son, and their daughter-in-law-to-be, more often.

The wedding day arrived. A simple wedding for the families. Then afterwards, the reception. The groom's family, meaning Petró, was to pick up the tab because the wedding was in the groom's, not the bride's, hometown. An old custom.

Petró rented, for the afternoon, the same dance hall where he first met Svetlana—and later married Olga—all those many years ago. Not inappropriate that he do so, for Svetlana's husband Viktor, the Party operator, was bringing drink for the festivities. Viktor was always close to the pipeline for surplus vodka.

Petró stood in the middle of the empty dance hall, wearing his brown suit, a white shirt, a red tie. On edge, he looked at his chronograph watch. Nine o'five in the morning. The wedding upstairs at noon, reception to follow where he stood. This had to go smoothly.

Across the wooden dance floor, the caterers put together tables where food would be served. Olga seemingly worked through the night on her contribution to the fare: dozens of cheese-and-potato pirogis. Well, he mused, she only worked late and got up early. She did sleep.

The bar would be next to the food, and Viktor assured him the beverage offering would be one of the best for a wedding in Gorod. What had Petró done for Viktor to deserve such generosity? He wasn't sure. What he did know was weddings brought out generous impulses in everyone. Petró had the niggling suspicion, down the road, Viktor would sidle up and say, Remember that favor for your son's wedding? Good. I have a small favor to ask.

And so, trading back and forth on the value of friends, relatives, and well-placed acquaintances, things got done.

"So, Viktor, how goes it?" Petró had walked across the empty dance hall, where Viktor directed burly Egor to wheel in a case of Pyatizvyozdnaya on a hand truck.

"Can I complain? I deliver the goods, see?" Viktor beamed, as only a member of the Party could. The pants of his black, pin-striped suit had smart, unbroken creases, as though to prove he'd not so much as kneeled to the floor.

Petró eyed poor Egor, huffing and puffing, taking cases out of the van, wheeling them inside. Egor was not doing this only to help. Like a good Party man, Viktor knew Egor's fondness: the vodka he wheeled in the door. Surely, Petró reasoned, labor would be rewarded: a bottle or two from Viktor. That was how Viktor operated: He knew everyone's levers, what to pull to get them moving, for him.

Petró swept his hand right. "Well, the food will be set up soon." He glanced at his chronograph again. Nine-twenty. "And warmers will keep things fine until guests arrive."

"How many people do you expect?"

"Oh, more than eighty." Yelena's folks and relatives, more than ten from Leningrad. Then Andrei's Air Force buddies. The neighbors in our block. I'm forgetting a lot."

"I'm sure all will go well." Viktor motioned for Egor to unload the second case of vodka by the first.

"Well, this is a big day for me. I finally feel like I'm letting go of little Andrei."

"Oh, won't they live with you?" Viktor joked, knowing most newlyweds ended up living in cramped quarters with parents because of the chronic shortage of flats and impossible waiting lists. Many housing blocks no longer took applications.

"No, that's the advantage of being an officer. Andrei gets married housing on the base. A great deal."

"I wonder if that had something to do with deciding to get married now—"

Petró laughed. Perhaps. He knew deciding when to marry was hard, but being married and not having your own place, you either accepted or put off the date.

He looked at his chronograph again. Nine-thirty. "Well, I'm glad things are coming together here. Thanks again. I must go upstairs. That's where Olga is setting up flowers."

A few hours passed, and Andrei and Yelena were officially man and wife.

Before long the crowd made its way downstairs to the dance hall with more than a few people Petró didn't know. Bride and groom, Yelena and Andrei were on the way. Petró looked over the milling faces and turned to Olga, whispering, "I'm glad we had but one child—I can go through this excitement only once."

"Oh, I love weddings," she replied, standing there in her best gray suit, wearing her favorite babushka scarf on her head. "But, yes, one of our own is enough. If someone else has to worry about everything, that's better."

"What a day!" Petró said in the direction of the older couple approaching them. "We lose a son, we gain a daughter," he laughed, knowing for the Gorbunovs from Leningrad, the arithmetic reversed.

"Oh, we hope you enjoy your visit," Olga said, even though she knew, without the wedding, Gorod was probably a destination deemed too industrial, too culturally deprived for their tastes. Both were fashionably thin, if middle-aged with graying hair. Olga took note of Gorbunova's fashionable blue satin dress. Quite Western. She recalled her first sight of Yelena, when Andrei brought her by, how she wore those Italian pumps.

She smiled as Petró made small talk, asked about their flight down from Leningrad. *Oh, those who live in Leningrad,* Olga mused, *so susceptible to the West, its fashions.* They had been like that since Tsar Pyotr the Great.

"They're on their way, no?" Petró turned and asked of a tall, thin young man, who joined them. Nikolay Volodin Mushinsky was Andrei's best man and would know the whereabouts of the groom, if anybody.

"Oh, yes, they're still upstairs with the photographer. He's having them in many poses as the newly married couple." Nikolay smiled mischievously. How Nikolay became Andrei's best man was a mystery, beyond Petró's ken. The two were so different. Andrei the helicopter pilot and Nikolay the perennial university student. In any case, Nikolay was an engaging conversationalist and a delight for Andrei, who said he enjoyed the long discussions into the night about things he never had time to think about.

Nikolay complemented Andrei's plodding ways with big picture stuff.

Before Petró could answer Nikolay, a collective gasp swept through the room, and in the doorway appeared Yelena, her hair topped with a sweptback, showy feathered veil, and Andrei, tuxedoed and beaming. They walked confidently and slowly, acknowledging the cheers of onlookers and headed to the food and drink tables in the rear of the hall.

They stood by the cake, and Andrei picked up an empty wine glass, tapped it with a fork. The ring stilled the murmurs in the crowd. "Thanks to all of you for coming to our celebration. Yelena and I want you to eat and dance and enjoy yourself this afternoon, the most important day of our lives." He glanced at Yelena. "So far!"

The caterer handed Andrei a broad serving knife. A photographer, holding up a corded flashbulb reflector in one hand, his other hand at the shutter button of his tripod-mounted camera, stood ready to snap the picture.

Andrei sliced off a big piece of the cake, placing it on a plate he held high for all to see. Then he took a fork and held out a bite for Yelena. She took the fork and gave him a bite too. Cheers went up, and and the photographer's flashbulb went white light, pop.

Nikolay held up his wine glass. Petró rubbed his forehead, studying the best man standing nearby, the suit obviously borrowed from a relative, for his socks showed too much below the cuffs of his pants. *Young Pioneers were skipped for him!* An amused curve shaped Petró's closed lips.

"I propose a toast," Nikolay offered. "To Yelena and Andrei: May their marriage be long and fruitful ... with little ones," he added, his words trailing off in a chuckle.

Hooooooray! someone yelled.

And so the wedding went. Petró took in the whirl of the afternoon, and by evening, he and Olga were pleasantly exhausted. Their Andrei had gained his wings and flown away, or something like that. As they left the dance hall and walked back to their flat, the newlyweds already departed for a destination unknown, Petró felt a bit older, maybe not wiser, but as though he'd reached another landmark in his life.

At twilight, Venus appeared in the western sky. A tiny, steady beam. He knew things would work out fine for Andrei and Yelena. The job with the Air Force was a career, and he would be in line for promotions from his second lieutenant status as a fledging pilot.

They reached their block, and Petró glanced up the side of the building. "Today, our little Andrei took a big step," he said.

"So did we," Olga replied.

30
ОРБИТА-2
(ORBIT-2)

That night, Petró relished his quiet meal back at the flat. Olga washed the few dishes, and he settled into the easy chair, ready to savor tea and catch up on news of the day.

No longer did he have to listen to the bulky Popov radio in its wooden cabinet. No longer would Petró have to wait out its sometimes reluctant vacuum tubes until they died and refused to glow orange. That was when he'd replace them. Now, for quick news, he had another radio, so small he could hold it in one hand, but its place was the little side table by his easy chair.

An Orbit-2 all-transistor shortwave receiver. Petró got stations everywhere, even though most of what he wanted to hear was jammed by relentless Soviet radio transmitters. He'd listen to Voice of America in Turkey, then *blaaaaaaaaaat*, a buzzing station at that frequency. He couldn't tune around it.

Most of the time, he just went to Radio Moscow. The news, no complications.

"Today, in America, we learn of the death of U-2 spy plane pilot, Francis Gary Powers," the newsreader intoned gravely.

Petró sat up. *Can this be?* The years came back. He and Ivan driving out to the U-2 wreckage in the taiga. *That pilot's name, Powers, I remember.* He looked over to Olga, busy drying off a dish with a towel. Could he tell her now, what he'd seen in that wreckage so many years ago? *No, it's only for me and Ivan to know these things.*

"After serving a prison sentence in Vladimir Central Prison for his espionage overflight of the Union of Soviet Socialist Republics on May 1, 1960, Powers returned to the United States where he later found work as a private pilot.

"Yesterday, the helicopter Powers was flying for television station KNBC in Los Angeles, California, crashed after he reported on widespread brush fires in Santa Barbara County—"

Petró suddenly felt dizzy. So much happened since he and Ivan went to the downed spy plane and started the nonstop work on reconnaissance cameras.

Little Andrei, a mere toddler. Now, married. An Air Force officer. Also a helicopter pilot.

Petró could tell him about Francis Gary Powers being killed in a helicopter after surviving the crash of the U-2. He bit his lip. *I better not. That jinxes with words.* Andrei might find out from others on the base. But then, maybe not.

31
КИНЕЗИОЛОГИИ И АМИЗДАТ
(KINESIOLOGY & *SAMIZDAT*)

Andrei's best man, Nikolay Mushinsky, was more than a professional student. He had a job too. At the municipal library in downtown Gorod, an antiquated, ramshackle building far too small for the many casual piles of books stacked in the aisles between loaded shelves. Seemingly, every book the library acquired, even if unread, found a home for eternity. Nothing was tossed. The library staff who worked there could only guess what was where in the unshelved piles. One of those staff was Nikolay, the doctoral candidate, reluctant to finish and given to contemplating "sabbaticals" from further progress on his thesis: "The American Reformer Henry George as an Influence on Leo Tolstoy." What sort of assigned work could he expect outside the university knowing *that*, if his still-pending two years of military service didn't come first?

Nikolay Mushinsky's work at the Gorod Central Municipal Library was on the second floor where he sat at a desk by a Nadjakov photocopy machine. The machine, no more than a few years old, was prone to jam with paper. Besides clearing out jams,

Nikolay approved all photocopies as proper and legal. He was the photocopier operator.

He stood at his desk by the copier, waiting for an approaching library user with a thick bound journal in hand. The reader had inserted his thumb between pages of evident interest.

Nikolay looked every bit a photocopier operator: thin, standing tall, wearing a white shirt, wool tie, dressy—though ill-fitting pants—and shined shoes. Small, rimless spectacles clung to his ruddy face.

"Hello, you've something to copy?" Nikolay asked the reader.

The reader set the open book on the desk. "Pages two thirty-four, two thirty-five, two thirty-six. I want to copy those, yes." The reader was an older man, and why he would be interested in this journal about applied kinesiology was more than Nikolay could imagine, except perhaps the doddering man before him had some idea he'd recapture some spry moves from his youth if he exercised, first knowing a few scientific principles.

"Okay, let me see the pages."

Nikolay took the bound journal, open to page two thirty-four, and gave the text a once-over. He had to make sure the photocopies would not be violations under uniform Soviet law.

"Just a minute," he said, and he opened a drawer and took out the exhaustive compilation, *Prohibition Guidelines to Be Applied to Photocopying of Restricted Materials*. "I need to check if kinesiology is sensitive, photocopying not allowed."

He opened up the loose-leaf binder, looking under "K" to see if there was an entry. As often was the case, there wasn't. He flipped pages for related terms, like "anatomy," that might apply to the three pages the older reader wanted.

"Hmmm. I don't see applicable guidelines—" Nikolay scanned the second-floor public area for another staff member with whom he might confer about whether to let this go. Nobody was around: They probably were on break, taking a smoke, drinking coffee in the lunch room, something like that.

"Just let me glance this over." He plunged into the article, descriptions of different arm muscles and ligaments to the shoulder and what the dynamics of contraction and release did when one, for example, threw something with the left hand, and how a fluid, forward motion was achieved. Nikolay looked up at the doddering reader, not sure he, if anybody, could be interested in such an appallingly dull medical treatise. Reading pages of that would put him to sleep or at least age him, so no secrets of youth hid in these paragraphs and, most important, no State secrets that under any circumstances were ever photocopied.

"This is okay," Nikolay told the reader with pleasant directness. "Where are your tokens? I need three."

The old man handed over three tokens he'd obviously bought at the front desk on the first floor. Five for one ruble. Nikolay took the tokens, put them in a drawer in his desk, where he took out a key, then placed the journal face down, page two thirty-four on the glass surface of the photocopier. He turned the key clockwise in the switch, and the machine sprang to life. "Warming up," he told the old man.

Then he pressed the green button, and a bar of light under the glass began moving, leaking out each side of the cover flap.

Such requests for photocopying were typical of Nikolay's work day: An old pensioner, who had the free time to spend in the municipal library, would wander up to the desk and ask for photocopies of material that could not be removed from the library. Bound journals were common candidates for photocopying.

As a rule, Nikolay was able to honor the requests, but many

included topics in the Permission-to-Photocopy-Denied category. Anything having to do with State spending by the government, even though published, was not to be photocopied. Or if the production total for some rare mineral appeared as bragging rights in a mining journal nobody ever read, the State decided there was no "need to know" among the general population, so why let the figure circulate freely?

Nikolay had long ago given up on trying to figure out the logic of the prohibition list. Even though he thought listing certain subjects silly, he acted as if he took it seriously. Nobody, not even his shadow, was to think he didn't perform his duties responsibly. He didn't want to lose such an easy job. An elevator operator was far busier.

Besides, if he had to deny someone the right to photocopy, there was nothing to prevent them from taking the journal back to a carrel and copying out what they wanted on scraps of paper. Nothing. Nikolay called that "Finnish photocopying," and if they were as slow as a Finn, they'd also have to come back the next day.

Few readers asked for photocopies, however, given the comprehensive list of prohibited subjects. Thus, Nikolay's work day was filled with plenty of idle hours. But because Nikolay had such an active interior life, this was not an overwhelming drawback to the job: Boredom seldom arose. He wrote most of his doctoral thesis—so far unapproved—sitting at the Photocopy Reservations Desk at the Gorod Central Municipal Library. Nikolay didn't consider this dereliction of duty. Sure, he could have left his desk, walked about and tidied up books on shelves, or got to know some of those books stacked in the aisles, but he also felt the assignment at a low-activity library desk was an unacknowledged stipend, of sorts, for his academic pursuits.

His thesis was about the property reforms first proposed in

America by the great Henry George: Abolish all private ownership of land and place it in the hands of the State. Georgian reforms were heartily endorsed by the illustrious Soviet novelist Leo Tolstoy.

So Nikolay's doctoral thesis, an examination of how someone rooted in the capitalist model of the West could endorse public ownership and responsibility for all land and natural resources was, for him, compelling.

Nikolay knew the grand workers revolution had gone off the tracks. The Soviet economic engine sputtered on with rife inefficiency. Marx was wrong to focus so much on taking over the "means of production." What are the means of production worth, if nothing feeds it? No, Nikolay felt a true revolution would give the means of production back to whomever wanted them. Only the State could own the land and natural resources needed to feed factories.

Others came to the same conclusion. Tolstoy illustrated the problem of land ownership in his short story, "How Much Land Does a Man Need?" Typically, Nikolay ran into like minds in a downtown tea house close by the Municipal Library. Hot, steaming black Yunnan tea was their beverage of choice. Unlike vodka—the leisure drink of the nonthinking man—chai, for Nikolay and other tea-house habitués, cleared the mind and made productive thought for doctoral dissertations possible. Dmitriy Lyutenkov was one such familiar face.

Dmitriy lived at home with his parents, spending days in and out of tea houses, writing in his journal. He had opinions galore, but after failing to qualify for military service—his eyesight so bad, he was deemed legally blind—he realized he might better go through life developing skill as a freeloader until he could reform Russian society. Which he was intent on doing.

He and Nikolay, in that regard, were kindred spirits.

One day, Dmitriy of the thick glasses, black felt beret hugging his brow, approached Nikolay's desk in the library. "What do you have to photocopy?" Nikolay asked, eyeing the omnipresent journal he carried in one hand.

"I finally have it done." Dmitriy whispered, looking around. Two or three library visitors sat at tables, asleep or reading. Nikolay could never tell.

"What?" Nikolay answered, searching Miya's proud, nervous eyes behind the thick lenses.

"My manifesto. How to reform the corrupt system once and for all." His eyes darted about, electric with alertness. "Now I must publish."

"Publish?" Nikolay whispered. "Where's the money for that?"

Dmitriy slowly turned about and stared long at the photocopier beside Nikolay's desk, a smile warming his face. "That's beautiful," he whispered. "A beautiful means of production."

"Reproduction," corrected Nikolay.

"A beautiful means of reproduction. I stand corrected," he whispered.

"We cannot talk of such things here," Nikolay said. "Our study group meets at a new place this Tuesday evening. You come here." He took a piece of paper from the desk and scribbled the address for the next meeting of Advance Front, a gathering of "refuseniks" who got together to voice dissatisfactions with the social order and to come up with schemes for disruption and eventual reform of the Soviet system.

He handed Dmitriy the address. "You read your work there," he said, pointing at the journal in his visitor's hand, "And we'll decide if we can help you distribute your writings."

"*Samizdat*," Dmitriy said. No official publisher would touch his writing. He had to go underground. He gave the photocopier a last look, turned, then quickly walked away from Nikolay's desk.

32

Ф6.3, 1/50 C.

(F6.3, 1/50 S.)

Andrei and Yelena had but a few months of honeymoon before the morning when Andrei's new assignment took him away.

Petró's gut ached as the four of them stood in the front room of their flat, hesitating about good-byes. Andrei's duffel bag sat, unmoving, on the rug.

Helicopter pilots were fighting guerrillas on the Afghanistan and Tadzhik borders. That's where Andrei was going. He'd lost married housing at the military base, and Yelena was moving in with them.

"Be sure and write." Yelena looked up at Andrei's face, the flight cap on his head with the two stars of a full lieutenant. "Often," she added.

She clutched at Andrei's camo military jacket, as though reluctant to let him go. He was assigned for two years to the Afghan border station, but she knew, from their talk, these assignments could be extended. As Andrei openly speculated, If a helicopter goes down, why would they let another helicopter pilot return to the Motherland and leave the fighting?

Petró knew war was war. All he could hope for was no bad news. No pine box.

That was why Petró's gut ached, even though he stood ready to carry his son's duffel bag out for the bus ride to the train station.

Andrei had long hugs for Yelena and Olga. "I'm ready," he said briskly, as if the sooner he left, the easier to keep moving to the destination that put him on edge.

"I'll take your bag," Petró offered. "You'll carry this far too much where you go," he said pointing to the Air Force-issue duffel bag. "The least I can do."

Out on the sidewalk, they waited for the bus. "War is what we military do," his son said.

"Yes, of course. And this is not an easy war. Those Muslim mujahideen, they're armed by the Americans. Well, we'll show them," Petró said, a flash of memory tugging him back decades: the smoldering wreckage of that American U-2 spy plane in the taiga of the Urals, he and Ivan arriving in the GAZ-63 truck. *Yes, we shot it out of the skies, we made the Americans look bad then.*

They got off the bus at the train station. Then walked across the terminal's expansive floor to where Andrei read the schedule posted overhead. He'd take the train to Stalinabad in the extreme south. From there Andrei was to go to a military base with the helicopters.

Andrei had to be on Track Two. The Stalinabad train arrived in twenty minutes.

"No time to sit and drink coffee, let's go out there and talk," Petró said. He reached over to take the duffel bag again, but Andrei firmly grabbed it.

"You feeling nervy?" Petró asked, once they stood on the

raised, concrete platform running between the track beds. Overhead, a bank of feeble canopy lights shone down with a pallidness that failed to brighten the overcast skies beyond. Behind them a long train, Moscow-bound, took on passengers.

A hubbub of loudspeakers implored people to board the train on Track One, and passengers were yelling to keep their parties together. Andrei yelled, too: "Of course, but I'm also concerned for you. Now Yelena lives with you. Oh, she didn't want to go back to Leningrad, her parents."

Petró's face blanked, not understanding. "Why not?" He was sure the Gorbunovs had plenty of room for their daughter.

Andrei shrugged. "She says our family is her family. As my wife, she wants to stay in Gorod."

Petró gulped, hesitated. They would be a bit crowded in their two-room flat. Poor Yelena would sleep on the sofa in the front room until Andrei returned to stay, or she found another flat, which for one person of modest means was difficult.

"We're glad our Yelena lives with us," Petró said though without irony. This sharing quarters with family and relatives was typical, given the chronic housing shortage. Nobody would so much as blink an eye if he introduced his daughter-in-law and said, Our son's away, flying helicopters in Afghanistan.

"You know, one thing before you go. One favor I ask. Your picture, may I?"

Andrei smiled, for he knew his papa mostly took pictures on holiday. "But of course."

Petró reached into his large overcoat pocket and extracted the scuffed leather case holding his beloved Fedka.

He unsnapped the front leather flap, gripped the lens barrel, extended the lens outward, then rotated it a quarter turn to locked position. He was ready for pictures.

Andrei stood erect in military fatigues, duffel bag at his feet. He couldn't remember when his papa last took pictures of him alone.

Petró glanced at the sputtering overhead lights, cocked the shutter, then decided an f-stop of *6.3* was right. Then he moved the shutter speed dial from the *Z*-rest position to *1/50th*. "There," he said.

Andrei smiled bravely.

Petró snapped a picture. Another. Then another. Possessed almost, he stopped talking and kept taking pictures until the train pulled alongside them. He hugged his son, who boarded the train, and he walked beside the train to take more pictures once Andrei leaned out the window and waved. Then the train wheels squealed forward, like a cornered pig.

It had been a long time since Petró felt his face wet with tears, but that Saturday at Sokolov Station he did.

33

ХЛЕБОВ

(LOAVES)

Even though Andrei had been gone less than a month, Yelena wrote him day after day. But Yelena, Olga, and Petró got only one letter, one obviously delayed—given the original postmark—the letter seemingly having to survive terrible mail service over the Caucasus and the inevitable Soviet military censors, who, Petró speculated, read everything.

Still, no news was good news, and mostly what Andrei mentioned was the food and primitive living conditions. He had yet to fly a helicopter mission over enemy fire. He said he could wait on that.

Petró noticed Yelena must have read Andrei's letter at least a dozen times. Each time she picked it up, Did she read something new between the lines? Whatever it was, he knew his daughter-in-law hungered for another letter soon.

When the next letter came, weeks later, Petró sensed Yelena was relieved and more accepting about the separation. It was her trial to endure. Andrei's commitment to the defense of the Motherland decided so much for them as a newlywed couple.

Still, Yelena needed work to occupy her days. She couldn't sit around, waiting for Andrei to return. He was gone for years. She would go stir-crazy, eat wall paint. So she said. On her own, she volunteered to help Olga at the neighborhood bakery, about a kilometer away.

The other choice wasn't appealing: waiting in queues, filling out forms with the Ministry of Employment. Then the probable disappointment of being assigned a job on the other side of Gorod in a cheerless warehouse with punishing travel back and forth.

Far easier, Yelena figured, to see if Olga could take her on as a "free apprentice." If she worked out, perhaps arrangements might be made to pay her. In the meantime, she would learn everything she needed to become a baker.

Olga always set out early, shortly after six, and soon Yelena joined her.

She stood at the kneading table, getting ready to mix up ingredients for black bread, a best seller every day. She had a large vat in front of her, big enough to make dough for twelve loaves at a time—all their oven could handle. She put in two kilos of the dark rye flour, powdery plumes rising above her hands like small ghosts.

Next, she poured in the first of the water, after adding a bit of molasses. She knew from having done this under the tutelage of Olga, she would use all the water, but only if she added it gradually.

Slowly, she pushed her hands on the wet dough, folding in the dry flour with yeast and salt until the dough ball began to take on a fleshly reality, unlike its ghostly powder beginnings. Her mind drifted at such times, working her hands in the wet dough, grabbing a handful of dry, powdery flour, then working that into the wet mixture. Over and over, her hands massaged the dough, almost as if she was silently talking to it, asking it to come to life.

She had been sick that morning. Again. Needed to rush down the hall to the bathroom, where she tossed. This was happening every morning. Olga—who worked at the counter, handling customers at that hour—told her she could do little about the sickness. She had to ride it out and hope her body adjusted.

Yelena pushed harder into the dough, paused, then added a bit more water from her pitcher.

All those intense nights with Andrei, after he came back from a hard day of helicopters, training, flying, whatever he was asked to do. Then they moved to Gorod, married, and too soon, he left. Now, what remained?

She coaxed the dark mass of flour into a living, pulpy being. Imagined the same within her now.

What will it be? Boy—a little Andreika—or girl—a little Lenochka?

She had almost all the flour wetted, had most of it in one hulking mass and no water left. She got it right and would simply knead hard a bit more, then form loaves and set them out to rise. Then she could bake.

She had to be careful, Olga said, and not lift anything heavy. Have someone else move sacks of flour. But other than that, she could keep working. But the heat. She wiped her brow, knowing some loaves in the oven had to be taken out soon. The timer went off. Peeking in the window, she saw what was to come out. She would later slip in a new batch on her baker's paddle.

The baked loaves cooling, she reached over and grabbed her baker's tray and began forming her twelve loaves from the dough. She had a good eye, could judge how much each got. She felt nothing in her tummy yet. But she felt different, as though something was happening to her. As though she, too, had one in the oven.

Will Andrei be surprised!

34
ОЛИМПИЙСКИЙ ФАКЕЛ
(OLYMPIC TORCH)

The years passed. Nearly three and, as Andrei wrote, the war was dragging on endlessly and kept him there. He mentioned that fighting the mujahideen seemed as impossible as eradicating a fungus. Even if they won every battle with the guerrillas, the enemy seemed to live another day and always popped up elsewhere.

He wanted to get away. If only for a few weeks, back to Gorod, but his commander wasn't authorizing leaves. They were always short helicopter pilots.

But when Petró read that letter, he surmised the morale of Soviet censors must have been sagging too: Unlike Andrei's early letters, this one had not a single black expurgation.

Still, Andrei was sacrificing for the Motherland, as was the family who never saw him after he left for combat. The family of his wife, Yelena, his parents, Petró and Olga, and importantly, his son, Gleb Andreyev Kravets—the son he only knew by pictures Yelena mailed every month. Gleb would have his second birthday in a month, and more than the daily mayhem of war, not seeing, not holding little Gleb kept Andrei awake nights.

Weekends with no daycare meant toddler Gleb had to be watched over, which Olga would help Yelena do. But, on occasion, Petró pitched in, leaving Yelena and Olga free to do something together, away from work. Last Sunday, they'd seen a movie.

That Sunday, however, in early June of 1980, Petró and Olga left Yelena with Gleb and set off for the Plato Cinema downtown.

After walking from the Metro Pobeda stop, they joined the queue outside the ticket booth. Petró glanced at the marquee. *Countryside Love.* "What?" He pressed his palm to his temple. Olga and Yelena had just seen the picture. "You're seeing this again. Last Sunday, you saw this!" he said.

"It's okay." Olga paused, nodding toward the woman in front of them. "She says the picture this week didn't arrive. So they play this again. Held it over."

"Held over?" Petró didn't know what to do. He had no desire to see *Countryside Love.* A movie for women. Romantic, gushy.

But what else would they do on the Sunday afternoon, if he got stubborn? Olga didn't mind a second time. Last Sunday, she and Yelena were still talking about that movie when they got back to the flat.

"It's fine," Petró said, realizing he'd only create more trouble than what he had to endure. What were a few kopecks for tickets anyway? They'd spent fare for the Metro and would have to pay to go back, so what if they spent a bit more for this stale entertainment?

Before long, in comfortable balcony seats, Petró left to get popcorn and fizzy drinks.

When he got back, the lights had dimmed. People distractedly munched away on handfuls of popcorn. In the dark, Petró let his mind drift away from his usual Sunday worries about Andrei in Afghanistan.

The last lights went out, and the projector started up, the curtains pulled apart, and numbers, counting down, flashed on the screen.

SUMMER OLYMPICS IN MOSCOW. The title of the first newsreel, out-sized letters flooding the screen. Petró's chest swelled with pride. This was what the Motherland waited for. The Russian people were playing host to the most important sporting event in the world. Petró beamed. This was not *Countryside Love!*

Strains of the National Anthem of the Soviet Union, then the newsreader excitedly said, "Wednesday, in Moscow's Luzhniki Stadium, specially built for this year's Summer Olympics, the opening ceremonies featured Sergey Belov, a member of the Soviet Olympic basketball team, who lit the Olympic torch—"

On the screen, a runner raced out a stadium portal onto the chalk-striped, oval track, holding the flaming torch on high, and circuited the entire stadium. The newsreel camera zoomed in, capturing his face, his pure elation.

Petró glanced sideways at Olga, no big sports fan. Then catching her eye, he smiled. This was still a Russian moment for the history books.

How could he have been at the stadium up there for this? Where would he have gotten tickets? They were so hard to get. Perhaps Viktor could have helped. He was sure Viktor managed to go with Svetlana. They both were sports fans.

He slumped in his seat, munched more popcorn. He had to be content to miss out on Moscow, so glorious for the Motherland. Instead, he was stuck in an audience for a romantic movie coming up.

His mind turned wistful.

"Notably absent from the Moscow Olympics, with more than one hundred of the world's nations participating, is the United

States of America. American athletes have trained long and hard to be here in Moscow, and they wanted badly to compete, but at the last minute the American Olympic Committee pulled its athletes out.

"President Jimmy Carter announced as long as Russian troops are in Afghanistan, no American athletes would go to Moscow.

"TASS was curious about how the American athletes felt, so we called one on the phone. Here is Jamal Jordan from Berkeley, California:"

A photograph of the dark-complexioned American runner filled the screen.

"What is your event, Jamal?"

Yellow subtitles paused along the screen's bottom.

"Oh, you call me J. J. Yeah, I run the hundred meter."

Petró stared at him, at how his bushy hair seemed as wide as his shoulders. *How does he run with hair like that?*

"And how do you feel, J. J., about not being able to compete in Moscow?"

"It's a slap in the face. We all trained hard. Why we be singled out? Man, do I look like a puppet for U-S-A foreign policy?"

"Are you saying you're not proud of your country's action?"

"No, how could I be?"

"Why do you say that?"

"Uh, it's not like America always does right, know what I mean? This boycott is stupid."

"So, J. J., you think it's wrong to mix sports and national politics?"

"I don't think anything Russia does with Afghanistan is anywhere near what my country done. I mean, how do you spell Vietnam?" The speaker on the other end of the phone laughed.

As did Petró.

The American runner had it right. His country was wrong-headed to stay out of the Summer Olympics because of Afghanistan. Petró shook his head.

Afghanistan.

If Andrei wasn't in Afghanistan, how he would have liked to have been at this Moscow Olympics with him—even little Gleb too—up there in Luzhniki Stadium for just one event. To feel that electricity, that Russian pride, surging through the air, the crowds, their feet stomping the stadium floor boards into a crescendo, into a deafening roar.

Petró looked over at Olga again. *Oh, women, they have not the interest in sports like men. They want beauty, the human side of it. How graceful is the gymnast Nadia, that sort of thing, but as for following the competitions, that's for men.*

"Russia is expected to do well in these Olympics," the newsreader said over more clips of the opening ceremonies, the Olympic flame burning brightly on an elevated platform at one end of the stadium, the panned shots of the crowds cheering, and the mesmerizing chalked, parallel lines that ran around the track.

Petró let the screen images sink into his memory, as if by doing so, he might save them for Andrei too. A tear welled in his right eye. The parade of athletes began, each country's team led by one of their own—two hands, extended arms—presenting their national flag. The teams marched through the stadium entrance around the striped track, Greece first, then one country after another in alphabetical order. Russia, however, was saved for last. As host country, the finale, always.

"The Russian Olympic team is made up of four hundred eighty-eight athletes," the newsreader said. Petró peered intently, as if he were in the stadium, not sitting in a theater seat, munching popcorn. The Russian flag, hammer and sickle of the working man, held aloft by Boris Guzunov, weightlifter, was in front. The tear rolled down Petró's right cheek. How he would have liked to have Andrei standing beside him in that stadium, both of them yelling away into the roar of the crowd for the Motherland's greatness to host such an event.

The National Anthem of the Soviet Union rose as the newsreader made a final comment and signed off from Luzhniki Stadium in Moscow. Hands waving on a sea of faces lingered in Petró's eyes for the longest time, knowing he could have been there, if only Andrei had a military leave, if only he had persuaded Viktor to get him some tickets with his *blat*—his pull—if only ...

The camera drew back and rose, taking in all Luzhniki Stadium, holding more than one hundred thousand strong that late afternoon on Saturday. The camera climbed higher, taking in the skyline of Moscow, the Kremlin towers, St. Basil's patterned bulbs looming in the distance, and then the clouds.

The billowy white clouds.

35
КРАСНАЯ ЗВЕЗДА
(RED STAR)

The cumulus puffs floated like buoys in the pristine blue sky, pierced only by the jagged peaks of the Hindu Kush range.

The air stopped moving. No breezes. Just the insistent hiss of flames licking at his fractured Mi-24 gunship. The chopper took an incoming missile seconds before. Exploded and dropped like a stone to the floor of the mountain pass. Foreign voices in the trees, unsure where. Came down with a *thump*. Releasing himself from the seat belt and rolled off the pilot seat. His gunner, seated beside him, a bloody pulp of raw meat. He almost puked. The missile hit the side of his ship, on the red star emblem painted right over the oil tank. That's why.

The flames hissed, licked at the wreckage, leaped higher. Fuel was leaking from the tank. Soon, the full nineteen hundred liters of kerosene would ignite. Those foreign voices were waiting for the finale. Waiting for the explosion. His gunner should have opened fire at the glint they saw on the side of the mountain, above them, but he ignored it. A glint from rock mica, he'd said. Then they knew otherwise. Must have been a shoulder-launched missile pointing down at them. Should have fired and wondered later.

They ran out of luck. But his comrades would fight on. The mujahideen were no match for Soviet military might. He would be sitting the fight out for now. Lying in a hospital somewhere. But he didn't send out an S-O-S.

He needed the medics. A warm wetness wept under the flight suit across his chest. He felt odd.

His head turned sideways. Not more than five meters away, he saw some of the casing of the missile. The rear fins, three of them, a tripod of ailerons. One had a flag. Red and white stripes, white stars on blue. America.

He wanted so badly to get home, to see Gleb, to see Yelena. But that would wait. He had to sleep a while. His jaw loosened. His eyes went dull.

36

ОТКАЗНИК
(REFUSENIK)

A few weeks into the new year 1981, a winter storm brought heavy snow and made walking Gorod city streets punishing.

On one such street—a spot of dark clothing moved—a solitary man stepping through the night over the icy whiteness.

An outsider in more than one sense, he trudged through the forbidding night, his feet nervy about a slip, his wary eyes knowing not a soul shared the walkway with him. A few pairs of headlights passed, tires slushing; a bus, too, with but a handful of passengers, its tire chains clanking into the heavy silence of the black night.

But the steps of Nikolay Mushinsky had purpose. He was bound for a meeting, and he was late, the others surely there.

He and the four other like-minded spirits, among themselves only, cheerfully bandied the appellation of refusenik, for they truly believed hypocrisy had corrupted their Marxist-Leninist society, destroying its soul, leaving it unclean.

Crunch, crunch, crunch. His steps broke thin ice.

Yes, he and his group wanted to set right a Soviet-style communism that too easily yielded to the temptation of elite fascism, giving the Party a domination over the proletariat that rivalled anything power-mad Hitler and his Third Reich Nazis did. Stalin's bloody purges, coming to light, had the unbridled efficiency of Dachau and turned the Jewish legacy of Karl Marx, for what it was worth, on its head.

Again, *crunch, crunch, crunch.* He wrapped his arms on his chest. When a government of the workers oppresses them, then it must rot from within and become ripe for invasion from without. Wasn't that what history testified? Didn't centuries of Tatars and Muslims pillaging the Motherland by sword prove that? Could the fighting on the Afghan border now with those Muslim mujahideen be otherwise?

Nikolay winced. Only last summer, he got news his childhood friend Andrei died flying a combat helicopter there. He had been best man at Andrei's wedding three years ago. Although they—Andrei and Nikolay—differed greatly as adults, their bond from childhood, as always, was unbreakable.

Nikolay felt sorrow about Andrei. He only hoped what he did from then on was for a just society in which Andrei would have proudly lived.

He stepped down the stairwell to the basement entrance and knocked.

He went inside.

They'd taken to calling themselves Advance Front and met in a windowless, basement storeroom of a public housing block. The room was unheated, cold, and musty. But away from observers who might have noted comings and goings, an anonymity Advance Front wanted.

Five were present: Dmitriy, Stas, Misha, Kostya, and Nikolay who would lead the meeting. Before Nikolay said a word, however, he took a cassette player from his shoulder bag, set it down, then started playing loud traditional folk music.

"If we're bugged," he joked.

This precaution was needed. The KGB couldn't plant an informer in a group of five, who met for years. The KGB had other ways, a popular one being the deployment of "little listeners," electronic listening devices placed anywhere. On telephones to tap the line. Or another kind, on ceilings, broadcasting to an outside receiver manned by a KGB operative.

Advance Front moved its meetings every few months to keep the KGB guessing where to plant "little listeners." And if members ever wanted an unscheduled meeting, it was always in a public area, away from crowds. They'd meet briefly—ten, fifteen minutes—casting a wary eye about while they talked in hushed tones. The public zoo and the national cemetery were favorites for these quick chats.

"Advance Front exists," Nikolay began, "solely to change the minds of the common worker. How do we do this? We do not have a radio station, we do not have a television transmitter, we do not have a printing press. Are we only to stand in Great October Park and yell out our ideas to passersby? No, we would be taken in for questioning by the KGB—"

He paused, looking over each of his fellow dissenters, committed enough to sit on the concrete floor, no thought given for personal comfort. The cassette player wailed away with heart-wrenching lyrics, *Midnights in Moscow* with accordion accompaniment.

"No, we won't harangue people in Great October Park. No minds would change anyway. The same people walk there every day. Not a good use of our time. The way to reach many minds is not easy—"

"Didn't we," narrow-faced Kostya with the beard said, holding up a pamphlet, "publish Dmitriy's manifesto? Aren't people reading *that?*"

"Yes, *samizdat*. We did that. I made fifty copies at the library. But who did we give them to? People who would change their thinking? Or people who agree with us because they know us?"

"Kolya's right," Dmitriy said. "We distributed fifty copies. Maybe they read them, maybe not. Maybe they gave them to others to read, maybe not."

"A lot of work to make those pamphlets," ruddy-faced Misha added wistfully, "and maybe nothing happened."

The cassette player was not to be upstaged: A singer drew out a sustained note of joy.

"I'm glad you bring up Dmitriy's *samizdat*, Kostya. Something we can do, but probably not yet," Nikolay said. "So I thought about a clandestine radio broadcast. We could get equipment and reach countless people; many might be interested in our ideas—"

"But there's so many risks," blond Stas said. "They find those pirate stations all the time, shut them down, lock up the operators—"

A smile slowly slipped over Nikolay's face. "Radio is good and reaches many, but risky, and after every broadcast, the station has to move. So I agree with Stas. Radio has problems. So I say, back to *samizdat*—"

"I thought you said that didn't work," Dmitriy said, apparently willing to separate pride about writing his manifesto from failure to get many pass-along readers of his *samizdat*.

"This time, we publish differently." Nikolay rubbed his hands together. "You know the way to reach people minds hasn't changed since Gutenberg invented the printing press and made hand-written manuscripts a thing of the past. Cheap printed copies brought down the religious hegemony of the Roman Catholic Church everywhere. You know why?"

"Sure, people read for themselves, they no longer needed to be read to—" Dmitriy said.

The cassette player went silent. A long pause between songs. Then the squeeze box took over.

"Dmitriy's right. Everyone can absorb the words into their mind, can read them over, understand them. And it's cheap. My position at Central Library gives me the gift of Gutenberg. I'll make copies for Advance Front."

"But *samizdat* for Dmitriy's manifesto went nowhere," Stas said.

"Yes, so we'll now publish differently." Nikolay took from his shoulder bag photocopies for everyone. "A summary of Advance Front's demands for government reform." He handed them out, smiling: They'd talked about these many, many times, but by boiling them down to one page, Nikolay felt he'd done something important.

"What I've written out is the first bulletin from Advance Front. Read this over, and we'll reach agreement on what it contains. Please."

"How's this *samizdat* different from Dmitriy's?" bearded Kostya asked. "Shorter?"

"Yes, but also the distribution," Nikolay answered. "We'll go post in public places, sure to be read by many, not like a manifesto in one pair of hands—"

"So now we'll approve?" Stas asked.

"Yes, we need consensus. Then I'll make one hundred copies, and we'll go post—"

"We'll work together—" Dmitriy said.

"Yes, I thought the same," Nikolay said. "Two's good: one to hold the can of paste, another to put the bulletin on a wall. Any wall you can find. The side of a housing block is good. Passersby see it and read.

"But we must do this unnoticed." he added. "Early morning hours. The night policemen sleep on the job anyway. We'll get up before sunrise, and we can put up many—"

"The entrances to Metro are best," Kostya interjected. "Many people go there, but go early, before police come out, ready for pickpockets—"

The discussion dribbled off, and they quickly approved *Bulletin No. 1.*

The cassette finished, and Nikolay flipped the tape over. The strains of *Go Home, My Cow* rose to drown out their hushed voices.

What happened next was surprisingly quick and easy. In downtown Gorod, one hundred copies were pasted on walls of subway entrances and other places where people might stop and read. Nobody was seen, caught, or called in for questioning.

Nikolay thought what they had done miraculous, but then he knew it would work. On days to follow, when they saw everyday Gorod citizens standing before their Advance Front bulletin and devouring their words, the refuseniks knew it had happened.

Advance Front gained a public identity, but nobody, not even the KGB boys, knew who they were.

37
ИГРУШЕЧНЫХ СОЛДАТИКОВ
(TOY SOLDIERS)

On that same winter night Nikolay met with Advance Front, across town in the Kravets' family flat, Petró, Olga, Yelena, and Gleb finished a pelmeni dinner.

Gleb played with toy soldiers on the rug. Petró sat in the easy chair after putting on his slippers and preparing a mug of steaming Georgian tea, his after-dinner ritual. Olga and Yelena had washed the dishes and stood ready to leave by the door.

"We'll go now, see Anya on the first floor," Olga said. "She had a tooth pulled. We'll see if she needs anything." Both women smiled at Petró, then slipped out.

Before taking his first sip of tea, however, Petró studied little Gleb lining up figures on the Afghani rug, its figured earthy browns looking oddly like battleground terrain. Methodically, studiously placing each, Gleb set out two opposing lines of toy soldiers. "Who're the ones in blue uniforms, Glebka?"

"Don't know, Papa."

"*Papa!* I'm not your papa. I'm your grandpapa," Petró shot back.

"Yes, Grandpapa. I don't have a papa. You can be my papa too."

"You have a papa, let me show you."

Petró set the unsipped tea down, got up, then went to the back room and pulled out a small box under the double bed. "In here," he said, returning to see Gleb follow his every move.

Back in the easy chair, he took the lid—*Андреи* printed on top—off the shoe box, placing it beside the tea mug on the side table. He let his fingers flick the top edges of dozens of snapshots.

He had pictures from the day Andrei was born. They were all there, and they all still fit in one shoe box.

Petró gazed at Gleb, busy moving about the toy soldiers, then looked back at the shoe box. It held hundreds of photographs to show Gleb he had a father like other boys his age. *But why is he gone?* Gleb would ask.

Petró didn't know what to say, what to tell Gleb other than some words about his papa making a sacrifice to protect the Motherland from the Muslim invaders in the Caucasus, more of the endless conflict that went back to the days of Genghis Khan.

Gleb's to understand this?

Petró sighed. The problem of the Muslim horde was still with them.

Gleb had to be spared this.

He pulled out one picture. One of the last. Andrei stood in his camo uniform, shouldering a duffel bag, ready to take the train from Sokolov Station. His Fedka camera had taken the picture, a roll of pictures, finishing with ones of Andrei leaning out the window from the rail car.

Tears welled in Petró's eyes.

Why should he even show Gleb the pictures? How would that prove he had a papa?

The photographs were just images. Gleb was too young to understand death, especially the death of a soldier, an aviator like his papa in the Mi-24 gunship brought down in the Hindu Kush. Or that once in a while the toy soldier falls and never stands up again.

In the photograph, standing on the train platform, Andrei smiled, but Petró saw it might have been for show. As though Andrei was unsure he'd see his papa again. That doubt weighed on his lips, bringing a lie to the smile.

A tear tracked the right cheek of Petró's face. He jiggled the photograph, but the image, fixed in the silver halide emulsion, stubbornly refused to budge. Lifeless. The moment frozen when Petró last saw him alive.

No, he'd put the shoe box away. Gleb was too absorbed in the soldiers advancing across the rug. He had no interest in pictures.

Petró took a deep breath. *Better to tell Gleb stories about his papa. Let his young mind imagine what his papa was like. When he's older, perhaps he'll understand sacrifice for the Motherland, but not now.*

He's too young.

The next day, not a working Saturday, Petró again kept little Gleb company while Olga and Yelena left for the flower seller Irina on Chernozem Street, then caught the bus out to the War Heroes Cemetery. They took flowers to Andrei's grave, as they did every month.

Olga watched Yelena, holding the flowers, step off the bus. The cemetery in Saltykov Park Preserve was vast, and today they would go to the newest section, where Andrei was buried. They began walking the roadway to the left, away from the old, original cemetery with the graves of Olga's uncles and Petró's father. They would take flowers there another day.

The sun was out for a brisk winter day; they trudged along, mostly silent, wearing coats, simple house dresses, and scarves.

Soon they stood before the snowflecked tombstone they knew so well: ANDREI PETROV KRAVETS 1956-1980 AVIATOR HERO OF THE SOVIET UNION.

"He was doing what he wanted to do," Olga said. "He always wanted to fly, even as a child."

Yelena fussed with the poinsettias, as though arranging them for a more pleasing presentation. She took the green metal cone of a flower holder Olga picked up from the wooden bin at the cemetery entrance. In it, she slipped the flower stems and again rearranged. Kneeling, she then pushed the spiked end of the holder into the cold ground before the tombstone. From her pocket she took out a small plastic bottle, unscrewed the cap, and poured some sugared water she'd brought from home.

She stood up beside Olga, bowing her head in a moment of evident reflection.

"You knew him as a child," Yelena said, turning to Olga. "I knew him for only a few years."

Olga could see Yelena's eyes had gone teary. She hugged her.

Yelena nodded. "You'll have to tell me more about Andrei, when he was young."

"Yes."

"So I'll know him better, even though he's gone." Yelena bent down and fussed with the flowers one more time. She looked up at Olga and smiled. "There, we can go."

"Yes, until next month."

38
КРЕСТЬЯНСКАЯ ЖАЛОБА
(PEASANT COMPLAINT)

A morning like many others, Petró went off to work. A blustery day that made him realize what never changed: Winter was winter. He pulled up the fur collar of his heavy coat, instinctively keeping the top of his ear-flapped *shapka* into the wind, his gaze stubbornly down, almost as if leading his shuffling steps across an open square fronting the Metro entrance.

The subway entrance on Narodniki Prospekt at Gorkii Stop had a cold cheeriness. A public space of iced-over benches that, during sunnier months, Petró remembered were for eating lunch al fresco. The usual public art on display, dominated by a statue of Lenin, holding his proletarian cap on high, as if saluting workers on parade before him.

Petró knew, despite the changes in new technology—satellites in orbit and whatnot—what wouldn't change was weather. The snow in his path said as much.

Winter winds gave the small park a scrubbed look. Municipal cleaning crews swept out the subway entrance, too, and, with wire-bristle brushes and soapy water, removed a blizzard of bills pasted on the walls.

Petró paused to admire the clean renewal. But his eye caught a fresh, solitary bill that must have been posted recently. Such an opportunity! He couldn't resist reading the only bill on that wall. He walked straight to it.

He stood there—letting others pass into the entrance archway—and studied the bill. Nothing for sale. No lost dog. No, a political screed, an ordinary rant of complaint.

Advance Front. What's this? Petró scratch*ed* his right temple and rocked on the balls of his feet planted on the miserably cold concrete. *Bulletin No. 1?*

Petró read quickly. *What do they think, this call for revolution? Again?*

He had seen similar postings before. This one was no different: The Revolution of 1917 had gone wrong. Instead, it only brought to power a new ruling class to exploit workers.

Petró knew the promise of 1917 hadn't been delivered. Still, like most people, he pretended for the higher-ups that with enough sacrifice from everybody, the worker's paradise would eventually be theirs. And he sacrificed: He went off to work dutifully every day even though his efforts hadn't brought him the comforts people in the West took for granted. No worker in Russia drove a car. But in the West, so many had private cars. Where was the failure of capitalism Marx promised?

This Advance Front says the Politburo in Moscow has to go. A fairly elected Duma, the solution. A government of the workers, by the workers, and for the workers.

Good luck.

Petró turned away from the bulletin, sure to attract other posted bills, soon leading to a cluttered, eyesore wall. Six months away, another work crew would return with wire-bristle brushes and hot soapy water and put muscle into uncovering the clean wall again.

He descended the subway stairs quickly, the fleeting thought in his head, *Who's Advance Front?* How could they be worth his attention? Or was that group just some lone reformer, who had too much time on his hands? Sitting around, thinking up subversive ideas, writing them out, making copies, *samizdat*, and going around posting the bulletin where people couldn't help but see it? He was sure that's what it was. Advance Front might be nothing more than one person. One serious crackpot.

People complained about everything in Russia. That was how they got through the winter, that was how they got through the week, that was how they endured. Petró was wise to that. But often, relief by complaining might bring something worse. Were farm peasants more miserable under the Tsar or under the collectives the Revolution gave them?

But some things Petró could depend on and not complain. The subway: dependable transport and out of the cold weather. He got on the car that halted beside him.

39

ОВИР

(OVIR)

The attention paid *Bulletin No. 1*, posted around central Gorod, emboldened Nikolay Mushinsky. Because nobody knew he was a founder of Advance Front, he had the satisfying pleasure of watching a passerby, who otherwise might have been briskly walking on his way, stop to read the bulletin, arrested by words Nikolay personally wrote.

Part of Nikolay wanted to go up and introduce himself as the author.

But he was content to let the *samizdat* speak for itself. That was as it should be: In silence, the seeds of reform were being planted in an individual mind.

He went about his rounds for the next week or so, walking across some public spaces where Advance Front posted its first bulletin. People were still reading the post. But the lone post had begun to attract other paper companions. Announcements about free kittens, veterans' charity sales of used goods, a blurry photocopied picture of the young husband who disappeared, and upcoming dances whose dates came and went. A concern gnawed at Nikolay: Were people possibly ignoring *Bulletin No. 1*? Was their first posting sure to be lost in a blizzard of others before cleaning crews came back to clean off the walls?

He did what they had to do to keep getting readers: He wrote *Bulletin No. 2*.

Again, in early morning hours, Advance Front went out in pairs and surreptitiously posted. Often the sole posting on new walls. Again, readers drifted by and read.

Nikolay was happy. Advance Front once more had attention, was making a name for itself.

But he couldn't resist wanting more.

At first, he'd merely go up to a reader and comment on the post. Before long, though, if the onlooker had time, they engaged in a spirited discussion about Nikolay's words. He wasn't about to admit, however, he was the author. He simply had a preternatural understanding of what the bulletin said, or so the unknowing reader might have thought.

As weeks went by, the inevitable happened: Nikolay attracted crowds. No longer was he having a happenstance discussion with a passerby, but instead he was shouting to dozens of listeners.

On a clear, nippy afternoon, he stood in Great October Park, by the wall honoring the Revolution of 1917. Nearby, a statue of Comrade Lenin towered atop its stone base. "What do I have here?" Nikolay asked, reaching into his coat pocket. "A rock?" He held it high above his head, not unlike Comrade Lenin's upraised hand holding his worker's cap.

"No, even more special, this is not a rock. It's a fossil of a long-lost marine life. See how this shell has an outside, all pitted?" Everybody could easily see what he was talking about.

"See, this is what happened to the ideals of the Great Revolution. Workers of the world unite? Where did this lead us?

We're united, waiting in line for bread. We're united, waiting years on a new refrigerator. In countries of the West that refrigerator is delivered the same day. Why?" That Nikolay identified with those who wanted more material goods was not contradicted by his ill-fitting tweed pants. They stopped too short of his shoes and showed off his socks.

"I'll tell you why. The Great Revolution has become a fossil of what it was supposed to be. The great Soviet social experiment, the idea we'd reform our political structure when we took control from the Tsar has gone wrong. It has ossified. It's this rock-hard fossil I hold up before you."

Nikolay, never one to shy away from speechmaking, could easily talk like this for an hour, but took care to keep his speech to generalities about a return to true Revolutionary ideals. He never would attack the Kremlin, or a leader in Moscow. That could only lead to charges of sedition and an extended vacation in a psychiatric hospital: the standard treatment for political dissidents.

Not once, moreover, did Nikolay mention his link to Advance Front in public. He assumed KGB tracked Advance Front. Because Advance Front was anonymous, authorities knew, unless proved otherwise, it must be intent on harming State interests. Anyone willing to associate with such a group would surely be interviewed at length.

Nikolay let Advance Front, under the cover of darkness, do the *samizdat* circulation of ideas, and he could, in broad daylight, stand up in Great October Park and speak openly of his general dissatisfactions, his fossil prop in pocket always ready.

One day, however, he thought his public speaking might end. A policeman, who'd walked up, waved his rubber cudgel and shooed away the listeners. He took Nikolay aside.

"I see you come here often," the black-uniformed officer said brusquely.

Nikolay was shocked at how the policeman could scatter his listeners as so many sparrows taking flight. Not undeservedly, people took to wryly calling the rubber cudgels waved about by policemen *democratizers* for how they were freely used to break up public discussion of democratic ideas.

"I've done nothing illegal."

"Possibly. A magistrate might not agree."

What is this about? Nikolay hung his head, not willing to challenge the policeman. Not when he had the power to arrest him.

Then Nikolay happened to glance at his wristwatch. "Oh, I must be off to my assigned work, or I'll be late."

"One minute. Don't move. I must first make some notes about this encounter—" He took out a notepad and began what Nikolay knew well would be a detailed description of how he looked. For future reference.

A long two minutes, then the policeman dismissed Nikolay with a wave of his beefy hand.

Nikolay walked a few blocks. Then ahead, the thin figure of Kostya—the macaroni—walking slowly, seeming ready to fall into step with him and talk.

"Sorry I left you with that bully waving his *democratizer.*" Kostya's narrow, bearded face broke a smile.

Kostya turned his head, checking for any possible eavesdropper. "Certainly, we mustn't be seen talking—that's why I left."

"Even worse would be if the authorities identify us with Advance Front."

"Oh," Kostya smiled. "For that I have eyes on my back."

"But did you hear about Stas?"

"No, what?"

"He was out with Misha, walking by the Narodnaya Metro stop. They had a few bulletins left to post. They see an idle cop walking across the plaza. So they leave each other, quick as a fart." Nikolay laughed.

"Yeah, good thinking."

"Sure, but Stas then takes the bulletins, folds them, stuffs them, his inside pocket. Okay?"

"Did the cop see that? Talk to him?"

"No, but when Stas walks to avoid his look, the cop calls him to stop."

"He complied?"

"Yeah, just some daft questions he answered, but the bulletins stayed hidden."

"Good, but if you keep talking like you did back there at the park, the dirty cop will write you up as a *refusenik*, for sure."

"I don't care."

"As long as they don't link you to Advance Front?"

"Yeah. But I tell you I'm thinking of becoming a real *refusenik* and leaving."

"No, not a Yid!"

"Yeah, I'm sure I have a Jewish bloodline somewhere. I'm thinking about emigrating."

Nikolay knew his days in the Soviet Union were numbered. He had a profound dissatisfaction with staying. He studied for a doctorate in economic history, but would that take him beyond overseeing operation of a photocopy machine in the Gorod Central Municipal Library on the second floor?

Even that job was no sinecure, not if he was ever caught red-handed making *samizdat* photocopies for Advance Front, a clear violation of work rules.

Not that stealing State materials wasn't rife in most workplaces. Everyone seemed to take to heart the Marxist adage, From each, according to their means, to each, according to their needs. No one got more than sorry wages, so everyone figured stealing to satisfy their needs had to be expected and surely okay.

But Nikolay knew Advance Front would never reform the Soviet Union. How could it challenge the Politburo that each May Day would truck missile after missile past parade crowds, displaying its military might in Red Square and every other public square across the Soviet Union? Gorod was no exception. On May Day, the Politburo of the Communist Party of the Soviet Union showed off the iron fist in the velvet glove. Nikolay was no fool.

For Nikolay, for Dmitriy, for the others in Advance Front, their *samizdat*, their subversive activities were but a way of keeping their sanity. A way out. Publicly, but anonymously, refusing to give their soul to the apparatchiks of the Communist Party who worked so hard to brainwash everybody. No one went for it, unless, as Nikolay knew, they wanted to advance in the Party and then lord it over everyone else.

Nikolay would have none of that.

If there ever was merit to the grand experiment of communism and the social ferment before 1917 that included the likes of the great Leo Tolstoy, who embraced public ownership of land as proposed by the American reformer Henry George, Nikolay knew those reforms were long lost in the economic hard times that swept the world in the 1930s. The ongoing dictatorial brutality imposed by Josif Stalin to keep his power, and then the challenge of survival that came with the Great Patriotic War, made the true intellectual amalgam of Leo Tolstoy and Henry George in

Nikolay's still unpublished doctoral thesis an irrelevant, though interesting, historical footnote. He knew he had no Soviet future.

Then, for Nikolay Mushinsky, a door opened. A way to leave.

For several years, the Soviet Union allowed its citizens, upon application approval, to emigrate to Israel. This was because of international politics with worldwide Jewish groups asserting people of their religion and ethnicity were being mistreated in the Soviet Union and so should be allowed to leave.

Nikolay knew he barely qualified. He was not a practicing Jew. Well, why go to synagogue in the Soviet Union anyway? Those who did, did so surreptitiously. He knew he had a Jewish bloodline somewhere in his past. What about that great-granduncle, whose name was Hyam? His babushka grandmama told the story of how Uncle Hyam had all the kosher chicken trade back in Gorkii, the days of the late Tsar. He was sure he could show his relationship to Uncle Hyam, if he could get to Gorkii and find records.

He stood in front of the OVIR—the Office of Visas and Registration—and pushed back the door and went inside to see a line of people waiting to pick up forms, to take home and finish, to return and have their answers questioned, answer new questions, then wait.

Nikolay stood patiently in the queue. He chewed on his thumbnail, nervous that once filled out, the application with his life history, was sure to be copied and sent anywhere the apparatchiks wanted. He could not turn back. If his application for an exit visa failed, the rest of his life would be the special torment given one who rejected the Soviet Union, a lower circle of socialist hell for the unpatriotic.

Could he accept that? He gazed at a fly buzzing on-high, close by the ceiling, seemingly oblivious of the upper window, swung open at its hinges for fresh air. The fly must've come through that window. Would it go out too?

"Here are the papers. Please fill out and bring them back. You can fill them out now, if you have the information and documentation with you."

"For that, I don't."

"Then take the papers with you and bring them back completed and the necessary documents."

"How long to approve a visa to Israel?"

"At least a year. Another office must approve those applications."

"Oh, then I must wait and make my plans later."

The OVIR clerk nodded her head no more than a centimeter.

Nikolay turned to leave, unsure what, *much later*, was to happen.

40
СОН КОСМОНАВТА
(COSMONAUT DREAM)

Petró got around to showing Gleb his papa, Andrei, in pictures. With a five-year-old's eye, Gleb picked out his favorite. Wasn't even one from the shoe box full of glossies Petró took with his beloved Fedka. But he could accept the logic of his five-year-old grandson's mind that went to the last known picture of his papa, mailed from the front months before his death in the Hindu Kush. The snapshot, doubtless taken by a buddy, showed Andrei in flight suit, standing next to the Mi-24 gunship he'd easily jump into and take whirling away, aloft.

That the picture of his papa, the pilot, had a lasting influence on Gleb was clear one Sunday when the two went off to the same Pioneer Park of amusement rides Petró had enjoyed with young Andrei years before.

A bright afternoon in May, the place was packed with kids, parents in tow. Incessant screams, undeniable pleas from all directions.

Beyond the entryway and PIONEER PARK arch, a Ferris wheel loomed and towered overhead. To the right, undulating, pitching, spindly tracks of a roller coaster and everywhere, crowded lines snaking away from ride after ride, each a wait for the chance to enjoy thrills too.

Gleb, beside Petró, was speechless.

"Know what ride you want?" Petró asked.

This was Gleb's first time at Pioneer Park. He probably didn't understand the importance of choice. For some popular rides, he might have to wait far, far longer than the ride lasted.

"Look, there—" Petró pointed left. "The merry-go-round has no line. You ride now and take more time to make up your mind about the others."

"Okay, but I want to ride them all," Gleb answered, crossing his arms, his eyes tight with determination.

"Oh," Petró said, surprised Gleb quickly understood the admission ticket let him go on rides as many times as he wanted. "You'll be here into the night," Petró said, laughing, "or you might poop out and get hungry."

Gleb ran over to the merry-go-round. He followed. Then Gleb stopped, his eye caught by something else: two spaceships with blinking lights, whizzing by on rotating struts, scissoring up and down.

The near spaceship flying past had two kids, a boy in front, a girl in back, her long hair streaming in the breeze. "What's that one?" Gleb asked.

"A new ride," Petró said confident, at least, the last time with little Andrei, the spaceship ride wasn't there. "Cosmonaut Ride," he added, eyeing the arcade sign studded with colored light bulbs above the engine swinging the rockets around in their orbits. The gasoline engine sputtered, backfired, and the spaceships came to a rest on their metal arms.

"That's the one I want, the one I want." Gleb rushed away, leaving Petró to follow, leaving Petró to wonder if that last picture of Andrei—the pilot—beside his gunship, a black-and-white memory on paper exerted its pull on little Gleb years later.

He joined Gleb in the long line. "You pick the most popular ride, you wait twenty minutes—" He paused, studying Gleb, whose mouth hung open, as though pondering his choice. "Or more."

"I want to sit in a spaceship. I want to sit in front and pilot the spaceship!"

"You might sit in the backseat—"

Gleb looked at him, unbelieving.

"You might not be first in line. You might be second and have no choice. Then you'll sit in the backseat."

"Oh." Gleb's brow furrowed, as though this problem had to be solved. His face slipped into a smile of mercurial quickness. "That's easy. I'll give my turn to the next person. That way, my turn, I can sit in front."

Petró patted his grandson on the back. "Smart, wait an extra turn, then sit in front."

He shrugged about his young grandson, who simply had to be the pilot, no matter what. Was that the price of having lost his papa? That he had to be a pilot too? Surely, Petró hoped, Gleb didn't want to join the Air Force, but then maybe the curse of going off to war would not skip a generation, as it did for him. Maybe Gleb wanted to follow his papa in every way. For a moment, Petró didn't hear the children about them, screaming their lungs out with joy.

That October, Petró, Olga, Yelena, and Gleb were off to Leningrad. This was over Constitution Holiday, so they took four full days. The Gorbunovs were especially happy to see Yelena and Gleb again. But whether they realized Yelena had settled into Gorod and wouldn't live closer was an open question. Seeing how her mother Gorbunova pestered Yelena with questions, then advice, Petró figured Yelena enjoyed her mom at a distance. Once-a-year visits would suffice.

The second day there, Gorbunova suggested it might be a good time for the "ladies" to go out shopping and have tea. "But no shoes for you, Yelena." The women chuckled at that remark. Petró knew it had been a long time since Yelena bought those high-fashion shoes she was wearing when Andrei first introduced her back in Gorod. Petró smiled. Yelena had no use for Italian shoes working in the bakery.

"Alas, if the ladies go shopping," Gorbunov said, "I wish I could show you and Gleb around, but soon—" he said glancing at his wristwatch, "I have a meeting that will go through lunch and well into the afternoon. We're working on the appointments list. This must be done with the entire committee there." He gave Petró a look of resignation, as though he had no choice in the matter.

"Well, Glebka," Petró said, brushing the locks of his grandson, "it looks like we're on our own."

They soon were out walking along Nevsky Prospekt and saw on side streets the town houses where Dostoevsky lived and where Nabokov grew up. They kept walking, reaching Old Town where Petró and Gleb went inside the Hermitage and wound up in a room on the second floor devoted to Impressionist paintings of the great French masters.

Gleb stopped and stared at the distant ceiling, the ornate moldings and the bas-relief on walls everywhere, painted delicate pastels. "Did someone really live here?" he asked in disbelief. "Or was this just for paintings?" He turned his head toward Petró, who smiled fondly at his grandson's questions.

"No, most of the paintings here came after the Tsar and his

family left this palace—" *Left this palace?* Petró paused at his misleading way of putting it, but for little Gleb, he was not about to detail the gore that brought down the Romanov royal family. Let Gleb learn that in school.

"But if he lived here in all these rooms, why'd he leave? This is nice. Nobody lives like this in Gorod!" Gleb shook his small head, his tousled hair in need of a combing, but that didn't worry Petró.

"You're right, the Tsar and his family, the Romanovs didn't want to leave, but they had to accept the Russian people didn't want a royal tsar anymore. So the Tsar, his family, they all left Russia—"

"Left?" Gleb said quizzically, looking out the room, as if this had happened recently.

"Yes, they left quickly, they didn't take anything—

"And not all these paintings were from here," Petró continued. "Once the Tsar took off, people brought paintings from his other palaces." Petró waved at the walls with countless paintings, room after room, where Petró knew they could spend years, day after day, and have only a minute for each work of art—or so someone calculated.

"Oh, you mean he lived in other palaces?" Gleb's jaw hung slack.

"Of course. The Russian Empire is huge, more than a quarter of the earth. The largest country in the world. So when the Tsar travelled about his empire, he liked to have his own place to stay, that's why he built several palaces—"

"Were they all like this? This is like in a fairy tale."

"Yes, the Romanovs lived a fairy tale with many palaces like this. But this one, the Hermitage, was the biggest, the one with room for all the paintings."

Petró sighed. He was glad to sidestep the questions Gleb was sure to ask once he found out Nicholas the Second met his end in a bloody basement room one July night in Yekaterinburg. But not now. Gleb seemed more struck by how where he lived in a concrete block differed from the splendor of where they stood.

"This painting," Petró said, pointing to the Millet in front of them, thinking he might distract Gleb. "'Man With A Hoe.' See he's a working man, like all good Russians."

"But, Grandpapa, why did he leave? He had it nice here. Didn't the people want him to be happy?"

"Well, yes, the Tsar was their leader, and they liked their leader to live well, but when they—like this common worker with a hoe—didn't have enough to eat, they turned against him. See?"

"Then he and his family left?"

"Yes, it's a little longer story, but, yes, they left. The people wanted everyone to have something to eat. They couldn't have a rich tsar if everyone else was starving. That was how communism started, to give everyone a share."

"I'm glad they left the palace here for us. This is nice." Gleb's eyes took in the room, his head turning about slowly, as though meditating on what survived from Russia's days of royalty, which now was for everyone to enjoy.

"You know, someday I want to live in a nice house too. Not this big, but just nice." Gleb gave Petró the convincing look of the innocent. Petró smiled, knowing what his grandson had yet to learn: He wouldn't live like that if he wanted to be a pilot in the Air Force, or even a cosmonaut.

41
МАШИНА ДЛЯ ОТЖИМАНИЯ БЕПЬЯ
(WRINGER)

Yelena traded off the chore of washing clothes with Olga. So one Saturday, while Olga stood in lines for meat and other groceries, Yelena did laundry. It was her turn. Use of the laundry room on the third floor was by signup, and the Kravets household seemed to get along fine with washing every two weeks.

Yelena faced two sinks. One for soapy water and one for rinse water. She filled the first sink with hot water, dropping in her bar of wash soap.

Yelena took a shirt out of the basket of dirty clothes. One Petró wore last week. She held it to her nose: It had a week's worth of wear.

She tossed it in the sink to let it soak.

She then reached over to the basket and took out a skirt, one of hers. She smiled at the last time she wore that.

When they went to Leningrad Constitution Holiday last week. She tossed the skirt in the sink too.

Yes, Glebka had a good time. With Petró, of course. Things, they're good here. Even though Mother wants us back in Leningrad.

But why?

She didn't have much to wash. She picked the rest out of the laundry basket and put everything in the hot water to soak. The sink was half full. Then she read her magazine.

An article or two later, she put down the magazine and took the washboard off the wall, then put its feet down the side of the sink after first rubbing her bar of soap over the board's ribs. She rubbed soap on both sides of that first shirt of Petró's and pushed it back and forth on the washboard to loosen up whatever could be washed out.

Petró, he's so good to Gleb. We go to Leningrad, my father never has the time for Gleb, not with so much Party activity.

Then she wagged the shirt in the hot soapy water before cranking it slowly through the wringer mounted between the two sinks, letting it fall into the empty sink on the right.

Next, she took out her soaked skirt and gave it the same scrubbing up and down on the ribs of the washboard, then wound it through the wringer too.

Before long she was done with the soapy water and washboard. She had a pile of wet clothes in the empty sink. She turned on the cold water and let the sink fill.

Some clothes seemed to float about in the rising water. She put her hand in, idly stirring them.

No, Mama wants me back, wants something to do, someone to order around. Hah! But I'm not her little Lenochka anymore.

She'd let them sit while she read more of her magazine. Ten or so minutes later, she was ready to wring them out.

She first took one of Petró's shirts, twisted out the excess water, then ran it through the wringer and dropped it in her laundry basket.

Soon, she had everything—socks, underwear, shirts, skirts, dresses—lying wet in the laundry basket. It was heavy.

We belong in Gorod. Yes. Petró and Gleb. Me and Olga. We get along. Almost like she's the older sister I don't have.

During the summer months, she would take the wet clothes outside to hang on the lines in the breezy sunshine. The best possible way to dry clothes. But rainy weather had set in, and she would carry them down to the clothesline in the boiler room.

In the basement, someone was late taking down their clothes. No room to hang what she had washed. But the clothes on the lines were dry, so she simply unclipped them and piled them on the laundry table next to the lines, where she'd put her basket of wet clothes. This was okay if a neighbor was late getting their laundry.

She put the clothes up, dripping wet. They would be dry tomorrow.

42
HP 12C

A different Russia seemed in the offing. Petró just wasn't sure what would get better, what would get worse. More and more, people waited in long queues at the food stores of Gorod for the most basic foods: milk, eggs, bread. The news told him the social order was growing restless everywhere.

Paradoxical or not, Petró saw the tight controls, the legacy of Josip Stalin, were nothing more than—like so much frozen ice—paralysis in the Kremlin leadership. The world changed too fast.

Things were falling apart, the ice was breaking up.

He never expected to hear from Voice of America that the workers at the Lenin Shipyard in Gdansk had gone on strike. But workers led by Lech Walesa openly defied the Polish government and playfully called their movement Solidarity. Petró couldn't trust his ears at first: The same worker solidarity that was to sweep away capitalist exploitation of workers had its first crack.

Could workers openly reject even token acceptance of communist authority, defy its leaders?

As if the Gdansk news wasn't confounding enough for Petró, America had a new president. A movie actor, no less. He had it in for Petró and the Soviet Union. The American president called them the Evil Empire.

That year, visiting Yelena's parents in Leningrad, Petró and Gleb watched a bootleg copy of the American movie *Star Wars* on Gorbunov's new Sony videocassette recorder. Gleb, of course, loved the outer space stuff, the battle against the Evil Empire, but why would the American president use the same derogatory name for the Soviet Union?

Petró was uneasy about this American actor president who wanted so badly to put satellites in outer space to shoot down Russian missiles. The American president called *that* Star Wars.

Was the world coming to this? Worker strikes among Polish comrades and an American president who thought the world should live out a movie script?

Petró bit his lip, sipped his tea. *Ronald Reagan, take your movie fantasy to the babushka here in Gorod waiting in line for a loaf of bread to buy!*

If change elsewhere in the world unsettled Petró, the change that brought him joy and restored his spirit was watching how grandson Gleb kept growing. The hand-clutching toddler, dependent on Yelena, was gone. He was now a little person Petró enjoyed.

He'd watched his own Andrei grow into a young man, and with Gleb, he was only too happy to step in for Andrei and see his grandson turn into a young man who would have made his papa proud.

Especially on his days off work, Petró found time—while Olga and Yelena shopped for food, cooked, or washed, ironed clothes, and the like—for Gleb.

Sometimes they'd go to a movie at Plato Cinema downtown. Gleb liked Tarkovsky's *Solaris*, though Petró wasn't sure how much of that old film went over Gleb's head. But more often, on the winter days of snow and ice, they kept busy indoor. He didn't want Gleb watching TV, as some let their youngsters do. If anything, he wanted Gleb staring at a chess board.

One sunny winter afternoon, however, Petró was out walking with Gleb. They ran into Victor Zhzhyonov.

"Oh, it's Petró and his grandson," boomed Viktor, wearing a natty suit. "How goes it?"

"Quite good, Viktor. How can we not like this weather?" he said, his hand sweeping out at the sky.

"And you're—?" Viktor asked of Gleb, "Forgive me, I sometimes forget names."

"I'm Gleb, son of Andrei. This is my grandpapa." Gleb laughed.

"Yes, your father is a true Soviet hero, and I'm sure he'd be proud of his fine young son. You must be in beginning school?"

Gleb nodded.

"So what do you like to study, if I may ask?"

"Oh, arithmetic. My favorite."

Petró smiled at his grandson's quick answer.

"Is that true? I've something here in my pocket that might interest you—" Viktor said teasingly. He reached into his inside coat pocket and pulled out a slip-cased device. "This electronic calculator comes from America. Called an HP 12C." He turned it over. "Yes, made in Corvallis, Oregon, USA," he said with a chuckle. Petró grimaced at how confused life had become. Now lusting after Western consumer goods was okay. Even a steadfast Party hack could show them off openly.

"Very nice," Gleb said. Petró could see his grandson had a keen interest in Viktor's calculating device. Only someone in a privileged position could get something other than their own Elektronika brand and afford it too.

"How many rubles?" Petró asked.

"Oh, I'm not sure. This is used, but like new. A gift from a colleague who goes to Europe all the time. I suppose in the West they sold for one hundred U. S. dollars. Something like that."

Gleb knitted his brow, peering at the calculator as Viktor pressed the ON button. An *0* in dark gray showed on the tiny LCD screen. "So how do you use it?" Gleb asked.

"All the time, I do percentages. Some restaurant wants to renew their license for alcohol, I need to know the square meters of the restaurant. Say it is twenty meters by fifteen. I multiply like this." Viktor quickly pressed buttons. Dark gray digits—*3 0 0*—appeared on the little rectangular screen.

"Then I need to calculate my service fee from the square meters."

Petró snapped his head back. *If the arithmetic is in rubles, Viktor does it between his ears.*

"Just a one-time fee," Viktor continued. "I put in: *4, 5, %*, like so, he said pushing the keys, and that's it. The fellow pays me hundred thirty-five rubles, and everything is taken care of. Fast track approval." He beamed at his apparent indifference to the bribe he just calculated.

Gleb knitted his brow again, "Oh, you do reverse Polish notation, not algebraic entry—"

Petró knew Gleb read popular technology magazines nonstop, but from where did this come? Viktor and Petró gave Gleb a double take, as if he were an alien intelligence newly arrived, who made an observation impossible to follow.

Viktor, as the capable Party functionary, quickly recovered. "Yes, yes. I have read the user manual, so I do the calculations accurately every time." He beamed; he slipped the HP 12C back into his coat pocket.

43
АНГЕΛ (ANGEL)

The white, high-wing, single-engine Cessna skimmed over Red Square not more than ten meters above the heads of visitors to Moscow's most revered public space. The open faces of the spectators were awe-struck and must have wondered, Is this a movie stunt?

Gliding past them, its engine noisily pulling it onward, steady as an egg-beater, the Cessna headed for the bridge to onion-domed St. Basil's, where the plane touched down, soft as a bunny hop. The aviator climbed out, and the spectators who approached him saw that he was young, no more than a teenager. Their curiosity led them to learn he didn't speak Russian.

Finally, one who spoke English asked where he was from. "Germany," he said. "West Germany," he clarified.

He said he was a messenger and he wanted to talk with Secretary Gorbachev about world peace.

Petró sat down in his easy chair, *Pravda* in one hand, cup of tea beside him on the side table. He snapped open the newspaper to read more about what everyone was talking about: a West German teenager landed a private plane in Red Square yesterday, May 28, 1987. The black-and-white news photo on page one showed a small white plane, propellered nose in the air, sitting on its tail wheel, domes of St. Basil looming in the background.

Petró plunged into the report: *The pilot, 19-year-old Mathias Rust, reportedly flew his Cessna Skyhawk from Helsinki, Finland, and landed in Moscow's Red Square without incident. Why he did this brazen act, intruding in prohibited airspace of the Union of Soviet Socialist Republics is not known at this time.*

Petró sipped the tea. So this teenager flew into the heart of Moscow without so much as a scrape? He chuckled, wondering where the Soviet air defense was, asleep at their radar screens?

He read more. *Informed sources are convinced a teenager could never plan such a flight over Soviet territory without accomplices. More likely he was not supposed to succeed. Informed speculation believes Rust was a fall guy, a prostofilya. He was expected to be shot out of the sky, and his sponsors—the American CIA a prime candidate—would use his sacrifice to trigger an international confrontation.*

Petró would have kept reading, but decided nobody knew what happened. This was not Francis Gary Powers in 1960 on a spy mission to photograph Soviet military targets, something Petró knew well. He sipped more tea. *No, this young idealist had the luckiest flight of his life—born with his shirt on, as the saying goes. This only proves Soviet defense is confused, like too much in this country.*

44
СИНИЙ СВЕТ, КРАСНОЙ ШАПОЧКЕ
(BLUE LIGHT, RED CAP)

Wanting more of the material comforts of life touched even Petró's hallmate Egor Bok, who usually was content with the ferment of the lowly potato, vodka. One Wednesday in June, leaving the Metro in downtown Gorod, Egor saw across the street, parked by a ministry building, a stately, black ZIL motorcar.

Only high-ranking Party members rode in such a fine car. Always with a chauffeur driving.

Burly Egor patted the flask of vodka in the chest pocket of the blue overalls he wore everywhere, then he stopped walking and stared at the ZIL. *Where is the chauffeur?* He peered in disbelief.

He thrust his right hand in his pant pocket, found his folding knife, the one with the ten-centimeter blade. The knife, basic as a screwdriver, never failed him.

A sly grin slipped over his face.

Egor was good with his hands, knew how things worked.

What he had to do was simple.

He crossed the street and stood no more than twenty meters from the parked ZIL, its roof topped with a blue light. He squinted, looking for the distinct red cap of the chauffeur. Those guys could be seen a block away. He scanned up and down the boulevard. In front of the tobacconist store, the red-capped chauffeur took a smoke, talking with someone. Then both went inside.

This was his chance.

He walked briskly, but not so as to call attention to himself from passersby. Stood next to the driver's door of the ZIL, pressed the handle down, then opened up, jumped in the seat. Yanked the door shut to. *Whoooomp.* Silence cocooned him. A well-made car. The leather seat massaged his lower back, his shoulders. His nostrils quivered at the smell of good tobacco. *This is just for Party members.*

The back and side windows were tinted for anonymity, all to the good for Egor. He took out his pocket knife, flipped the blade open, confident if any passerby wondered what he was doing, they'd probably think he was a mechanic working on a balking, hard-to-start ZIL. He smiled as his dexterous fingers went to work behind the ignition switch, feeling around its mounting on the dash, nestled under the pressboard cover. With his knife, he pried away.

His fingers probed feverishly, working back and forth with the unseen wires. Then he put the knife, the flask of vodka, and his wallet on the passenger seat. He slid off the driver seat, scrunched up on the floor in the passenger footwell, his neck cradled on the driveline hump to see what his fingers felt. Two big fat wires. He wanted those. One black. One red.

He wiggled the connectors off the ignition switch, and two wires hung below the dashboard. He sat up again in the driver seat. His chest swelled at the next task: His knife blade scraped insulation off the wires he kept apart. When he had several centimeters of bare wire on each, he knew he was ready.

He jiggled the gear shift lever on the steering column into

neutral. This was a three-speed automatic. The knife went in his side pocket. He picked up the flask of vodka. Took a sip. Peered out the windshield to see where he'd go.

He tugged his handkerchief from his back pocket, folded it over several times, brought the sparking wires together and twisted them tight.

Vrooooom. The big eight-cylinder engine roared out its throaty command of the motorways from under the gleaming, long, black hood. The biggest smile crossed Egor's face, but then fell away like a dropped cup, when out of the corner of his eye, out the front door of the tobacconist—the red cap. Running his way.

Egor gasped. Reached over his left shoulder and pressed the door lock.

"Thief, thief, thief." The pounding steps.

He took another swig and chuckled. The chauffeur left the ZIL unguarded. He slipped the column gearshift lever into first and gave the accelerator a light toe. Egor studied his rearview mirror: The chauffeur's red face grew small.

Egor surveyed his domain, felt his power. Other than buses and taxis, light traffic. He reached over to the dash and flipped on the blue light.

He drove carefully, mindfully, aware his powerful ZIL could overtake any vehicle on the road. Down Vorontsov Prospekt he motored, taxicabs moving over to the right as he approached. He smiled. *So this is what it's like!* Being respected as a member of the Party and a high-ranking one at that. If any bus or cab dared to slow him down, why—they might be hauled in for questioning!

He wasn't sure how far he would go. He just wanted to get away. He reached down beside him, took another swig. Yeah, if the police wanted to stop him—and why would they stop a ZIL with the blue light flashing?—well, he'd show them the eight-cylinder ZIL's arse! He toed the accelerator more, passed a stupid slow-poke taxicab. He was leaving town.

He'd run until the gas gave out. Then he could always walk back. Or hitch on a truck.

After a few days, residents of Public Housing No. 17 on Chernozem Street realized Egor had taken an unexpected vacation or was missing. For starters, two interview officers of the KGB commandeered the television room on the first floor and called in anybody who might know Egor Bok. That included Petró, who was not only inconvenienced by not being able to watch television news on Saturday evening, followed by reruns of *Stierlitz*, his favorite spy show, but did not enjoy being cross-examined.

Petró sat on a bolt-upright metal chair, facing the two interviewers, who had a pot of tea and a pitcher of water on the fold-up card table, at which they sat ready to catch any resident in a slip-up about where Egor Bok might be.

Petró was offered nothing to drink, while one interviewer calmly poured tea for the two. Sitting on his hard chair, Petró felt on edge, even though four meters separated him from these information-hungry KGB types, two women in dour, black attire.

On the card table, Officer Shelepin placed and toyed briefly with what she said was Egor's wallet, doubtless with ID. "When Comrade Bok abandoned the ZIL motorcar he stole, he did so at a bridge where he jumped into the river below. The pursuing officer assumed he drowned and didn't try to find him or his body in the river."

Her words paused, and she tapped the wallet, allegedly Egor's, a few millimeters sideways, then withdrew her left index finger and rested it momentarily on the septum of her broad nose. She spoke again:

"So, first question, Petró Kravets: Has Comrade Bok been in

touch with you since one o'clock Wednesday at any time? Has he been around here, has he called you, has he had a message conveyed to you through a third party? Any contact?" Officer Shelepin took a quick sip of tea, then patiently waited on Petró.

Petró drew himself up straight, to appear, at least, sincere. "No. No contact. None whatsoever. I didn't know he was missing. I've been working. Today, I was busy with my grandson. I don't see Egor that much." Which was true. They weren't close.

"This is understandable. No contact the last few days. But please, you have spoken with Comrade Bok in recent months, is that not true?" She flashed him an engaging smile.

"Well, yes, but not that much."

"But you and Comrade Bok once took it upon yourselves, I understand, to fix a toilet two floors above us."

A wave of unease came over Petró. His face reddened with panic. *Who tells them that? They talk to everyone here?* "Yes, we fixed the toilet, but years ago. Comrade Bok is good with his hands."

"So you and Comrade Bok talk. Did you ever share his vodka?"

"A sip or two, when he offered. To be polite. But no drinking together, no." Petró glanced away from his inquisitors, not wanting to reveal more than needed.

"Okay, you and Comrade Bok shared drink, talked together, as you say. Tell us, at any time, did Comrade Bok express to you wishes to drive a Party member's car—like the ZIL he stole? Consider this question with care: Did he ever say anything to you that showed envy of Party members who use motorcars?"

Petró slid down on his metal-frame chair, sure this was a trick question. Who had these interviewers talked to who might have told them differently, who might have suggested Egor went around telling *everybody* he hated the Party members and the ZILs they rode in? Who? He rubbed his forehead, as though trying to come up with the right and true response. "No, to be honest, I never heard anything like that from Comrade Bok."

His inquisitors looked at him intently, as though certain to pounce if Petró said something incriminating. His instincts told him to not say anything. But then if he told them something they already knew, what was wrong with that? "To be honest," he continued, "I think Comrade Bok might have done it for, how do you say, just for *kicks*."

"For *kicks*?" Officer Shelepin shook her head slightly, smiling. "Why do you say that?"

"As you must know, Comrade Bok's military service was as a truck mechanic. He's always been good with his hands and likes motor vehicles. Still, after his military service, he couldn't get work assigned as a mechanic. Anywhere." Petró looked them each in the eye, having made an admission. "I think that bothered him," he said softly.

"So you think Comrade Bok stole the ZIL because he wanted to drive a car, wanted to start it up without a key, wanted to prove his mechanical skill. You think he did this for a thrill?" Officer Shelepin looked over at Officer Aliev, who wrote furiously.

"Possibly. I cannot know inside Comrade Bok's head. I know, however, he's good with his hands and talks fondly of days when he worked on trucks and got them going. He liked to say he knew how to make truck engines roar like a lion." Petró laughed. The two interviewers chuckled too, but in a perfunctory way, and seemed satisfied Petró kept nothing back.

A keen sadness pierced him, as he waited for more questions. None followed. Officer Shelepin gave a dismissive wave. Petró stood up.

So sad how Egor couldn't find work on trucks or cars or buses or even tractors. So sad.

45

НЕТ БРОВЕЙ
(NO EYEBROWS)

A week went by, and with neither sight nor word of Egor, Petró assumed his neighbor was a goner. Egor's wild ride in a stolen ZIL must have ended badly.

The following Saturday morning, however, while Petró finished up his breakfast, he heard a commotion outside in the hall. He put his fork down, glanced over at Olga, Yelena, and Gleb; then got up and went out. Several other tenants had surrounded a woman and excitedly asked questions, one after another, not giving the woman a chance to respond. Petró joined them.

The woman facing her inquisitors wore a coarse peasant dress, and her head was wrapped in a baggy red babushka so loose fitting that Petró saw her hair was shaved off. Even her eyebrows were shaved off—instead she had some brown pencilled lines there. But when she looked away from the harassing inquisitors—*Who are you? Why are you here? Why won't you leave?*—and glanced his way, Petró knew instantly. "Egor," he exclaimed. The dark, coal eyes were his neighbor, long lost Egor Bok. Subject of the man hunt.

"I'm trying to get in my place. Why're they bothering me?"

"They don't know who you are—" Petró said. The others went quiet, stood back from Egor, sensing they'd find out something about her, or him.

"That's good. They'd like to turn me in."

"For borrowing a car? Hah!" Petró looked at the three others, the inquisitors who might have recognized Egor, if they weren't so intent on keeping the supposed stranger from burgling a flat.

"Oh, let him in his flat. So he can get in some comfortable clothes!"

Egor went to open the door, but did not have a key. That must have been lost in his escape the same way his wallet and ID got left in the ZIL, finding their way into the hands of the KGB. Having no key momentarily slowed Egor. He reached into his pocket, took out his trusty knife, unfolded the blade. Then pulled out a bit of string after inserting the knife blade in the strike plate of the lock. Then pushed in the string and worked it around with the knife until both ends stuck out. He took the ends of the string and yanked.

Petró gasped as Egor calmly opened the freed door.

"So how you been?" Petró asked.

"Come in, I'll tell you." Egor turned around, however, eyeing the three inquisitors who wanted to hear more. "Oh, not you too. Petró's okay, but not all of you." He grimaced at the three, then closed the door.

"Oh, one probably rings up KGB, I'm sure, so why tell them more?" Egor said, resignation in his voice.

"So why did you come back, dressed like a woman?"

"I got tired running around. I knew they hunt me down like a hound, but with this," he said pointing to his scarf, "nobody sees the man they want to find."

"So you came back because you're going to give up?" Petró asked, not sure why Egor would decide to quit if his disguise as a woman threw off the police.

"I got hungrier and hungrier. I stole food at night. I worried about the police. No identification; I'd be detained. I figured it best to come back here, even though it's hot-water time."

Egor pulled off the babushka scarf, revealing his shaved head. His bald head had plenty of nicks.

"So you shaved your head, did you?"

"No, some farmer, but he did a bad job. Then he wanted money for the sorry food he fed me. I ran away. Some help he was."

"Where did you get the dress?"

"Oh, the farmer's wife. She was dead. He hadn't thrown out her clothes, so he happily gave me this dress."

He pulled it over his head and stood there, wearing only underpants, an undershirt, and heavy boots. He grabbed a shirt from a pile in the corner and put it on. "Now, the pants, where did they go?" He sifted the pile, picked a pair of coarse tweed trousers, took off his boots, and slipped on the pants.

"But your eyebrows, you shave them off?"

"Yeah, looks like a woman, no?"

"But the grease pencil marks, will you wash them off?"

"Yeah, everything grows back, few weeks. Hair, I grow fast."

Egor then clutched his temple, as though recalling something unfinished; his heavy boots thudded across the room to a cabinet door he opened. "Aha, what I missed." He pulled out a half-empty bottle of vodka, uncorked the top, then took a swig. "Ahhhh. I missed this so and lost my flask. Here," he said, offering Petró the bottle.

Then, on the other side of the door, a knock.

Petró held the vodka, and Egor opened the door. Petró wasn't surprised to see in the hallway KGB Officers Shelepin and Aliev.

It didn't take long, a few days later, until Egor found himself standing before the regional magistrate downtown, hearing criminal charges read against him. His bald head had grown a stubble, but his bald eyebrows had yet to come back. In short, he looked comical.

"Bok Egor Kuzmin, you have been charged with theft of State property," Magistrate Nikonov announced, still busy with papers he shuffled. Egor blanched with fear. "Specifically, you stole a ZIL eight-cylinder sedan, manufactured only last year, that was parked in front of the Ministry of Non-Ferrous Metallurgy on Vorontsov Prospekt in Gorod about thirteen hundred on the afternoon of June 4, 1986."

The magistrate continued, "You were seen by many witnesses stealing this ZIL, and you were chased by the chauffeur assigned to the car, who repeatedly yelled 'Thief' as you drove away and failed to stop."

Magistrate Nikonov paused, looked up over the rims of his glasses. "Are those statements essentially correct, Comrade Egor Bok?"

Egor had spent the last several days being exhaustively questioned by the KGB interview officers, who had him sign a statement admitting everything the magistrate recited. After he was questioned by Officers Shelepin and Aliev, he was locked up in solitary confinement with the barest of comforts. He didn't want to go back to that. He nodded his head, hoping the magistrate might take pity on a defendant who didn't protest.

"Your whereabouts were soon unknown," the magistrate continued, "and the Gorod police were unable to give you chase. But you were seen driving erratically near Diryevnya, fifty kilometers east of Gorod, where a local police officer thought you, the driver of the ZIL, must be drunk, even though the car, obviously assigned to government use, had its roof light flashing.

So the officer gave chase on his motorcycle and tried to halt you.

"You continued to drive erratically at high speed down Diryevnya Road until you reached a bridge and stopped. Officer Tomsky reported you then got out of the car and jumped off the bridge into the river below. He didn't see you after you leapt.

"Are those reports consistent with what you know happened?"

Egor, standing there in gray overalls, felt vulnerable, as though he were still trying to elude the police. Who was he to argue with the magistrate? A harsh sentence would surely follow. That was the power of the Supreme Soviet Justice, whom any city magistrate represented. And this was the regional magistrate. That much more important not to anger him. Egor nodded his head, with emphasis, so the magistrate would see he agreed and was possibly contrite.

"Very good. What happened next was, the following Saturday, you were discovered in the hallway of your residence at Public Housing No. 17 on Chernozem Street. Your neighbors were shocked to discover you dressed in woman's clothes, wearing a babushka scarf, with your customary hair and eyebrows shaved off.

"Is that not true?" The magistrate's eyes fixed on him, as though daring him to disagree.

Egor said nothing. How could he argue?

"Of course, it is true. That is why you are here. But tell me, why were you dressed in a woman's clothes, why did you shave your head, why did you do this?"

"So nobody knows me," Egor said in a small, unsure voice.

"And yet you went to the one place where people would probably know your face, know your voice, and recognize you despite your attempts to disguise your appearance. How can this be?"

Egor shrugged.

"Your actions are not those of a reasonable man," the magistrate said gravely. "Some behavior, such as rashly stealing the ZIL for a joy ride, might be understood as drunkenness. We found a flask of vodka in the car—emptied, but still wet inside. But everything, afterwards, the woman's clothes, returning to your flat, this is not reasonable to do. You would have been far more reasonable to simply turn yourself in at a police station. But no, you first tried to elude everyone and then still went back to the people who know you.

"The mandatory sentence for theft of State property valued at more than one thousand rubles, the ZIL is worth far more, is a year in prison at hard labor. But my magisterial judgment is that this would not reform your behavior. Unlikely. I think your problem needs to be treated scientifically."

Egor, rapt with attention, hung on the magistrate's words. *I don't go to prison. How can this be?*

"Bok Egor Kuzmin, I sentence you to report to Ivan Pavlov Psychiatric Hospital for extended evaluation. Your accommodation there will be indefinite until a treatment plan is proposed and found acceptable to this court, so you will not become a menace to the social order as you have been the last few weeks. Is that clear?"

Egor shifted his weight in his heavy boots and looked up, then quickly away. If he went to the hospital and the doctors took over, he could not drink vodka. He knew that. His life was finished. How would he ever find comfort in his hard life, if he couldn't drink? He took a deep breath. "Yes," he replied to the magistrate.

The magistrate brought down his gavel with a thud. "Officer of the Court, please take the defendant from the room and arrange for his transport to the hospital."

46
АГАТ КОМПЬЮТЕР
(AGAT COMPUTER)

If Egor was a poster child for deviant behavior, Petró felt his grandson was, by example, the opposite: fitting in and doing remarkably well in school. Gleb was profoundly interested in the world around him. He especially liked learning anything technical and could while away what seemed like a half hour or more asking Petró how reconnaissance satellites worked. Petró knew much of what he said Gleb probably didn't understand, but apparently what little he did was enough to keep him asking more.

Petró noticed Gleb also had much of his curiosity satisfied, if not stimulated, by his Young Pioneer Club after school. Of late their projects centered on the science and technology for which Gleb was so keen.

Still, he was surprised one evening, before they started eating, by Gleb looking up from his clipboard of papers, excitement plain in his face. "Grandpapa, guess what I did at the club today?"

"Don't know, you do another electricity experiment?" Petró thought of the time the club leader brought a handcranked Tesla coil. Gleb touched an electrical bolt a meter long, but felt only a tingle. What could top that?

"No, we did something far better. A computer. I got to put my hands on the keyboard of the Agat. A microcomputer. Little, all on the table. I pushed the keys, and letters came up on the screen, tiny, green letters on that black screen." He flashed his broadest smile. "I'll get to learn how it works. I can't wait until tomorrow. I go Saturday too!"

Petró had heard of the Agat microcomputer before, having read an article in *Pravda*. But he had never personally seen and touched an Agat, Russia's first microcomputer, available in 1981, and a fairly close copy of America's Apple II from the late 1970s. Petró wondered how the Young Pioneers got one for kids to learn on, but most likely it was a discard. After all, everybody wanted the IBM personal computer from America. A Russian factory cranked out PCs by the hundreds. He'd read IBM went ahead and let any manufacturer copy their PC.

"So, you'll learn how the Agat works, then learn programming, no?"

"Oh, yes, our leader said tomorrow we'll use BASIC and teach the computer to count to ten—"

"What's BASIC?"

"B-A-S-I-C. It's Beginner's All-purpose Symbolic Instruction Code. That's how you tell the computer what to do."

"And you're learning to write this BASIC?"

Gleb paused. Yelena was setting down his plate of hot pirozhki. He slipped his clipboard of papers under his chair, giving his mom an embarrassed smile: It was time to eat. Petró could see that the excitement at Young Pioneers left Gleb hungry. "Yes, I have something to study after dinner to be ready for tomorrow."

Olga brought over the plate of cooked turnip greens they

would share.

"You know, if it's okay, I'd like to come by Saturday," Petró said, taking his first bite of the pirozhki. "Take a picture of you at the keyboard of the Agat. This is an important occasion. Such a picture of you at your first computer will be one you would like to have many years from now—"

Petró looked over at Yelena. She nodded.

"I have some fresh film in the Fedka. Yes, I should come by and take your picture."

"And take pictures of the others too?"

"How many in your club?"

"Oh, thirty, maybe."

"Well, perhaps a group picture. Everyone can stand beside the Agat. I will get several copies, so you can keep one at the club."

That Saturday—not a working Saturday—Petró went to Yezhov Primary School nearby and spoke with the Young Pioneer leader, Comrade Kissin, about taking pictures.

"That's fine. In ten minutes, we take a short break. You have time to get ready," he said.

Soon Petró stood by the side wall, the Young Pioneers having gathered about the Agat. He saw a low-light situation. He didn't want to use a flashbulb, though that would work, but it never looked natural and was hard to control. He took out his meter and saw he had to keep the camera rock-steady for a long exposure. Another table would do the trick. He'd cock the shutter, set the f-stop for *3.5*, set the shutter speed for *1/20th*, put the camera on the table, focus and compose the picture, then click.

Two weeks later, when Petró got back his developed prints, he saw he succeeded. In one, Gleb, next to the Agat, hands on keyboard, radiated a confident smile he was about to tell the microcomputer what to do.

Before long, all Gleb seemed to want to talk about was the Agat. He would talk about the computer in detail, as if it were in the room. It, of course, wasn't. The grandson had everything about its inner workings stored somewhere between his ears.

Petró knew that the Young Pioneer leader must have wanted time-outs from the persistent questions with which Gleb surely pelted him.

And if there was a point to microcomputers like the Agat for Gleb, it was more than just playing games like PONG. Far more. He wanted to write programs because he was learning BASIC.

One night after dinner and after the women went to visit a neighbor, Petró was left with Gleb. He looked over at his grandson, who wasn't about to do his homework. He should've been cracking a book, getting some reading assignments done for his history class. But no, he sat on the floor against the wall, under the lamp, and on his lap rested the familiar clipboard loaded with paper. He chewed on the end of a pencil, as if figuring out what next to put on the sheet of paper.

Petró resisted the temptation to ask Gleb why he worked at such nonstop intensity. He knew his grandson would be only too happy to tell him in exquisite detail, giving Petró the benefit of learning programming one step at a time, as thoroughly as Gleb knew it.

That was the problem. Petró didn't want to program computers, not even microcomputers. Maybe he was too old to learn something technical besides optics. Or maybe he felt Gleb's destiny was to learn microcomputers the same way his was to learn cameras. Whatever the reasons for not disturbing Gleb, he knew his grandson would be only too responsive and tell him what he was doing. But that interruption would also break the train of thought going through his grandson's blond head. He especially would not want that, for it would waste precious time Gleb needed to finish up and get on to reading history before bedtime.

A few days later, after spending most of Saturday at Young Pioneers, doubtless with the Agat, Gleb came home and held out a cassette tape for Petró.

"What's this? Music?"

"No, this is for the microcomputer. My first program."

"So I can't play it for music?"

"No, only goes in the computer. See, I put this cassette into a player, and that's connected to the input port of the Agat, ready to read into memory. Random access memory of the computer."

Petró stood back, as though to be sure what he saw in his nine-year-old grandson was true. This youngster was programming computers? "So you tested this program," he said skeptically.

"Oh, many times. Had to be sure each step was okay. Simple program." Gleb looked up at him, as though he knew he finally did something his grandpapa didn't understand, and yet something that was important. Something that was new and would change things.

"So tell me, what does your program do?"

"Easy. It asks two questions. You type in answers on the keyboard, and then the computer calculates and tells you what you want to know."

"Really, what does it tell you?"

"How much you weigh." Gleb had a smug smile.

"It tells you how much you weigh? How does it do this, if you don't stand on a scale?"

"You don't. The program estimates your weight. Always close."

"How?"

"Easy. It asks your height in centimeters. You answer that. Then it asks your waist in centimeters. Then it calculates how much you weigh."

"Does it take long?"

"No, the Agat does fifty thousand mathematical operations each second. Takes no time."

"And this program works?"

"Yes, guessed my weight to one kilogram."

"But how did you come up with this program?"

"Oh, I read somewhere about the correspondence of height and girth to weight. But it's not linear. I needed my program to solve a second-degree equation."

"You learned this, and you're only in fourth grade?"

"Sure, it's fun."

"Hmmm. I don't think you will go off and work in a commune like me. You will work with computers, I'm sure."

Gleb shook the plastic cassette in his hand with pride. "Oh, I hope so. That would be great."

And over the next few years, Gleb's interest in personal computers did not let up. If anything, it got stronger, and he often said he couldn't wait to have one of his own. Petró worried, though, this continuing obsession with computers might take too much time away from Gleb's studies, but paradoxically, his grandson seemed to have more energy, if not time, to tackle his other studies with dispatch and get back to programming.

47
ЁЖ20 (HEDGEHOG20)

Life in the Kravets' household steadily changed. Gleb grew taller. Age eleven, he was still busy with Young Pioneers and learning all he could about computer programming. The Young Pioneers at school had a home-grown version of the IBM PC called an Agat-II. Gleb loved that it allowed him to do much more than the "slow Agat" ever did.

Petró felt Gleb was right to follow his passion for computers. Such proficiency could only benefit his future. He knew Andrei would've liked where his son was headed. Also encouraging to Petró, as he watched his grandson become a young man, was Gleb's interest in the larger world, although that, at times, could annoy.

"What are you listening to?" Petró yelled across the room at Gleb, hunched over the Sony shortwave receiver on which Petró spent a small fortune to replace the Orbit-2, when he heard how the Sony ICF-7600D, with integrated circuitry, not transistors, pulled in even more stations from the West. But he kept his old wooden console radio with vacuum tubes, its only use—perhaps out of habit—for listening to Radio Moscow. He couldn't part with it. The Popov radio in its wooden cabinet was like furniture, gave him an at-home comfort he'd never felt for either the Orbit-2 or the Sony in their plastic cases.

Well, now that's all right, mama. That's all right for you. That's all right, mama, anyway you do ...

Petró went back to watching the new Rubin color TV he got after his name sat on the delivery list for so long. And that was after making payment of the full price. No longer did he go downstairs to the television room, though many of his neighbors still did.

He was listening to the news broadcast from Moscow and got up to fiddle with the rabbit ears to get a sharper picture.

Again, he glanced at his grandson, who seemed absorbed, seemed to understand the English lyrics, though how anybody understood such pop songs from the West was beyond him. Maybe he was getting old: He was in his sixties, but future retirement was out of the question. How could he ever afford to live as a pensioner? So he hung on to his job, dutifully doing anything supervisor Aleksandr—who'd taken over after the welcome retirement of Maksym Belenko—said.

"This is a pirate station," Gleb said. "Here in Gorod."

"And they play that rock and roll?"

"Yeah, they get cassette tapes from the West."

"The authorities will find this radio station soon and close it down."

"Sure, Hedgehog20 knows they will. So he moves. Often. Even broadcasts from public places he tells us about later." Gleb gave his grandfather a broad smile, as though he had sympathy for the disruptive *samizdat* of the airwaves, Hedgehog20 doing his underground subversion of Soviet culture by bringing inside Russian borders the programming the government relentlessly jammed for decades.

Babe, now you don't want me, why not tell me so? You won't be bothered with me 'round you no more ...

Petró went back to the television news. The newsreader was going through the obligatory evening report about the economy:

"The Ministry of Mines today reported that the last six months' production of coal for 1988 has set a record, up more than five percent from the same period in 1987. This news is welcome as is the price of petroleum, which continues to rise and is an important export of the Soviet Union. Coal continues to be a mainstay in the Soviet Union for electricity generation, unlike Western European countries, which rely too much on natural gas and nuclear energy because they are not blessed with ample natural resources, as the Soviet Union, having more land area than any other country in the world—"

He rocks in the tree tops all day long. Hoppin' and a-boppin' and a-singin' his song ...

Petró shot a look back at Gleb. "You learn this Western music, but you won't forget your Russian 'Motherland Hears,' no?" Petró said this with wistfulness, as though he knew young Gleb was on his way to wanting a larger world, one bigger than the Russia that survived the Great Patriotic War at enormous sacrifice when he was not much older than Gleb. Everyone seemed to have lost a father then. Now Russia was trading so much with Europe. Plus, as reported by Moscow News, everywhere, nations wanted to buy Russian oil: The Middle East was too unpredictable.

It was all different, and his grandson was growing up in a world where survival and war were fading memories. Change was in the air. Petró saw that in the Levi's Gleb wore, the American blue jeans his grandson cajoled Yelena into buying—used—as the "gift for all his birthdays."

He started going steady and bless my soul. He out-bopped the Buzzard and the Oriole ...

"The Ministry of Mines also reported today aluminum production set all-time records with notable results from the new bauxite discoveries in the steppe regions of Outer Mongolia contributing to much better than expected results. Up eighteen percent from comparable production a year ago—"

"I like Western music," Gleb said. "It's a fun change from study. Makes me happy. Russian music," he made a grimace, "so much sadness. It's not happy music."

Petró had a long face. *If only he knew the tough times Russians survived and those songs, from the heart, helped people get by. Not this.*

Go rockin' robin. 'Cause we're really gonna rock tonight ...

"The world is changing," Petró said philosophically. "You'll learn more about the West now. This is what Pyotr the Great wanted." He mused at his Russian namesake, what he would think about his country now.

"Oh, yes. I need to keep learning about the West. Soon, you know, our computers will talk to each other. No matter what country—"

"Why do you say that?"

"They do today, in America. Computers talk to each other. It's called the Internet. We, too, will have it soon. Can't stop the computers."

48
ПОТЕРИ ЛАЙКА
(LOSING LAIKA)

That same year, Petró saw a familiar face from the past. What caught his eye was a burly, younger man walking toward him, but hobbling like an old man. His shirt untucked, he could've used a cane to steady himself. They drew closer.

"Egor, Egor, that isn't you … is it?" Petró asked. The words tripped off his tongue. The doddering man lifted up his face.

"What's happened to you?" Petró's eyes stung with the recognition. He had changed back to his old self. Unlike the last time he saw Egor in court—shaved head, shaved eyebrows—now, bushy eyebrows and the untamed bird's nest of hair.

"You're, you're—I don't know. Sorry," Egor said in a weak voice.

"Petró. Petró Kondratovych Kravets. You remember me, don't you?" He frantically searched the coal eyes in Egor's face for anything. Petró shook his head.

Petró turned to his right, hand outstretched toward the expansive façade of Public Housing No. 17, most of its seven-story east side painted with a mural depicting farmers: a man holding aloft a scythe and a sheaf of wheat; a woman clutching an infant boy in her arms. "Back there, those flats, don't you remember? Third floor, you lived there too."

Egor gave him a stare, void as a pocket turned inside out.

"We fixed the toilet together, no?"

Egor's face stayed blank.

Petró knew Egor couldn't help himself anymore. He probably was forced to swallow strong medicine in the psychiatric hospital. They put medication in his food. They made him take *vitamins*. A nurse watched him. Wrote it all down.

Petró felt a chill creep over his back. *If only he recognized me.*

He bit his lip. *Wasn't he the good-with-his-hands man, vodka-cheery fellow back in Public Housing No. 17?*

Petró rubbed his temple. Stealing that blue-light ZIL was his doom.

"Don't you recognize me, Egor?" At the mention of his name, his once-was drinking pal flashed brief recognition in his eyes. Then, again, the void.

"No. Never saw you."

Petró didn't know what to do. He couldn't reach out and shake the hand of someone who thought him a stranger. Or could he? Shake his hand and start over, as years ago they once did in Public Housing No. 17? *But his brain,* Petró grimaced. *They've wasted his mind. And surely, no good with his hands anymore.* Petró knew whatever mechanical genius was left in Egor's hands probably would have to be retrained all over, just like a child.

He reached into his back pocket, felt the flask of vodka he happened to have. He wanted to, but couldn't take it out, unscrew the cap, and offer Egor a sip. No sips of vodka could ever change the torturous chemicalization of Egor Bok's brain.

A lump grew in his throat. His hand left his back pocket. This was the authority of the State.

Petró understood, with his lost hallmate in front of him, why so many took it upon themselves to find a way out of the Motherland. The State only wanted to stay in power. What they did to Egor was too close to home.

Egor stood there, seemingly unsure whether to start walking again.

Petró never wanted to think such seditious thoughts about his country. But now, here was an inarticulate witness for the thoughts that increasingly Petró would not surrender.

He reached out and patted Egor on the shoulder, then walked away and knew why he mustn't look back.

Petró wept: The glory of Sputnik-1 had died. As surely as that brave cosmonaut mutt, Laika, never had a chance to return from her heavenly orbit.

49
МОЗГИ БИТЬ ХОЛОДЕ
(BRAINS BEAT BRAWN)

For Petró, arriving at work several weeks later on a Wednesday seemed like any other morning arrival. Even with the bonus of greeting Ivan outside the manned security gate, where they both held up their IDs in a perfunctory way—practiced thousands of times—avoiding the guard's strict gaze, but never failing to take notice if a new face was at the outdoor gate inside a furry *shapka*.

Once inside Building A's tunnelly hallway, they strode purposefully toward the employee commissary. No need to exchange more than morning greetings. The chatter could wait until Ivan had his coffee and Petró, his tea.

They turned at the hallway intersection.

"What is this?" Petró said. A line of employees snaked out the commissary front door. The line wasn't moving, or if it was, hardly.

Petró walked around the line, to see what he could glimpse going on inside. Past the doorway, he saw, above the cash register, a new sign. A huge sign, larger than the one it replaced, with bigger, impossible-to-ignore prices to match for the breakfast items a lot of workers had been buying at modest prices.

Petró gave the sign a double take: prices—yes, prices—for tea and coffee!

"I don't believe this," he said, rejoining Ivan in line.

"What's the hold up?" A look of uncertainty crossed Ivan's face.

"It's bad, so bad. They have new prices, higher prices, for everything. No more free tea and coffee!" Petró shook his head. "I don't even have kopecks—twenty kopecks—for a cup of tea. Can you lend?"

"Twenty kopecks for tea? What happened?"

"Don't know. Everybody must be giving the cashier a hard time."

They stood like that for a few minutes, the others in line grumbling as Petró and Ivan had before they sized up the situation. They waited patiently and the line moved slowly forward. Only a scattering of workers inside were enjoying the breakfast they had bought with new prices.

Others gave up, discovering they were short pocket money, or simply upset, and turned around and left the commissary line, muttering mild obscenities about the uncaring State.

When they got to the top of the line, Ivan asked the cashier, whose flush face and askew hairnet suggested she was already exhausted from work, "People been telling you about the new prices?"

The cashier nodded, as if talk about the new prices had gotten old fast.

"Okay," Ivan said, "we'd like one coffee, one tea," he said glancing up at the new menu board. "My colleague here, however, is financially embarrassed about the new charge for tea, so I'll pay for both."

Petró grinned sheepishly.

After she pulled the coffee and the hot Georgian tea, they took their cups and headed over to an empty table to figure out what happened.

Ivan scanned the tables that at that time would normally be packed with workers and said, "I don't know. This new policy seems pretty drastic."

"You're telling me," Petró replied. "Charging for tea? I know things have been slow for us. Our boss Aleksandr says budgets are being trimmed. But are they cutting back the food subsidies too?"

"Looks that way. See, eggs and toast, two rubles. Used to be eighty kopecks."

"I wonder what Aleksandr has to say. This and the military budget falling apart. They can't afford to feed us workers, we who do important work to defend the Soviet Union."

Petró took a sip. Not free, but the tea tasted the same. "It's hard to watch. Our military is failing. We lost in Afghanistan. I lost Andrei there too."

Ivan blew across his coffee, sipped.

"Where is the Soviet pride that defeated the German fascists?" Petró added.

"It's the Americans, Petrush, the Americans. The Star Wars and armed satellites in space, all that. The Americans spend so much on defense, the Soviet Union will go bankrupt trying to match them."

"We can't keep up. Our technology is getting old."

"Yes, they were the first and only ones to get to the moon. We always have better, bigger rockets, but Americans have computers."

"Yes," Petró said, with a sigh. "Brains are beating brawn this time."

"And so here, our comrades pay two times, three times what

they paid for breakfast last week—"
　"And no free hot drinks," Petró added.
　"Of course not."

50
БЕРЛИНСКАЯ СТЕНА
(BERLIN WALL)

The fabric of Petró's socialist society continued unravelling, as if ordinary working people everywhere in the Soviet bloc, like Jews earlier, wanted to leave, to take their families out and not come back.

One evening, he was enjoying his after-dinner mug of Georgian tea and listening to the little Sony that pulled in BBC broadcasts.

Usually, the evening newsreader presented his reports in a droll, quiet voice, as if he knew the power of the British Broadcasting Corporation's radio transmitters alone were enough to move his words around the globe to settle on every radio antenna caught in its commanding sweep. Tonight, however, the newsreader was excited, shouting:

"What is happening now is something many of us never thought we'd see in our lifetimes: The Berlin Wall is coming down! Yes, the Berlin Wall is coming down!

"Okay, broadcasting live from our studio in Bush House, London, let us go now to our correspondent in Berlin, Mitch

Rallison—"

"I don't believe this," Petró yelled to Olga across the room. Yelena and Gleb were gone for the evening, so Olga would be his only witness that what he heard was not an auditory hallucination.

"Yes, Mitch Rallison here. I'm standing in West Berlin as we speak, right in front of the Berlin Wall, near the Friedrichstrasse Crossing, an enormous wall, four meters high, which up until last week was topped with the barbed wire East German work crews have this past week been busily removing—"

"And what is happening now?" the BBC newsreader fired back.

"It's one big party. The East Germans know they are free to leave their country for the first time in most, if not all, of their lives—"

"Do you know what this means?" Petró asked Olga.

"No, what?"

"This chaos in Germany, our Russia might be next," he said, not sure if he was ready for *that*.

"The East Germans are out in force, and hammers, chisels, and sledgehammers are the tools of the hour. Men and women alike are passing sledgehammers back and forth and taking ceremonial blows to the wall, standing atop it, broken blocks falling to the street below—"

"Now, Mitch, surely the wall is not going to come down with sledgehammer blows by manual labor. That would take months—" the BBC newsreader broke in.

"Yes, absolutely right, Ian. Very true. No, what we're seeing here, under the klieg lights playing across the length of the Wall here at Friedrichstrasse, is celebration, a party. People chipping off souvenirs of what will soon be only a dark memory.

"Of course, in the days ahead, bulldozers will show up with the dump trucks, and authorities plan to take down all of the Wall in the most efficient way. But for now, it's, as I said, one big party."

"Fabulous," newsreader Ian Toalster back at the BBC World Service in Bush House said. "What we see now with our own Mitch Rallison on the scene is the parting of the most visible symbol of that Iron Curtain Prime Minister Winston Churchill spoke about in chilling tones back in 1946. Ah, yes, 'From Stetin in the Baltic to Trieste in the Adriatic, an iron curtain has descended across the Continent'—that was how the great man put it. And what we're experiencing today, the removal of the literal wall, expressed in concrete cinder block and stretching for miles, dividing East Berlin from West Berlin—why, Sir Winston himself must be applauding from his grave!"

Petró sat in his easy chair, dazed, unsure what would happen next.

Freedom. Freedom. Freedom. People could talk of nothing else. And it came down to this, the Berlin Wall. First the shipbuilder strikes in Poland. No communist country ever had labor strikes. Unthinkable. Workers of the world unite! and go on strike. Crazy. But it happened. Now the Berlin Wall. How could the rest of the Soviet countries not want to go free too?

For Petró, he was too old—or not old enough—to understand why this was happening. Yes, for Petró, it had been one small world: taking the Metro back and forth to work, living in Public Housing No. 17 in the one-bedroom flat he glanced about, knowing he probably would die there too, and occasionally, a vacation down to the Black Sea. That was his life. Or so it seemed.

"Olya! I think Russia's next. That Gorbachev *perestroika* isn't enough. We're going to be open to the West again, like the old days, before I was born."

Olga gave him a perplexed look.

"Yes, before Comrade Stalin went crazy with the power to his head," Petró said aloud, something he would never have said in earlier decades. "Back then, Russians were free to come and go to the West."

Olga smiled. "Oh, it's good, I won't have to wait in line for meat—"

"No, Olya, it's Western goods coming here, not meat!"

"So Gleb buys new Levi's, no problem?"

"Sure, we'll be free to buy Western goods, but where's the money?"

"Maybe Gleb keeps buying used Levi's," Olga said and went back to drying the dishes with her blue towel.

51
ΛΟΚΑΥΤ (LOCKOUT)

The Berlin Wall came down. East Germans began streaming across the border into prosperous West Germany. Some pulled up alongside BMWs and Mercedes Benzes in their two-banger Trabant autos, a sure sign of impoverished socialist origins the Trabant drivers were only too happy to abandon in the nearest welcoming ditch. Or so Petró heard the cynics say.

Talk started about "brothers and sisters." Would East and West Germany reunite, as before the Great Patriotic War? Petró wasn't sure what to make of the news, week after week. Were the Baltic countries of Estonia, Latvia, and Lithuania next to break loose and free themselves from the Russian bear hug?

Petró had strong memories of how Russia put a stop to an earlier insurrection. In 1956, Russian tanks rolled into Budapest, the Politburo saying a mutual defense treaty held by all Marx-Leninist nations must be honored.

What was different now?

Russia seemed unwilling to object. Was fear of international opinion the difference? Or was it a lack of military might to enforce what the Motherland wanted? Petró was now sure it was the latter.

Yes, Petró saw at work how Russia no longer had unlimited money for anything justified as defense. He and Ivan had to think about retirement. Petró thought he'd work another year or two, then start taking what was probably going to be a pitiful State pension. They'd show up for work, day after day, but not like the old days, the two responsible for helping put the first reconnaissance sputnik into orbit, working closely with Dr. Natalya Dezhnyova. Those exciting projects were written up in the history books.

Ivan returned to their workroom, a broom in hand.

"What do you have there?" Petró said, knowing the room with their workbench had been swept only the night before.

"A broom. Thought I'd give it a once-over."

Petró rolled his eyes. "Sure, like you did before we left last night."

Ivan liked keeping busy, even if resweeping what he'd swept only hours before. Petró would have none of that and was content, instead, to write out a report to give Aleksandr about the past month. A status report of what amounted to an inventory of reconnaissance sputniks OTS had worked on and that were in orbit and the operating status of each. Mostly, Petró wrote "Unchanged." But every few months, one sputnik would deorbit, come back to earth, and that ended its life aloft.

Petró could spend days working up such reports. Still the thought often occurred to him he could simply photocopy the report from the month before, cross out a few entries, and squeeze in updates as called for—*sputnik deorbited*—and be done. But Petró liked drawing it up from scratch, printing it out neatly.

That took more time and was more interesting than manning a broom, searching out debris to dispatch.

The two had so little left that needed doing.

Petró knew if he and Ivan were younger, they would have been told about their eligibility for a new work assignment—voluntary or not, he wasn't sure. But their age made transfer to a new job meaningless. They would not work long enough to learn the job well. So they were stuck at OTS, two of the last optics technicians who personally helped launch an age of reconnaissance satellites, now numbering hundreds. What they once did was done in assembly plants off in China. Petró had seen a newsreel: Row after row, twenty-ish women working tirelessly, their nimble fingers putting together compact modules, much as Petró and Ivan labored not that long ago.

There was nothing for them to do. Except look busy and not embarrass Aleksandr by openly goofing off and drinking tea and coffee in the cafeteria all day.

Petró glanced over at Ivan, saw his colleague pushing the broom around, polishing the bare concrete floor. *How has our working together come to this?* He winced at the thought, so many, many years ago, the two of them hunched over their work benches in the commune in Kharkov, patiently fitting together the minute parts for one FED. Was it age that kept them from working so intensively like that, what his memory gave back to him, one more time? Had age taken away their work and given it to those nameless young women in China, hunched over their work benches? Who in profile probably were not unlike teenage Petró in Kharkov.

"What do you think is going to happen?" he idly asked Ivan, who seemed too willing to stop the sweeping.

"I don't know. We have little to do. I look around, others seem not so busy—" His voice trailed off.

With no urgency to their work, they saw less and less of their supervisor, Aleksandr Levada, who seemingly was avoiding the embarrassment of having no assignments for them.

One afternoon, however, he appeared at their doorway, catching the two by surprise. Bearded, younger by a generation than Petró and Ivan, the best to be said about him, they agreed, was he was not Maks.

"That broom holding you up?" he asked Ivan, who immediately went to mincing sweeps about his feet. Petró picked up his pencil and pretended to double-check the log entries.

"You're not paid for standing," Aleksandr said with some evident relish for commanding his seniors.

Ivan paused. "Must've been working too hard, got ahead of myself." He smiled as if he didn't want a confrontation.

"Oh, good," was the reply. "Well, I'll see if you're in the budget next year."

Petró's clenched his pencil, and the pencil lead broke. He looked his supervisor in the eye. "But Ivan's worked here more than thirty years—"

Aleksandr puffed up. "Every year, January first, the Ministry of Military Aeronautics receives a new budget with staff adjustments. Out of my hands."

Petró stared at his papers, the broken pencil point. He was as vulnerable as Ivan.

"Until then, keep busy." With those parting words, Aleksandr left.

The two had no choice but to work like that for months. Showing up, going through the pretense of being employees, even though it was meaningless. Aleksandr would never come out and say how bad things were. He kept saying approval for project budgets was taking longer than usual. That the MMA was having to set new priorities and devote more effort to other goals.

For Petró, such gibberish was to keep him and Ivan off-balance about their future.

They kept showing up for work. Daily. The winter of 1989 came, and the snows descended on Gorod, settling in for the season.

One of those winter mornings, one in the first week of the new year 1990, Petró came out of the Metro, ready to brave the elements aboveground and walk the kilometer or so to the only entrance for the OTS compound. Dressed for the weather, he had on boots, wool pants, a thick down-stuffed jacket, and his fur-lined *shapka* with the ear flaps. And gloved hands, one holding his lunch bucket.

Moving stiffly in the cold, his aging bones not fully awake, he looked the picture of the typical Gorod denizen, soldiering on over the whiteness to get to work. If it was an unavoidable chore to walk the icy sidewalks and risk falling, the prospect of some hot tea in the company cafeteria cheered him on.

As did the sight of Ivan's characteristic gait.

"Vanya!"

Ivan stopped, turned around. Dressed warmly like Petró, he stamped his feet a few times in the snow, as though outwaiting a numbing chill. His breath was foggy white. "One year ends, another begins," he called out, as Petró walked closer. "I think I get up in the morning out of habit. What is there to do anyway?" he said, dissatisfied he had a goldbrick job, even though in past times, he didn't mind loafing for pay.

"Yes, it has to change. We could get a new project to start the year. Perhaps that is why they have us waiting about so much,"

Petró said, finally falling in step beside his friend, as the two continued on their way down the snow-clad sidewalk that led to Korolev Drive, home to the OTS buildings.

They walked most of the way to the plant in the characteristic way people of Gorod walked about on snow: silently. Talking in such weather took energy better devoted to moving ahead and getting out of the cold. Still, they walked slowly and knew they probably had a long, empty work day ahead of them. Their work as optics technicians had lost its sweetness and become more like pickled cabbage.

"I hate going to work today," Petró said, breaking the silence.

"Bad way to start the year."

"Yes, that's it."

Then more silence. The familiar plant entrance loomed ahead. A group of workers stood at the front gate, which was not open.

Petró peered in disbelief. *What time is it?* He glanced at his chronograph. He was on time, just a few minutes early. He stopped, looked at Ivan, who looked back at him. Neither knew what to make of this. It never happened before, that they got to work before the front gate opened.

The three other workers, already there, hung their heads down against the cold and walked away. One, coming past, said, "Bad news."

Now Petró and Ivan were engaged. What was at the gate? They walked quickly and saw chains and padlocks, as though this was not an overnight closure, but something permanent. A printed sign was bolted to the bars of the gate, a message delivered during their holiday time off, to be sure.

01 JANUARY 1990

THE MINISTRY OF MILITARY AERONAUTICS, GOROD OPTICS

Losing Laika 269

TEST STATION WILL BE CLOSED AFTER THIS DATE BY ORDER OF MARSHAL DMITRY YAZOV, MINISTER OF DEFENCE. WORK OF THIS PLANT WILL RESUME IN OTHER LOCATIONS TO BE DETERMINED. THERE ARE NO PRESENT PLANS FOR REASSIGNMENT OF PERSONNEL IN THIS PLANT. IF YOU HAVE WORKED IN THIS PLANT, YOU WILL BE NOTIFIED BY REGISTERED MAIL OF WHAT ASSIGNMENT, IF ANY, THE MINISTRY OF MILITARY AERONAUTICS WILL OFFER.–R. S. OLESHEV, DEPUTY COMMANDER, MMA

Petró stepped back from what he read. His lunch bucket dropped to the snowpack. His jaw went slack. "It's over," he said softly.

Ivan nodded.

Petró looked at him, then looked away, for he saw a tear forming on Ivan's face. Ivan's face, who went back to Kharkov and was with him for all the years, and now, this. He reached over and clutched Ivan's shoulder. At least, they got the bad news together.

The OTS complex stood before them, empty, no lights on inside, the hunkering one-story buildings foreboding in silence.

"This will all change and soon go to ruin," Petró said.

"How so?"

"Looters. The word will get out, and they'll show up and dodge any guards—"

"Looters always start by tearing out the copper pipes—" Ivan added.

"Anything of value."

Petró stared at the OTS complex, as if for a last time. Before long, graffiti would show up. Nothing of value would be left. The place was on its way to becoming a husk of the Optical Test Station where the first reconnaissance satellites took shape.

"This is not good," Ivan said. "We must leave. We'll share

vodka and talk of old times."

"Yes, we must do that," Petró replied.

With that, the two turned away from the locked gates and walked the snowy path back toward the Metro and a warmer place with plenty of reason to have sips of vodka at an hour they otherwise would be drinking coffee and tea.

52

СВЕКЛА

(BEETS)

Petró was home before anybody. What would he tell them? Petró wanted to tell a small lie, say he'd come home sick, even though he couldn't remember a sick work day in his life, unless from drinking hard when he was much younger. And if he pretended to go to work tomorrow, another cold January day, where would he get warm? The Municipal Library where Nikolay used to work? Even that was unheated these days.

Half past five, they came home.

Petró studied Olga's face: Her eyes showed concern. *She's sure something bad happened.*

"Why are you here?" Olga asked. She'd pushed open the front door and held an *avoska*, a string bag full of leafy beets. Yelena followed.

"Bad news. The plant's locked up. We're all laid off. Official letter's coming in the mail." He said it.

The beets fell to the floor. Olga rushed over to Petró and hugged him, tears welling in her eyes. "Oh, Petya, you've lost part of your life!"

"I'm okay.

"What do you mean? How can you be okay?"

Yelena bent down to pick up the string bag and, sidestepping the two, took the beets to the kitchen sink and went about cutting off the tops.

"You work forty years and lose your job. How can you be okay?" Olga asked again.

"My problem is not so big. I worry more about what's happening to our country. We always had the money for satellites. But not anymore. Our country must be broke."

"Who can know?" Olga said, not given to speculation. "You must do something with your time. Can you get another job?"

"Yeah, I could go downtown and see where I get assigned. But at my age, who wants to start someone sixty-two?"

"You've got experience, that'll help," Olga said.

"No, I'm sixty-two. They'll give me a broom and tell me to sweep the sidewalk beside the babushkas!"

Just then Gleb walked in.

Even though he was not yet twelve, Gleb could tell Olga's hand on Petró's shoulder meant something was wrong. He stopped, unobtrusively setting his bookbag by the wall, and waited to hear what was going on.

"Big change, Glebka. Our Optics Test Station is locked up and locked up for good. There's no job for Vanya and me." He smiled at his grandson, not sure if he understood having your life's work suddenly padlocked, ready to be bulldozed, was proof nothing would be coming back.

"Yes, I read in periodicals spending on military is tight—" Gleb dragged his index finger across his neck, but smiled.

"Yes, America's Star Wars, so expensive to defend against, not much left over for us—"

"Oh, I feel bad. You did so much. When I see a satellite at night, I know it's you, you and Vanya."

"Nothing lasts forever—" Petró said with plain resignation, thinking back over the decades, how that American spy plane shot down started so much of his work at OTS."

"When I was younger," Gleb said, hesitating, "I thought my best opportunity would be work in military computing, but now I'm not so sure. Perhaps something where there's more money."

"Well, I don't know what's next. I'll be a pensioner. The last money I ever get from MMA."

"I start cooking beets," Yelena, beside the kitchen sink, called out. "We eat in an hour."

53
ФИЛЬМ ЧУВСТВА
(FILM FEELING)

A few weeks later, Petró had to sign for a letter about leaving OTS. The usual opaque words Petró had come to expect Party hacks would write.

What mattered to Petró, however, was the last paragraph of the letter. What redundant employees could do. Nobody got paid anymore, so they were to report to the Ministry of Labor, Training, and Assignments Office. But—and this confirmed what Petró and Ivan knew—if the affected worker was age sixty or older, and Petró surely was that, then such worker could apply for a State pension. Petró decided taking the pension beat begging for an optics technician work assignment he would never get. Why settle for what the hard-to-place always got: taking up a broom as a Municipal Refuse Collector? Gorod had clean streets and clean sidewalks, even though many citizens excused littering to promote employment.

Petró went ahead and applied for his pension. After checking with the Ministry of Labor, Training, and Assignments, another office to visit: the Ministry of Worker Pensions, in the same

Stalinist, gray stone office building downtown. He would be paid for the first month after running the gauntlet for the rest of the day, sitting on a hard bench, clipboard on his lap, a leaky ballpoint pen to fill out form after form, each given to one of several clerks at the counter behind the glass partition, one of whom would, at last, count out one hundred thirty rubles.

He left the office elated. The pay, from then on, would be for doing nothing. A sunny winter day quickened downtown Gorod, and he was struck by how much time he had on his hands. The problem was a pensioner with one hundred thirty rubles a month couldn't indulge much in his new leisure time.

"Thank goodness, you still have your job," he told Olga that night. "And Yelena helps too."

Soon, Petró took his old Fedka to the back streets of Gorod. Somehow, shooting the camera in an unrushed way, taking photographs of what interested him—a park fountain, a passing bus, an iridescent, strutting rook—brought him back to what his working life had been about: images.

Images. He stood before the historic Church of the Sacrament. An imposing brick structure, whose colorful towers rose in the sky. The bulbous domes, swirls of green and cream, red and cream, each rose to a tip mounted by a singular gold cross with three crossbars, the bottommost aslant. In the clear night skies, Petró had walked past this church and felt its comforting shapes, its shadowy towers as so many candles gone dark in the night. The Soviets had no use for religion, and so the church was simply a cultural center, a medieval building preserved for Russian history. Nothing more. Although, occasionally, the church was available for weddings, always civil ceremonies; and music concerts.

He had to take a picture.

The Fedka rode in its original brown leather case, the strap going around his neck, so that when he was ready to compose a picture, he unsnapped the front flap of the case, unveiling the camera inside. He removed the lens cap, tucked it into his shirt pocket, and tugged on the lens barrel—which, when not in use, collapsed into the camera body—and extended, rotated, then locked it.

He saw what he had in the composition viewfinder. He frowned. The church didn't fit inside the frame. Not at all. He had no choice but to go across the street and take the picture at a distance.

Across the street, the church fit well within the frame: bulbous spires, imposing entryway, the fiery gold crosses riding on high. Even the occasional trolley bus passing at the bottom of the frame, well below the towering church, enlivened the scene. *Snap.*

He advanced the film and walked quickly up the street, trying to get more of a side shot. Once again, everything fit in the frame, but at a bit of a remove. Was he getting too far away? Still, *snap*.

He took a deep breath. What was it? He wasn't getting the *feeling* of the church, what he knew in his gut when he walked past and took comfort knowing it endured through centuries. Where was that power? How could he bring some of that feeling into his pictures?

He walked back down the sidewalk, stood in front of the church again, a trolley bus passing by while he stood there.

No, he didn't feel much of the church across the street. That distance—What, thirty meters?--took away its power. That was it. *I'll photograph right under it!*

He crossed the street and directly beneath one of the bulbous spires, saw none of it fit in the viewfinder. But that would not matter. He felt the church spire spilling down on him and his Fedka. Yes, as he focussed in the viewfinder, he confirmed what he knew: *The picture is right.*

His eye, caught up in the swirling colors of the spire, settled on the golden cross aloft. *Snap.*

He moved up and down the sidewalk, taking closeups of the spires, letting each fill the frame completely with bulbous swirls. Didn't matter if he couldn't get all of the spire. He was after the feeling. *Snap. Snap. Snap.*

Petró kept up his search for pictures to take, exploring Gorod on foot.

One sight he'd always liked was the Empire Monument in Great October Park. Built more than a hundred years ago, the stunning work of sculpture showed a thousand years of Russian history for the Empire. The monument was topped by a larger-than-life Prince Dmitry mounted on his battle horse, as if leading a calvary forward to engage the Tatars. Inscribed at the sculpture base, Dmitry's words: *I AM YOUR CHIEF. I WILL BE YOUR GUIDE. I WILL GO IN ADVANCE, AND, IF I DIE, IT IS FOR YOU TO AVENGE ME.*

Petró eyed the monument in the camera viewfinder. With such courageous words, they fought to victory.

Then Petró stepped back, taking in all of the monument, the historical tableaus encircling the base of Prince Dmitry's towering figure. *Snap.*

Another monument in Great October Park catching Petró's camera-eye was newer: a Great Patriotic War-vintage Army tank climbing the incline of an iron-plate and concrete slab, its silent turret pointed menacingly at the blue sky above. The drab green body had a serial number painted on it, preceded by the moniker

Losing Laika 279

WRESTLER. An easy shot to figure out, the tank was so compelling in silhouette and detail. He circled the tank monument, taking shots from every angle at which he could maneuver his Fedka. *Snap, snap, snap.*

Petró took a deep breath. WRESTLER had done its job: defended the Motherland. It earned its repose in the Park, but was also a reminder a sovereign homeland meant eternal vigilance.

The weeks went by, Petró doing little more than observing, seeing with his Fedka lens the city he knew for so many years only by rushing back and forth to the Metro and going to work. Weekends were for family. Petró had never spent time alone in the city, never let its sights and sounds and smells wash over him in a meditative way—until now.

Petró took many pictures. With twelve rolls of undeveloped film, he wondered about spending a good part of his pension developing them.

He procrastinated. Let the undeveloped film sit, unseen, in a bureau drawer. Rather than spending money on developing and having prints made, he simply went out and bought more film to shoot.

That only made his problem worse, he realized, when he saw the drawer had more than twenty rolls of film.

But after sharing vodka with Ivan one late afternoon, he saw a possible solution.

"You can develop film, make prints, not pay someone to do it for you," Ivan said, sipping his vodka with measured assurance.

"How can I do such a thing? No chemicals, no equipment!"

"Listen, I know a guy, Vasiliy." Ivan scribbled down an address on a slip of paper. "Here, talk to him. He's in some camera club, They do their own stuff all the time."

"Oh, I can stop by and see him on Saturday?"

"Yeah, if I see him first, I'll tell him you want to talk to him about the club." Ivan sat up with a self-satisfied smile: He'd solved at least one of Petró's money problems.

After meeting Vasiliy, Petró discovered the Russian Rangefinder Club had a nice darkroom setup because during weekdays it was for students at the Polytechnic High School. But after school hours, Petró and anyone else in the Club was free to use the darkroom.

Once Petró started printing eight-by-ten glossies of promising negatives, he was hooked on how great they looked. The print of the Church of the Sacrament he'd taken up close had, sure enough, the power of what he saw was there. He might shoot twenty pictures and print only one, but something like what he had in hands, good enough to frame, made him all the more enthused to take out his Fedka and keep shooting. He would stop worrying that his new leisure-time pursuit might take too much of his paltry pension.

A climactic finale to the larger social chaos arrived as the year ended in December, when the Secretary of the Communist Party, Mikhail Gorbachev, resigned, acknowledging he'd been outmaneuvered by the Prime Minister of the Russian Republic, Boris Yeltsin, who famously that September stood atop an Army tank across from Congress Hall and announced with a bullhorn a free, democratic society was on its way.

In mere months, Yeltsin's words bit.

"The Union of Soviet Socialist Republics is no more," the TV newsreader repeated emphatically. Petró stared in disbelief at his television screen that was bringing him bitter truth in flamboyant colors. *Does the Motherland go over the cliff?* He caught his breath, not knowing the answer.

"Yes, Ukraine is now a separate, independent country. Belarus is now independent too. Other republics are sure to follow. How did this happen? Why did this happen? Frankly, we don't know the details yet. Only that talks among the concerned leaders have been held privately for weeks and then this. Russia's Prime Minister Boris Yeltsin made the dramatic announcement only today—"

Petró turned off the television. Stood up from the easy chair, put on his slippers. He paced from one side of the room to the other. He had too much to think about. He rubbed his forehead as if to stave off a headache. He was glad Olga and Yelena were still at work. Gleb had yet to come home from school. He could be alone with his worries.

Surely everyone at the bakery will know soon. They'll have opinions. I won't have to break the news to Olga when she gets home.

Freedom. What does that mean if you have little money? Petró had no job to go back to.

In the new year, in all weather, Petró kept up his walks with the Fedka. He saw a lot besides subjects to photograph. He saw a flood of consumer goods from the West, and people felt free to buy what had been black market. Not only the new imported goods, but the price of everything else seemed to keep going up.

What this meant to Petró was that his pension was worth less, week after week. After a while, it was obvious he merely lived on the earnings of the two women in his house: Olga and Yelena. That was not right. He had not worked almost fifty years to become a bankrupt pensioner.

At first, when he and Ivan got together, they would sit in a bar in the middle of the afternoon and try not to cry in their vodka about their melting pensions. They felt enough betrayal for what had happened they would have liked to spit in their vodka.

What sobered them up was how bad things were going for Russians everywhere after freedom arrived. Had they really joined the rest of Europe? Petró looked around and didn't see that.

Too many bad apples thought they could get away with theft and looting, even robbery, and there would be no price to pay—no extended stay in a psychiatric hospital like Egor Bok, who came out a medicated zombie. Alas, bribe-happy police seemed to welcome the new "culture of crime," where strong-arm might makes right.

Petró didn't know what to do. He found the new breed of Russians hustling after Western goods and status symbols disgusting. Utterly disgusting and unlike the old days.

On one of his walks, Petró came across his old acquaintance Viktor Zhzhyonov, longtime Party hack.

"So how's it going?" Viktor, in his customary natty suit, called out to him. Petró had just emerged from Pozhar Square, near the Metro stop, where he was taking pictures of skittish pigeons.

"Oh, me? Just out walking, photography," he said, tapping the Fedka hanging off his chest. "I'm the same as last time we talked—retired, no job."

"But you're on pension?"

"Well, yeah, no point taking a babushka job, sweeping the streets—" They laughed. "This white hair, it was time to quit. But the pension is so small," he said, his thumb and forefinger barely apart.

"I confess my position changed too. I no longer inspect restaurants. I'm here downtown, that building over there," he said pointing to a concrete office with not that many windows, but a big Soviet Realism mural painted on its side. "I do plenty of paperwork. I don't know how long before I, myself, get the boot."

"So what'll you do then?" Petró said, feeling surprised even Party faithful like Viktor might suffer in the social upheaval.

"What'll I do? you ask. I've already started. See today's my day off. I've my own business."

"Your day off? Thought you work over there." Petró pointed back to the concrete bureaucratic tomb of an office building with the forty-meter high figure of a pioneer farm girl, sheaf of wheat in her hand.

"Yeah, I do, but they only give me three days a week. They cut me back."

"Oh, you worked longer hours, when you went around inspecting restaurants?" Petró said this half-jokingly, because an open secret was that Viktor's restaurant inspections were often leisurely meals with the proprietor, who might give Viktor a few choice cuts of meat to take with him for a favorable report to the Ministry of Public Health. Yes, Viktor's full-time work wasn't without cigar smoking and cognac-sipping moments.

"Absolutely. When I put out a favorable report on a restaurant, it meant I got to know who ran the place. I had to trust the proprietor."

Petró smiled. Sure, if he trusted the color of the rubles in the "little envelopes" slipped inside his coat pocket.

"So what's your new business?"

"Well, I've got more diversity of people I work with now—" he paused, as though gathering his thoughts. "I found many restaurant owners face criminal elements in our city who walk into a restaurant, pull out a gun, then demand money. Robbery."

"Yeah, I've heard that. Crime is way up. That's even in *Pravda*."

"So what do I do?" He hemmed and hawed. Typical Viktor evasiveness, Petró thought. "Yeah, I'm hiring some associates, muscle, you know," he said, clinching his fists, hiking up his elbowed arms toward his shoulders. "I offer a private security force for these restaurants. Some bigger ones always need someone there at night."

"So you must hire young muscle, not old farts like me," Petró said, brushing back his shock of white hair.

"Yeah, my clients want young men, you know, built like bulls, standing at their doors—to keep the bad elements away."

"I congratulate you, Viktor," he said. "You're in a growing business."

"Well, if you ever want to get another work assignment, let me know. I still have pull in a few offices downtown, but not much," he said, laughing.

54
РЫБАК
(FISHERMAN)

When Petró turned seventy-one in 1998, he, at last, felt the props of any order left in his life had been dismantled and sawn up for firewood. The new winners—trying to outdo any Western capitalist in their lust after money—spun out of control, goaded by red-nosed Yeltsin. Petró saw rude mobsters rushing from one drug deal to another in their Mercedes Benzes; Party hacks selling off State property, throwing people out of work, and retreating inside walled, guarded Italianate mansions; and, yes, even a bottom-feeder like Viktor Zhzhyonov living well by renting out his private security force.

Petró's retirement years were all the more cursed. What his pension would buy was melting, melting. Only Olga, still at Craft Bakery helping out, got them by.

They stayed put in their flat at Public Housing No. 17, the two of them. Earlier, Yelena moved to her own place. Gleb was living on the University campus. Ivan, whom Petró chatted with every week, was the only close, remaining voice, other than Olga's, from the early years. A past not without struggle, true, but shared. And given the sacrifices of his father Kondrat and his son Andrei, not one lacking heroism.

In his seventies, Petró wasn't looking forward to what change would bring next. He took temporary solace in his walks and looked for subjects to photograph. Pushing the shutter button on his little rangefinder camera was a thankful meditative pause.

One day, his leather-cased Fedka strapped about his neck, he was walking his frequent haunt of Great October Park, imagining a new angle to frame the fountain ahead, its waters spouting upward into the spring air, his legs moving stiffly, but ready to get to the fast-shutter, large aperture shots, then some tight-aperture, depth-of-field ones. Possible shots bloomed in his head, as he closed in on the fountain and splashing water, thirty meters away.

Suddenly, behind, loud running steps. He moved to get to the side, moved his neck to see who, but he was sluggish. He hadn't walked enough, hadn't yet shaken up his bones.

Didn't have time to turn about.

Two hands, unseen, slammed square on his back. His legs buckled. His body dropped sideways, the side of his head hit the hard, rough asphalt.

The dark, male hands yanked at the Fedka on his chest. The leather strap broke. Petró's eyes—shocked—saw the azure sky, nothing else.

Then the steps running away.

His head ached. Blood wetted his cheek. Petró levered himself up, eyes straining after his assailant.

"Roma," he muttered.

The swarthy youth stopped past the fountain, the waters jetting and falling. He stood there, leather-cased Fedka close to his face. Petró's heart ached for that leather case. The youth looked back at the fountain, then flung the Fedka like an egg skyward at its tottering spray and ran behind some nearby bushes and was no more.

Now on his knees, Petró felt relief the filthy Roma didn't want his Fedka. He could get it. He would get it. He would, even if he had to walk home with soaked clothes. He had to have his Fedka in his hands again. That leather case had his life.

Petró stood. A bleeding abrasion on the left temple. Pulled out a kerchief, wiped at the blood. He must look decent.

Stiff steps toward the fountain. He had to get the Fedka out. Before it filled with water.

Behind him came quick, but not running steps. He turned. Another youth, a Russian. Petró smiled. The young man's face had concern.

"Saw what happened, that robber, he knocked you down. I was back there, saw everything."

"Oh, I don't know why he knocked me down. Who would want it?"

"He threw it in the fountain."

"But I must get my camera. Even if I'm soaked."

"No, no, old man, don't do that. I'm here for you. I'll get it."

The young man stepped beside him, took his arm. They got to the fountain.

"See I don't care about water—" the young blond said. With those words, he sat down on the ledge of the fountain's low outer wall, yanked off his tan running shoes—German Pumas, Petró had learned—his socks, unbuckled his pants and let them fall, American Levi's—Petró smiled at the young man's taste, Gleb's too—then stepped out of them. Standing there in undershorts, skinny white legs, he was the novel sight in the sunshine, but didn't seem to mind. Petró was so joyful the young man knew how it was supposed to be. "This, I can't get this wet," he said, slipping off the cognac brown leather jacket he dropped on the Levi's.

Minutes later, the youth waded out of the fountain, the water having doused him, and held aloft a broken strap, and clasped in his other hand the Fedka and its leather case. As a fisherman displaying the catch of the day from his fly fishing, a prize-winning trout to show off.

When the youth handed over the Fedka, Petró asked his name.

"Andrei."

"I thought so."

55
ФИНСКИЙ СОН
(FINNISH DREAM)

Gleb, a third-year student at the University of Gorod, lived on campus in a shared dorm room. He studied Computational Mathematics, and though he did well, he wanted more.

Knowing his true yearning, he took his mom Yelena out for coffee one Sunday afternoon to talk about things.

They sat at a communal table in Rousseau, a new popular self-service patisserie, only open a year, a French import that, unbelievably, was affordable. Coffee and pastry: With the price of so much unhinged, something even a frugal university student could manage.

Yelena, her blonde hair showing strands of gray, took a fork to her buttery croissant, tilted her head sideways, looking Gleb in the eye. "So what are you saying, You're thinking of leaving the university?"

"I want to do as much with computers as I can." He sipped the French roast coffee, taken with milk, no sugar. The cleft in his chin defined resoluteness. "With our Internet computers at school, I've got so many ways to find jobs outside the country, now we're free to leave—"

Yelena's eyes were downcast, as though she faced another family loss, though not like Andrei. "Okay, so you have plans?"

"One company's interested in my experience optimizing math subroutines—low-level computer stuff. They want to interview me—"

"Yes, but what about the university studies?"

"I can decide that later. I forgot to tell you, they fly me to Helsinki next week for an interview."

Yelena's fork trembled in her hand. "You'll leave the country?"

Gleb's smile melted, his eyes giving away a sadness for any pain his dream caused her. "For the interview, yes. Then I'll have to see if they hire me. They want something specialized. But it's something I've done."

"But what about the degree? Your university studies. You've only a year left."

"I know. I've thought about that a lot. I decided the bachelor degree in computational mathematics is not worth much for a job here. Look around. Who's working technology jobs? Russia's trying to catch up," he said, waving his hand at the rest of Rousseau's interior, "with consumer goods of Western Europe."

"Oh, I know when I was your age, I liked Italian fashion. I had a small dream of going west, leaving Leningrad. But you think you'll leave the Motherland?"

"For the right job, yes, and with the World Wide Web, I look for jobs everywhere, no national borders."

"Tell me," Yelena said, savoring again a forkful of her croissant, "what this company does."

"They make cell phones. You know, mobile phones rich people carry about."

"But these cell phones, how do they work without wires?"

"Sputniks." He pointed up. "Plenty of them in orbit take telephone signals anywhere in the world."

"And you'll make those work?"

"Well, they work now, they want me to tweak things, speed up the interface for the user."

A flicker of confusion crossed Yelena's face.

"So when do you leave?"

"Next Friday, I fly out of Gorod for Moscow, then Helsinki—"

She brushed errant hair from her face, studied her son's strong facial features. He was younger than Andrei when he left for Afghanistan. But if Gleb got the job in Finland, at least she knew she would see him again. It's not as if he's off to war. It's not as if he's Kondrat, Petró's dad, who in the Winter War was killed fighting the Finns in Karelia. No, times had changed, were changing. "Good," she said. "You'll do well."

Not long after seeing Viktor, as chance would have it, Petró ran into Svetlana on one of his walks, Fedka camera strapped about his neck. She'd come out of the medical clinic on Spassky Avenue.

"Petya!" she called out.

His ears perked up, hearing his familiar name from an older woman he at first didn't recognize. He peered at her. *Is that Sveta?* He hadn't seen her in years. He couldn't remember when.

She hobbled toward him. In her right hand, she clutched a walking cane, helping her unsteady steps. Petró saw she still had her thin figure. She hadn't let herself go. But vivacious Svetlana, where was she, she who approached him with such a tired face? It was as though the effort to walk drained away what he remembered as her habitual smile.

Petró let go his momentary shock, then walked quickly toward her.

"Sveta," he said. "It's so long since we talked, and we're getting along in years, is it not so?" he asked, not willing to say anything about her cane. What he saw was obvious to even the most casual passerby. A woman in decline.

"Yes," she said. "But you, look at you, walking about looking like a tourist with a camera. You must not work today."

"Oh, work. That's finished. The Optics Test Station closed for good. All of us let go. And at my age, I could retire. I'm a pensioner now."

"Yes, I remember now; Viktor said something about seeing you and said you enjoy not working. So I see, out photographing."

"I must keep busy, but not spend money." He laughed. "The pension is so small, and these days, it seems, gets smaller every week."

"We all have changes to face." She smiled and waggled the cane out in front of her. This brought a brief smile to Petró's lips, knowing that she took her infirmity well, not openly complaining.

"The knee or hip?"

"Both, but mostly the hip. They give me better pain medicine today, so we'll see."

"Oh, the problems of getting older. So how's the son?" Petró asked, wanting to change the subject.

"Oh, Vladlen. He left for Moscow years ago. Busy, busy. He works in import-export. His own company now. Doing well, but still not married."

Petró had forgotten the son's name, but Vladlen brought it back. Who else but Viktor, longtime Party hack, would enthusiastically name his only offspring after Vladmir Lenin, Vladlen being a popular boy's name for a while. *But not anymore.*

"So," Petró said, looking away, "I don't want to keep you from anything. I'm just ambling about, looking for pictures to take—"

"Oh, so good I see you again after all this time. I'm not rushing. I'll catch the bus home now, get dinner started for Viktor. He and that security business, he is so busy, but I worry for him."

Petró did a double take. *She worries about Viktor?* These words from the same woman who said she was throwing away the best years of her life on a cold Party functionary? He smiled at the thought. Maybe the advancing years mellowed her.

"So tell Viktor hello for me. And I hope your medicine works."

"Oh, it has to," she laughed. "I tell Viktor if it doesn't, then he has to spend our money and send me to the West, so I can have a plastic-and-steel hip put in here," she said, patting her right side, the hip Petró years ago knew when he discovered the erotic mystery of life for the first time.

"And say hello to Olga," she added, a seeming afterthought.

They parted, went their separate ways, but Petró wasn't taking in the street scene about him, seeking out possible photographic subjects. No, the sight of a humbled Svetlana was unexpected, something he would never have contemplated in his younger years. But then, even now, not one to wear scarves, she wasn't about to become a babushka. He was sure she still thought of her days of glamour, and those memories must have kept her from settling into the more customary appearance of an older woman.

He turned on his heel and saw her standing at the bus stop down the street. Waiting for the bus. But not so far he couldn't catch her eye. He waved. She waved back.

He then kept walking, appreciating how years ago, their paths first crossed at the dance hall, the same dance hall where he and Olga married, where his son Andrei and Yelena married.

Yes, Yelena was married in the same dance hall he met Sveta.

Sveta, Yelena. He stopped walking, his fingers pinching his camera strap.

He paused in his walking about, but had no picture to take.

Sveta, Yelena. They were so much alike when they were young. He closed his eyes, rubbed his forehead, as if trying to summon images from those decades gone by. Might Yelena have been like Sveta when they were each nineteen? She once was glamorous, every bit as sleek as Sveta, and she had those Italian shoes. Fashion from the West captivated her, as many in Leningrad thought themselves European, not just Russian. But both women gave up the glamour and became dutiful wives and mothers, even though—to Petró's personal knowledge—Sveta wavered on the former. Yes, they both became good moms.

But unlike Sveta, whose marriage to Viktor was about survival, Soviet-style; Yelena lost Andrei. Oh, you could even say he left her at the altar for the Motherland and Afghanistan. She then had only Gleb. Yelena's life became the bakery, her son Gleb, and being the widow who took flowers to the War Heroes Cemetery every month.

Petró took a deep breath. The question was, If Gleb was going to Finland, as Yelena said, what kept her in Gorod? Were her life obligations fulfilled? Could she go to the West and re-discover that dream she had when she was nineteen?

The dance hall. Where Yelena married Andrei, where Petró married Olga, where Petró met Svetlana. He felt the heft of his Fedka in its leather case strapped about his neck. The dance hall was not that many blocks away. The midday sun was fine. Perhaps this was the day to photograph the dance hall. He never had. *Why not?*

He resumed his walk, but the steps were quicker, had urgency.

Gleb started his job in Finland, on the outskirts of Helsinki in a suburb called Espoo. He had his own flat. An efficiency flat, true,

Losing Laika 295

but a room he shared with nobody else. He luxuriated in the privacy, the ability to keep his own hours inside his four walls, without regard to anyone else's hours of sleep or schedules for work.

He wasn't allowed to bring much with him when he left Russia, but he did have Petró ship a box to him he had packed earlier. A box he took with him to work, a month or so after he was assigned his own cubicle. He was free to personalize the cubicle as he pleased. He decided the cabinet off to the side of his desk was the perfect place for what he had in the cardboard box that made it through the Soviet Postal Service and survived, rounded corners and all.

He pulled away the tape on the seams of the box. Lifted the flaps, pulled out the pages of *Pravda* used for packing.

"So what do we have here?" Jan said, standing up, peering over the divider between their cubicles. "A present?"

Gleb smiled. "Oh, a present from the past, from my childhood." He lifted out what seemed so small, but had such strong memories from when he first learned to write code.

The keyboard on the computer had Cyrillic characters, which Jan or most people around him wouldn't know. "My first computer. I was awarded this as a kid. This is the Soviet Agat with the old sixty-five-o-two processor. You know that?"

"Oh, yes, what we called the Apple. One of the first microcomputers."

"I'll keep this here for a while. An art object," he said. "But also inspiration, reminder of my roots," Gleb said with obvious pride.

56
СУВЕНИРНЫЕ БОЛТ
(SOUVENIR BOLT)

"Why don't they call us? They called those who came after us." Olga was at her complaining best and stood to her feet. Yellow babushka scarf on her head, she was ready to walk across the crowded waiting room of the OVIR, the Russian Office of Visas and Emigration, to shame whomever into calling them.

Petró tried to ignore her and sighed. *Things will never get better. Russia is shot.* His pension was nothing, another reason he and Olga decided to follow others out of the Motherland.

Gleb's unexpected transfer by his employer to California made the decision much easier. His name would go on their application as a sponsor in America, which the American consulate could not help but like as the reason to accept Petró and Olga's application for immigration, once Russia let them go.

As for Yelena, she would probably be going to America too. She just wasn't sure when or how. Everyday, she would spend time writing replies to American men who saw her picture and profile at an online marriage website.

Olga hadn't sat down.

Petró reached over and took her hand. "Don't—What does that do?"

"We've waited four hours, no lunch." She eyed the clock at the end of the room, mounted high on the ceiling, the little hand on the two, the big hand right behind.

"So no lunch. You want to stay here and starve?"

"What do you mean?"

"You know, go over there, make a fuss."

"Why not? They make us wait and wait—"

"They're slow."

"No, they want us to give up."

"Maybe, but if you go over there—" Petró paused. "The reviewer might just decide you're rude and stamp NYET all over our applications."

Olga looked at him blankly.

"Then we'll never leave and we will stay here and starve, no?"

He squeezed Olga's hand, and possibly what was at stake finally dawned on her—this was not standing in line for chicken at the butcher shop where if she was lucky, they would still have some for her. She sat down.

Petró was willing to indulge the State bureaucrats one more time. He wore his best brown suit for the occasion. But once the exit visas were approved, he would loosen his tie and then tell them to go kiss their arses.

"Glebka doesn't think we should go to California," Petró said, trying to while away the time until they were called.

"Why not?"

"He says it's too expensive there without a big job or plenty of money."

"We could live with him—" Olga smiled, not ashamed to impose. Gleb, after all, was their grandson.

"I don't know what his girlfriend, the Finn, would think—"

"Yes, the Finns, difficult people. Though I did like her picture. Did she say we couldn't live with them? Even for a little while?"

"No, I'm sure she said no such thing. Just when I talked with Gleb, he says we need to go where our money lasts longer."

"What'd he suggest?"

"Oh, he's found a church group on the West Coast of America to sponsor us where it's cheaper to live. He said Portland."

"Where's that?"

"Oregon, it's the state—like our *oblast*, next to California. We can see Glebka easily."

"But why there?"

"He said it's like Russia. Has snow. We'll like the weather. The summer is nice."

"If we can visit Gleb, it's okay."

Olga tugged the knot of her babushka scarf. She wondered how she would dress in America. It must be different.

Maybe she could not change. How could she after so many years?

"He says a community of Russians started settling in Oregon back in the sixties. Old Believers. Remember them?"

"Oh, yes, the Old Believers. I remember. They live the old ways."

"He said they have a good program that sponsors Russians. That's why he came up with Oregon."

Olga didn't respond, was looking across the room; a reviewer was out to call another name.

"Kravets. Petró and Olga, this way, please."

They stood stiffly to their feet. They had sat too long. A smile slipped across Petró's face. It would be okay.

Petró and Olga got their exit visas from OVIR in weeks. This didn't surprise Petró: The bureaucracy he'd learned to hate now showed off a newfound efficiency for rubber-stamping everything. Seemingly anyone with savings for a plane, train, or even a bus ticket out of Russia was trying to leave, and the applications overwhelmed OVIR. Obviously, the word came down at OVIR, if in doubt, let it pass.

The Kravets experience at the American Embassy was welcoming, almost a formality: They got visas to emigrate in a matter of hours. This put a glow on Petró's face as he left the downtown building where the Americans handled a long line of applicants with dispatch. Only a vodka toast would have him glowing more.

The value of the ruble fell weekly. Still, they scraped together enough life savings for a ticket from Moscow to Portland, Oregon, USA, with a bit left over. They went down to the Aeroflot office.

They would leave in a month, earlier flights out of Russia understandably fully booked.

It was time for good-byes. Petró never expected to see Gorod again.

"After all our work together, competition with America, you now go there." Petró's old friend Ivan laughed. They'd met for a walk through Great October Park, an especially sunny day and maybe one right for a last time.

"I'll miss this," Petró said with a sweep of his hand. "All I can do is take pictures with the Fedka and have memories." He tugged at the leather strap holding his camera about his neck.

As they walked, they were in a languorous mood and wanting to savor the last time. Petró and Olga would leave for Moscow the end of the week, and early next week, they would be in Portland,

Oregon, living with a church-sponsored family until they came up with more permanent arrangements.

They reached a fountain that the summer before always gushed skyward, water streams crashing down on the circular pool, and where the Roma ripped away Petró's Fedka and tossed it in the water for a splash that kept the lens from breaking. But not this day. The fountain was turned off. The standing water left had gone dingy with algae.

"See what happens here?" Ivan said.

"Like everything in Russia, doesn't work anymore!" Petró laughed.

"Look at that—" Ivan said pointing to a nearby bed of roses. The red-petalled flowers grew rampantly, unpruned—and so did towering thistles. "This place is going to the dogs. Maybe you're right to leave for America," he said. "But I'd have to study English like you—" he added, a note of regret in his voice, possibly, that he was staying.

"What will you do?" Petró asked, knowing full well Ivan's pension was probably the same as his, they worked at the same job the same years, and his financial embarrassment could be no less.

"I don't know. Now I don't work, I would like to leave the city, live in the country in a small dacha by a lake, spend the rest of my days fishing. But such a life, at my age, my wife gone, I don't think it can be."

"Well, let me get to America, and then I'll call you, see if you change your mind. I could find a place for you too."

Ivan gave a nervous look around. Petró had no idea of what kept him from admitting he'd like to leave.

But then some people are homebodies like house cats and don't want to leave home, ever. Petró shrugged his shoulders at the mystery of his best friend's mind.

"Say I've something for you," Ivan said.

"Oh, what? I hope it's nothing that cost dearly."

"No, free." He chuckled. "Look at this."

Ivan reached into his shirt pocket and took out a bolt. A couple of centimeters long, corroded with age, a relic.

"This is my present for going to America?" Petró asked.

"Yes, this is special. Here."

He handed it to Petró, who turned it over and over in his fingers, examining it for marks, like a good technician. "The thread on this, American three-eighths, sixteen. I see that. You know why I know that?" Petró said.

"Of course, we used that for the tripod mount on the old Fedka. We tried to sell to the English market—" Ivan screwed up his face in consternation: an American thread on the tripod mounting socket, everything else metric.

"So why is this bolt special?" Petró held the bolt high in the sunlight to see if his old eyes could pick out more under the corrosion.

"Remember we drove out to the spy plane wreckage, the American pilot was already taken away, and we looked over the camera—"

"Oh, the U-2, I'll never forget *that*." Petró's eyes widened at the bolt he held. "This is from that?"

"Yes, this bolt is off the U-2. I saved it, my souvenir, but now you go to America." He smiled. "It's good luck: The bolt wants to take you to its home safely."

"Oh, Vanya, you could not give me a better present—" He put his arm around him. "But now I must take your picture, okay?"

"Yes, of course." He smiled, but a smile to fade like water spilling off a table. Then it was gone.

57
ХРУЩЕВКА
(KHRUSHCHEV-ERA BLOCK)

The bolt Ivan gave Petró had a new home in his coat pocket. A talisman, he was sure, for safe passage to America. How could it not be? He tumbled the U-2 bolt about in his hand, showing it to Olga, who was busy picking things to pack.

"You must know what to take," she said.

"This certainly, my good-bye gift from Ivan."

"Then put it in your pile to pack."

"No, I'll carry it in my pocket."

"But you need to decide everything you take, we leave the day after tomorrow."

"You tell me that?" he said sharply.

"Sorry, I'm so nervy about the big change."

"It's okay. Gleb's already in America. But first," he said glancing at the lone window in their flat. "The afternoon light, plenty of shadows, I must walk, take pictures."

"Take pictures?" Olga asked.

"Yes, a last time."

"If you must," she said.

He had time to pack, and so he left, his Fedka strapped about his neck, for no particular destination. No Great October Park. No historical monument. Just open air and the side streets off Golitsyn Prospekt and many familiar ferroconcrete blocks of flats he would not see anymore.

He'd only walked about fifteen minutes, turned down a side street, when he stopped to study something he'd probably walked past countless times there and elsewhere: *khrushchevka*, a five-story one. All the blocks looked alike, and this was only one of many they tossed up in the years of the housing shortage. The early sixties, workers and families streamed into the cities for new jobs, and waiting lists for flats stretched out a year or more. Ol' Nikita put even more people to work, learning the building trades as they went, raising block after block of flats, always three to five stories.

The block walls seemed to crack smiles, welcoming new occupants. Still, patched walls, these buildings lasted long after most people expected them to collapse—though a talked-about few did. Petró's Public Housing No. 17 was built before the *khrush-chevki*. His block, from the Stalin-era, was often put down as a *stalinka*. So when he saw one of these blocks before him, he had no problem invoking the common pejorative: *khrushchevka*.

Petró unsnapped the case on his Fedka and extended the lens barrel. He brought the viewfinder to his eye. Aimed across the street. The building filled his viewfinder. All five floors, wall patches too.

The flats had cookie-cutter windowed balconies, each wide enough for no more than a few potted plants, but they also became improvised clotheslines. Guard rails bloomed with garments. This always caught Petró's eye.

The tenants in these newer flats had a communal laundry room that often included a dryer, but many who lived there, not long off farms, were superstitious. Petró knew the women might even resist panties and brassieres going through a gas-powered dryer. *Anything* that might contact their privates they wanted to dry naturally in the breezes and sunshine.

Or so Olya explained.

Camera to his face, the block across the street in view, he snapped a picture, full of the shadows tree branches cast across the far end of the building, but also an eyeful of women's undergarments, unavoidably cluttering up what the viewfinder framed. But then that was Gorod in a *khrushchevka*. What he wanted to remember.

He was sure he wouldn't see such a sight in America.

He'd keep walking, look elsewhere for shots.

But before he got to the next cross-street, he stopped, then turned about. He looked at the block he had just left.

A lone, white brassiere hung straight down from the last guard rail on the fifth floor. That ordinariness. Oh, he'd have to remember that.

What is it?

The building wasn't much. No entry for any architecture prize. But still, its ordinary façade was for the common man. The worker. That was true, as true as the worker commune in Kharkov where he built the leather-cased Fedka, strapped about his chest.

Oh, the ordinariness of socialist promise for the working man. In his gut, he knew that. He knew that humble five-story block at the end of the street showed a promise, a shared belief that helped the Russian people put in orbit the first sputnik, the first cosmonaut, and in his work for OTS, reconnaissance satellites that were still busy keeping tabs on missiles and military forces the world over from the heavens above.

Yes, that, and the other *khrushchevki*, though ordinary, had the dignity of a promise, even though broken.

Petró was saying good-bye. Good-bye to the lost dream of socialist equality for the working man. He was going to America. Petró's eyes were flat with resignation.

Yes, they were going to America because the dream was over. Crazy Yeltsin, lips wet with vodka, pissed away the promise of that dear old idealistic Jew, Karl Marx, in a capitalist orgy—*economic shock therapy* his advisor Gaidar called it—and destroyed any socialist aspiration once and for all.

What might have been. So sad. Petró shrugged and went back to walking.

58
TWENTY-FIVE DEGREES CELSIUS AND MUGGY
(ДВАДЦАТЬ ТРИ ГРАДУСА ПО ЦЕЛЬСИЮ, А ДУШНО)

Petró had to pack, and deciding what to take was sad and difficult. By terms of their exit visas, they were allowed two suitcases each.

He paced back and forth between the two rooms of their flat, trying to figure out what he wanted that would fit. Some choices were easy. Even though he waited years for it, he obviously could not take the television. Whatever he took had to be small.

"Olya, what clothes must I take?" he called out.

Olga stepped in from the other room, holding a scarf. "You'll take no clothes except what's on your back! This is way of émigrés, no?"

"Some of these clothes, they're important to me." He held up a leather jacket with a bear fur collar. "See this, it's my favorite. Once belonged to my papa. I cannot leave this—"

"Then take it, you must. But other clothes, you may buy in America."

"Oh, that's what you'll do?" Olga sewed clothes, so he doubted once in America, she would quit and buy in stores.

"Yes, if I'm in America, I'll fit in, wear clothes in the style of the West. Replace this," she said, waving her hand back at the rest of the bedroom, where she sorted through what was in the wardrobe. "What I'll take and wear is my scarves. They show I'm married. These I have a long time."

Some in their fourth decade, he thought. "I like my little Sony shortwave radio," he said. "It easily fits in the suitcase; do I need it in America? No outside world to find and listen—"

"Oh, take it anyway, it's so small, and you like it for the sentiment when you drink tea."

"Ah, yes, good you mention that, I must take my Georgian tea too."

Petró paused. "You think it's hard to find Georgian tea in America?" he asked haltingly, as if the question answered itself.

Her brow furrowed. She said nothing.

Petró settled down to deciding. A few underwear, shorts and undershirts. His pajamas. Favorite shirts. An extra pair of pants. The suit he had since he married. The only one he had. Soon the suitcase was full, and he started on the second.

"Of course, one thing I can't leave. I'll photograph everything new I see."

"Your camera?"

"Yes," he said, handling with tenderness the little Fedka encased in worn, brown leather with the thin, lanky neck strap he was about to bundle safely inside his knit wool cap. But first, he couldn't resist one last look at his treasure and went over to sit on the sofa, to relax, to meditate on what it had seen, what pictures it took in its long life, more than sixty years on.

He lifted the rear flap and flipped the front cover open. He turned it around toward him and pulled off the Bakelite lens cap with the letters ФЭД. The aperture was set at $f9$, his favorite. He

Losing Laika 309

extended the tube of the collapsible lens to its full reach and then rotated a quarter turn to lock.

The little Fedka had seen so much. He could let all else go. But this little camera, no, companion? Why he wanted to be buried with it. What he did at Kharkov proved Marx had a better way, when the scientific principles were followed sincerely and not corrupted by Party hacks, hungry for power and control. How else could a bunch of teenagers, he and Ivan included, have learned to assemble such an intricate camera like the FED, a people's camera, affordable for anybody? Thousands, hundreds of thousands, were made—for more than twenty years.

Some called the FED a shameless copy of the expensive German Leica II.

Petró held the camera to his face, peered through the viewer, and adjusted the lens to bring the window across the room into focus. He looked down at the distance reading. Three and a half meters. Accurate. Even today, the little Fedka rivalled a Leica of similar vintage. He knew that. Most Russians did too. Yes, the little Fedka might look like the Leica, but a copy? The question brought a smile to Petró's face.

Why was the first Leica II, the one in 1932 with the built-in rangefinder, an exact copy of the Russian Pioneer rangefinder camera for sale earlier that year? Originally, the Pioneer was developed in the secretive VOOMP labs of the Soviet military. Why would Russians copy defeated and bankrupt Germans? More likely, those losing Germans, banned from gaining military technology to fight again—which they did soon enough—must have sent spies to Russia, knowing about VOOMP's vaunted optics technology.

Petró knew that was the truth. The genius of the little Fedka was its Russian roots. He, Ivan, and all those young communards took to its assembly like ducks to water.

He gave the shutter knob a turn to cock the shutter, then pushed the button. *But no film.* He laughed.

A long flight. So long, Petró wondered if their Aeroflot Zupalov 250 with its four thirsty engines would run out of fuel somewhere high above the gray Atlantic ocean. He knew the pilots up front must have felt flying from Moscow to New York was no more difficult than driving a cross-town bus for too many hours. He just wanted them to do it once more. After that, he would let the air travellers who might follow him out of the Soviet Union put in their own worry-time like him.

The hours slipped by, and Petró drifted off in catnaps, each unsatisfyingly short. The plane was full of other Russians, all obviously plunking down life savings to get away from a Soviet Union lost to history. Petró sat in the window seat, right side, the back of the cabin. Olga beside him, the middle seat. She couldn't look out the window. She'd never flown before. Heights frightened her. Petró had flown, but only in small military planes, never in a big, comfortable jetliner.

"Ladies and gentlemen, this is your pilot speaking," the voice came on the loudspeaker, in Russian. "We're on schedule, and soon you'll see, on the right side of the plane, North America. That's Newfoundland, along the coast of eastern Canada. Weather in New York City is sunny and twenty-five degrees Celsius."

Seemingly, half the passengers in the plane pulled off their seat belts and stood up in the aisle to look out those right-side windows at the view Petró took in by merely turning his head sideways. *Green trees, that's all, many green trees like our taigas. No towns. So this is America.* The red hammer and sickle painted on the silver wing shimmered under the midday sun as Petró felt the captain ease up the engines, starting a descent into JFK International, named after the American president who stood down Khrushchev over the missiles in Cuba many years ago. Then he was assassinated. Petró knew, unlike Russia, Americans liked being able to arms themselves with guns in their own hands. Their rock-and-roll violence, Gleb would say.

Once they landed, once they filed off the packed Zupalov, only the air was theirs, however, in the land of the free: They still had customs to clear. Plus the air was muggy. Petró wondered when he could take off his suit coat.

"What customs? Can they send us back?" Olga asked.

"No, this is nothing. They look at our papers. Ask the value of what we brought."

"But everything we have is with us—"

"Yes, but it's old." Olga's face was worried, wrapped in her yellow babushka scarf. "We'll say nothing's new, nothing's valuable, and we've bought nothing." Petró bit his lower lip.

The several U. S. Customs officers were surprisingly jovial and casual when the planeload of Russian émigrés descended upon them. They kept talking back and forth, giving the most perfunctory of attention to the passports Petró handed over.

He scratched his head after they spent less than thirty seconds with the U. S. Customs officer, who said, "Welcome to the United States," and smiled broadly.

"Спасибо," Petró said, forgetting momentarily it was now English all the way around.

"Where baggage 4-A?" Petró asked aloud of any stranger. Olga had no idea, bewildered by the growing crowds, many of whom seemed less and less Russian, as they moved away from the U. S. Customs gate.

When they found the baggage carousel, they rejoined the other Russians from Aeroflot Flight 171, all waiting on luggage unloaded from the same plane. "Your suitcases look old," Petró said. "The ones with bungee cords. They stand out." Olga nodded. She knew her suitcases well.

The carousel's belted-surface lurched, began gliding past. From the rubber flaps at the far end, luggage emerged, a few, then a stream, one after another. Like a ready-to-swoop eagle, Petró watched each coming at them. Not one was theirs.

Finally, and only after he swore he saw the same tied-off trash bag make a second trip around, the two bungee-corded suitcases—Olga's—emerged under the hanging rubber flaps. "See, yours. I'll grab them."

But right behind Olga's belongings, Petró quickly saw his two suitcases, a set of old leather ones that were his father's—that old. Where had they traveled before? He didn't know. The suitcases sat around for years. Petró didn't use them on vacations to the Black Sea. No, he kept them around out of sentiment, but now they had been big enough for leaving Russia.

He reached over, yanked Olga's suitcases, one in each hand, dropped them beside her, stumbled around hers for his, but he couldn't move—the people beside him.

"Don't worry, Petya, they'll come back."

When Petró got his two leather cases, heavier than he remembered, he and Olga walked. But only as far as the inspection point to leave baggage claim. "Ticket stubs, please," the tall, uniformed woman said. Petró gave her the stubs Aeroflot stapled to their tickets.

After the young woman nodded, Olga walked out of baggage claim with her luggage.

Petró took the claim tickets back, picked up his suitcases, one in each hand. He lurched forward, then one suitcase struck the shiny, fixed pole by the young woman.

The blow of the metal pole on the bone-dry leather of the suitcase cracked it open, the lock came undone, the suitcase flopped open, and, for Petró and everyone else to see, stuff spilled out on the floor. "Wait!" he cried out. Olga turned, and shock took over her face.

Underwear, everything spilled out. Petró knelt down to pick up things. He didn't know what else to do. Who would help? His face felt flush.

Then he saw the old black knit cap. He slowly lifted it up. Opened it. In its fold, the brown leather-cased Fedka. It tumbled onto a soft bed of clothes. He smiled. Like falling into a splashing water fountain. The little Fedka had seen too much to break now.

Everywhere Petró turned, America was wonderful and confusing. So different from Gorod. Once they cleared customs and got their baggage, it was off to another terminal, so they could board the flight to the West Coast, Seattle, then Portland, Oregon. Petró had no idea what to expect from the Samilikovs, who would put them up for at least a few weeks, until arrangements could be made for their own place.

At Portland International, the thirty-ish Samilikovs, Boris and Tatya, greeted them.

"Long flight," Petró said, grumbling at what he endured to give up on Russia.

"Oh, you'll have a nice rest once we get home," Boris said.

Walking through the crowded terminal, Petró was struck by the prosperity of Americans. Everybody's clothes were fashionable, what his people might bring home from the West. He didn't know what to make of it.

They got their baggage and walked out to the parking structure and the Samilikovs' car. Boris put the four suitcases, one of Olga's bungee cords holding together Petró's suitcase that broke. Should he throw it away as worthless? After all, it failed him once he landed in America, spewing his stuff every which way.

But, no, it had been his papa's, and whose final sacrifice meant Petró could no more toss that suitcase than forget the sacred memory of his papa.

"Now, you'll see Portland," Boris said. "First, our freeways, we drive a distance to our house."

Petró eyed Boris' super-sized SUV. "You Old Believers have it good in America," he said with a faint chuckle.

"Oh, Old Believers, that's our parents. They still farm, follow the old ways down by Woodburn. Tatya and I, we're city folks, but we still have the faith."

59
HOMELESS REPUBLICAN
(БЕЗДОМНЫЙ РЕСПУБЛИКАНЕЦ)

Soon, the four were rolling down the road for a freeway on-ramp. They stopped at a light. Before them, on the median strip, a young man stood and held up a hand-lettered cardboard sign: HOMELESS REPUBLICAN ANYTHING HELPS GOD BLESS. The fellow, dressed in a black suit, a white shirt, and a tie. Far better than anything Petró ever wore. He begged for money and smoked a cigar?

"What is this?" Petró exclaimed about the sturdy beggar. "He should have a job. Do healthy young men in America not have jobs?" he asked. "This would not happen in Russia, we don't have beggars, we have people sweep streets if they need work."

"Oh, yes, this is America," Boris said. "That fellow doesn't want to work. He just wants people to give him money. Maybe he makes more that way. I don't know."

The light changed, and they slipped past the Homeless Republican.

"But what does that mean, Homeless Republican?" Petró asked, puzzled. "I've studied American history. Isn't that a political party?

"Of course. The party in power today. We have a new Republican president leading our country."

"So why does the fellow call himself Homeless Republican?"

"Not sure. Perhaps a sense of humor. Perhaps he wants people's attention," Boris said, picking up speed, merging, then changing lanes on the freeway.

"This is crazy. The man is not homeless. He mocks himself and the political party in power by these actions." Petró shook his head. "This would never happen in my country. Perhaps Lenin was right. Our people know when they are bad off. Here they pretend and don't work. That makes no sense."

The Homeless Republican was the first of several confusions Petró had about the American Dream, once he settled in and looked around. The beggars holding signs on street corners who couldn't or wouldn't work. He didn't understand this seemingly needless want in a land of plenty. He tried to keep his opinions to himself. He knew he was learning about the incredible freedoms Americans had to be themselves, to be different, even though, in Petró's eyes, they ended up looking like a Homeless Republican clown.

Although he and Olga enjoyed the hospitality of the Samilikovs, they didn't want to overstay. They were happy to see Gleb fly up from San Francisco. One thing led to another, and before long they'd moved into their own modest apartment.

At home in her one-room flat, Yelena sat down at the computer, an old Agat II Gleb left. She mostly used it for email. Nobody wrote letters anymore. Especially the pen pals from America with romantic interests she'd been cultivating.

They were too impatient for postal mail. They wanted those quick emails shot back and forth through the circuit of earth-orbiting satellites where speed approached that of light.

Her INBOX had an email from one such man: an American in Cincinnati, Ohio, whom she'd known for at least a month. He obviously was interested, wanted to know more about her.

Hi, Yelena,

Thanks for the picture, you by the subway entrance. You're most handsome and I've got my hopes up to one day meet you in person. But, of course, we first need to be sure we want to take that big step ;-)

But looking at this picture, your blonde hair's got a bounce that goes with your upbeat personality. Your figure's trim, not like many American women. I once asked if you'd been married and you said no. You also said no kids. So that might help keep your body looking great.

But as I said, before we take the big step and meet in real life, we need to be absolutely sure we really want this.

I must confess, something you said in one of your first emails put a small, nagging doubt in my head. You said as a child you heard Sputnik beeping in outer space over the radio. I didn't think much about it when you wrote that because frankly I wasn't sure how far we might be going.

But the other day, a disturbing thought hit me: Sputnik was 1957, 43 years ago. If you're 34, you wouldn't have been alive to hear Sputnik beeping.

So, please, I've one simple request.

Send a new picture. You holding the newspaper. That way the news headlines will prove all's up-to-date and A-OK.

I hope you don't take this wrong. That I suspect you or am saying you misled me. No, I sincerely hope you've been on the up and up and we can get together soon.

So if you can get that picture with the newspaper and email it,

everything will be fine and the clock will be ticking down until we can get together in real life ;-)
Mark

Yelena turned away from the computer screen, stunned. Why? Yes, she misled him, but not that much. She was forty-two, not thirty-four. True, she wasn't alive when Sputnik went up. She was born in 1958. Why does he assume I heard it when it happened? She and every other Russian kid heard those beeps many times. They were often rebroadcast on the radio, part of promoting Russian technology.

Why shouldn't she mislead him? She knew these Internet men. Oh, they were all ages—in their forties, in their fifties, in their sixties—but not one of them wanted to have anything to do with women unless they could have kids. The women had to be in their twenties or thirties.

If she didn't give her age as thirty-four and technically mislead them, she'd never hear from them again. They'd go looking elsewhere.

She stood and walked over to the bathroom and looked in the mirror. The lines appearing at the corners of her eyes. The tiredness in her face. But her figure. How had that changed from eight years ago? She was still trim.

No, she hadn't misled him. Just scanned an old picture lying around. It was her after all, not someone else. And her age. Why did women have to tell men their age, when women tolerated men of any age?

No, the small falsehoods she said—she was never married, she had no children, she was eight years younger—were what men demanded to even deem her worthy of another email.

She turned from the mirror, satisfied she was the same woman in that picture taken by the subway entrance.

What was she going to do?

Tell him about hearing Sputnik beeps on a radio program in the sixties? Where would that go? She'd still have to admit her age. Would she again deny she was a mother, had no Gleb? Of course not.

She didn't believe Mark's suspicions deserved a reply. It would be demeaning herself, but also the memory of Andrei, to answer such a request. A picture with a newspaper? Such a man is impossible.

If she heard from him again and she probably wouldn't—he surely was chasing others—she would delete his message from the INBOX. Not even open it.

60
FOOD CART
(ЕДА КОРЭИНУ)

For Petró and Olga, the Samilikovs made adjusting to American life so much easier. They introduced the Kravets to a larger community of East Europeans, who in numbers had settled in the inexpensive apartments of Portland's Mid-County, who almost every week had a get-together at somebody's house, an excuse to share food and stories of the Motherland, Petró and Olga enjoying the company of not only fellow Russians, but Ukrainians, Romanians, Bulgarians, Lithuanians; the countries the émigrés left seemed a roll call of the East Bloc.

Back in Russia, Yelena was cooling to the idea she'd find an American husband from being Internet pen pals. Besides, she had sponsors in America for a visa application: Gleb, Petró, and Olga. It didn't take many months of being alone in her Gorod flat for Gleb to persuade her she should complete the move of the whole Kravets family and rejoin them on the West Coast. Her only other choice, if she left Gorod, was to yield to the entreaties of her aging mom and move to what was now called St. Petersburg. Yelena quickly sized up the neediness in that plea and, without hesitation, said no.

With prospects of an American inviting Yelena to his country as his mail-order bride remote, she went ahead and bought an Aeroflot ticket out of Moscow. Gleb picked up the tab. He made the beaucoup bucks down in Silicon Valley.

Once settled in with Petró and Olga, Yelena looked for ways to make money. In America, only money was sure to get respect from others. She wanted to fit in. Fit in and buy fine clothes and possibly—just possibly—have a social life too.

She noted how other Russians in town made money. Like everywhere else, people had to eat, and if the food was good, spent plenty. She had baking experience from Gorod.

"So what will you do for this lady?" Olga asked Yelena, one Saturday morning.

"Daria, she has the food cart, a vacant lot on Foster. Busy, sells plenty of Russian food. The businesses around there send her many customers. So, I talked with her, heard how she came over from Ukraine, then asked her if she would like to add some pastries. She already sells coffee with food, so why not pastries?"

"What did she say?"

"She'll try it. Said if she doesn't make money, I don't make money. We must see if people buy."

"What are you going to make?"

"To start, I'll try ponchiki. Easy to make a batch here in our oven and take them over fresh early in the morning."

Yelena found the ingredients for ponchiki at the grocery. Making ponchiki wasn't a matter of exotic Russian ingredients, just common everyday butter, lemon, flour, a few other things. What was hard, what separated a bakery chef from amateurs was how Yelena deep-fried the baked ponchiki in oil at the right temperature for just so long. They always came out golden with mouth-watering crispness worth every bite.

"So how did you do?" Olga asked Yelena, off the phone with Daria.

"Nothing to pick up. By noon, they were gone. Daria wants more tomorrow. They're a moneymaker. I have to decide what else to bake. She wants to try something else with the ponchiki—"

"Ah, Lena, before long you'll be rising at three and working until daybreak, just to keep up with the demand—"

Olga wanted to bake again too. She was getting up with Yelena and helping out. Petró had seen the Samara Bakery, featuring fine Russian breads over on 82nd, and suggested Yelena might apply for a position. In a matter of months, both Yelena and Olga were working there mornings. Just like old times in Gorod when they worked together at the bakery. The owners of Samara Bakery were more than happy to take on the "Old World" recipes Olga and Yelena brought with them.

61
GLOBAL SALES
(ГЛОБАЛЬНЫМ ПРОДАЖАМ)

Petró also had to find ways to occupy his time. He needed a little part-time job to earn that lingua franca of America: the almighty greenback. But he didn't know what he could do, having worked for so long in defense optics.

In some ways, America was kind to the Kravets, extending them benefits similar to living in Russia. The apartment was Section-Eight subsidized, so they paid little for rent. They had lively, occasionally noisy neighbors. Mostly émigrés: Eastern Europe, but also Latin America, and Southeast Asia. A global village.

They got food stamps, so much of what they ate was free. And joining the Oregon Health Plan meant medical care was free too, if they didn't mind waiting at the clinic. The new life in Oregon was better than starving in Russia, plus, for Petró, he had an old Toyota that, surviving like a cockroach, was always ready to go forward with an unflappable motor, starting up when he turned the key and running flawlessly until he cut the ignition off. That old Toyota gave him a new freedom—driving his own car—he never knew back in Gorod. No common worker in the Soviet Union could jump in their own car and drive anywhere they pleased.

He didn't know how he passed the driving test, after the Sears driving school lessons—a gift from Gleb—but his eyes, sharp as ever, and a memory for detail got him by. Once he had that Oregon drivers license and once Gleb, up from California, went with him out to 82nd Street and helped him navigate those used car lots and settle on a *good* car, Petró was free to exult in his new wheels. He spent much of his free time simply driving around, getting to know his hometown.

His favorite hours out driving, while Olga and Yelena worked at the bakery, were making the rounds of garage sales.

Petró soon realized his prime hunting grounds for garage sales were the better neighborhoods. If he stopped near where he lived, he knew his neighbors of modest means only had modest goods to sell. Mostly clothes, old furniture, and a miscellany of throwaways.

So when he went out garage-sale hunting, he invariably headed for the better, close-in neighborhoods on the eastside: Laurelhurst, Dolph Park, Irvington, Alameda, or Eastmoreland. The garage sales tended to be on Saturdays, a big day at the bakery for Yelena and Olga, so Petró went alone.

Petró soon learned he couldn't take *garage sale* literally. Often, things for sale were in the driveway, where sunlight would show off used wares well. And often, if the sale was large, it would spill out into a nearby yard. Even sidewalks were pressed into service.

Petró hated most of what he saw. Tossed TV sets, portable radios, hair dryers—to his mind, so much plastic trash. None of which, once broken, could be fixed. If it stopped playing, a little Walkman cassette player was beyond repair. Put together by

Japanese robots, untouched by human hands, micro shots of glue holding it together: no metal screw anywhere. For Petró, the stuff was worthless, plastic fakery—maybe shiny and seductive when new—but still, in the end, couldn't be fixed.

But Petró soon bought a rickety night stand to set beside his bed. At least fifty years old, the thick varnish could be stripped, the wood refinished with a coat of linseed oil. Plus Petró knew he could glue wedges in the joints and make the table rock-steady. But most important, the wood was solid. Even the top had several small boards glued together edge-to-edge. No cheap veneer crap. Just the real deal.

The table had a price tag: four dollars. Petró, in his broken English, asked if the seller would take two dollars. He knew well the art of bargaining. She agreed because she just wanted to be rid of the table. He proudly took his acquisition home to show Olga and Yelena and made plans to fix it up "good as new."

But at most garage sales, Petró was content to not buy. Not that he was cheap, he simply enjoyed looking. He felt as though he discovered this window into the past, showing him for the first time what consumer goods Americans were buying all their lives, while his fellow countrymen back in Russia did without.

He wasn't wholly envious. As he saw over and over, most of what these Americans bought was disposable. The stuff refused fixing. *Why bother? Why buy such crap?*

Occasionally, however, Petró would stop not at a garage sale, but at an estate sale. Which is to say, Somebody had died. Petró figured the attic in the house was cleaned out. For his studious eye, a time capsule of honest treasure for sale.

At one such estate sale, his eye was hooked by the sight of an old folder film camera, one of those with bellows that popped out when the camera opened. An Afga. He picked it up.

Larger than his Fedka, a fine German camera, probably made before the Great Patriotic War. He looked for a price tag and saw none. His mind raced, for he knew by feel, sound, and sight if the camera in his hands was worth his time. The Agfa he felt was a treasure, one he figured, with the Tessar lens, was the top-of-the-line Agfa that sold for three hundred dollars US, new. At least. He decided to make an offer.

"This camera, how much?" he asked. "No price tag."

The woman smiled. "Oh, you name a figure. I'll say yes or no, okay?"

Petró was flustered, didn't know what to say. He was used to starting with a price and bargaining the seller down. Above all, he didn't want to offer too much. But if the camera sold for three hundred new and it was a good collectible camera, surely it could be worth a quarter of that. "Seventy-five," he said, unsure when he would be able to pay.

The woman's jaw dropped. "Oh, is that dollars or your money?" she asked, oblivious of the slight about his accented English.

"Oh, that's right," he said, realizing the woman gave him an out if his offer was much higher than she expected. "I forgot this is not rubles," he added, knowing the woman had no idea what the dollar-ruble exchange rate was, incalculable as it was, his homeland's money going down the toilet.

"I see," he continued. "Please, what do you think is a fair price?"

"What about five dollars?" she said, eager to wrap things up.

Petró stifled his impulse to tell her she was crazy to sell such a fine German camera for nothing. He closed his eyes and again, not thinking, took out his wallet, eyed his gas money and said, "What about four?"

"Okay, it's yours."

Petró couldn't believe his luck and had nothing but joyous anticipation for the rest of the day, scarcely containing himself at the prospect of going home and giving his new baby a going over, cleaning it off, seeing how it worked. And for four dollars?

Crazy. That's all he could think.

On later Saturdays, Petró quickly found out why nobody wanted old film cameras. Everybody had gone digital. These fine optical instruments, assembled with human hands, held together by tiny screws, in genuine leather cases, with glass of stellar optics could be had for pennies on the dollar, and they were, not lost on Petró, repairable.

Before he knew it, Petró had a table full of fine old cameras bought from the cleared-out attics of their deceased owners, who put them away decades before, as if to await Petró's discovery.

Petró felt like the bear at the honey pot.

He had been taking apart and putting together cameras all his life. At first, he looked over his growing collection of cameras, unsure what to make of them. The nagging thought came to him that they were obsolete. Was that why they sold for nothing? Yes, an old man and his old cameras.

He'd argue with Olga his collection of old cameras was a steal, that someday they would again bring top dollar. "From collectors," he blurted out.

"Silly old men like you," she replied.

Finally, he could wait no longer and did what he'd always done: fix cameras and tune them up to work like new. He took out the toolkit he kept for adjusting and cleaning his Fedka: the little screwdrivers, the adjustable lens spanners, the rubber air blower, the cotton swabs and went to the task of cleaning and adjusting one of his estate-sale discoveries.

Like an archaeologist at a promising dig, this was surprisingly relaxing, something he could do for hours. Every camera taught him something about how the camera maker solved the problem of focussing a lens on an image, which with just the right amount of time and light at the focal plane would change chemically that film strip emulsion embedded with silver halide grains, a fine granularity that escaped the naked human eye without powerful magnifiers. Like a microscopic mosaic of flip-flop tiles, those grains of silver halide, touched by light, would change from white to black once they got dropped in a bath of film developer.

Soon, Petró had repaired the dozen old film cameras sitting around keeping his little Fedka company. He looked them over and wagged his head in puzzlement. How would he ever get around to using them? He knew each intimately, having cleaned, lubed, and adjusted them until they worked within their boxed-out-the-factory-door specifications.

A clinker or two would be for parts only: Some would-be camera-fixing owner opened it up before Petró and made it unsalvageable: missing screws, broken levers, scratched glass. But usually Petró trusted outside appearances would show the care the camera got before it sat unused in an attic for decades.

One day, Gleb, up from the Bay Area to visit his mom and grandparents, noticed Petró's growing collection of cameras.

"So, what're you going to do with these?"

"Not sure. I pick them up at garage sales and enjoy fixing them."

"Must be like going back to work for you—"

"Yes, my eyes are strong, and I use a loupe to magnify the small parts, and my hands are steady. Makes me feel like a young man at work again." He beamed at Gleb.

"Why don't you sell them?"

"Sell them, I'm not crazy. They give them away at garage sales.

Who, except old men like me, would want these?"

"No, you can sell them. Specially fixed up so they work like new."

"But how, I know nothing about selling. Just buying cheap and fixing. That's what I know."

"Oh, you'll find buyers. You do this on eBay."

"What's eBay?"

"It's on the Internet."

"I know nothing about the Internet."

"But you have a computer here."

"That's only for email. Yelena does that. Yelena and Olga. Not me."

Gleb looked at his grandpapa. Hadn't his eyes seen technology advance? The launch of Sputnik, outfitting the first reconnaissance sputniks way back then. And he doesn't do Internet? "You know your buyers—people interested in these cameras are not just here in Portland—they're all over the world. They can find your cameras on eBay."

Petró looked at his grandson in disbelief and said nothing.

Gleb knew what that meant.

"I'll tell you what. I'll take the cameras you fix back to Mountain View. I'll sell them on eBay. I'll send you the money. How would you like that?"

"Oh, that sounds good. I'll take the money and buy more cameras."

"Certainly. But when I write these cameras up to sell, I'll need a bit of information about you, how you're qualified to fix cameras. Must be truthful. I want you to tell me about your experience working on cameras in the FED factory—all from the beginning."

"Sure. When do we start?"

62
DU
(ОБЕДНЕННЫЙ УРАН)

Years went by, Petró was in his eighties, and he lived alone. The loss of Olga was sudden and unexpected, but the fact she didn't endure an extended bout of suffering gave Petró solace of a sort.

As for Yelena, devoted as she was to family, she had left Petró and Olga. She could afford it, as a co-owner of another bakery where she worked. Then there was her social life. She moved in with a fellow—an American at that—and spoke about their "serious relationship."

With Olga gone, Petró discovered he wasn't much for keeping house or making his meals. He quickly went along with Yelena's suggestion they look over group homes, where he could have his own room, but share meals with other residents.

After Petró moved to Rentner Place, he found much to talk about with Fritz, a Swiss émigré from World War II days. Petró asked that he call him "Pete," which was fairly close to Petya, his nickname. When Fritz called him Pete, he felt their friendship grew closer.

One sunny afternoon, the two sat at an umbrellaed table on an outside deck, taking in some fresh air, chatting over glasses of iced tea, as if they'd each lived long enough and seen enough, to lounge about, wearing chinos and pastel long-sleeved shirts, unbuttoned at both collar points and cuffs.

"So you worked in defense optics?" Fritz asked.

Petró nodded. "Yes, all my life, nothing but cameras. Many satellites up there—" He paused, circling his index finger skyward, "that's our doing, in Soviet times, my group back in Gorod. At the Optics Test Station. We put eyes in many satellites."

"Ah, yes, I remember your Sputnik. Put some big fears in Americans. That was back when?"

"October 4, 1957." A broad smile slipped across Petró's face. He rewarded that memory with a sip of iced tea.

"The good ol' days of the Cold War," Fritz said, as if nostalgic, though why he'd have fond remembrance of hydrogen bombs and the "Balance of Terror" escaped Petró. Maybe he knew the joyous relief of living to talk about it.

"But you said something once, something about you were a physicist, worked for the government. You didn't work for defense, too, did you?"

"Yeah, I did, but I wasn't an employee. I had my own little company; I was a defense contractor. My only customer was the United States Army. I retired out twenty years ago."

"So what did you do, I mean what does a physicist do for the Army?"

Fritz turned his head, looking about to see who nearby might overhear. The others, elsewhere in the backyard, were at some remove.

"I had a top-secret clearance, never could talk about my work. Did ordnance research. That's all I could tell my late wife."

Losing Laika 335

"Oh, I had security clearance, too, at OTS, but so much of what I did is obsolete now. Who would care if I told you about optics in those early sputniks? All out of date, kaput—" he said dismissively, waving his hand.

"Well, what I did was a bit more controversial, and I'm not happy where it led—" He frowned.

Petró didn't know what to make of the "intelligence" to which Fritz alluded. "Well, surely, you could not reveal this stuff to the other side in our Cold War." Petró grinned, thumbing his chest. "You'd be accused of being a turncoat, a Kim Philby."

"Yeah, the Russians were our priority. My mission in life came down to one thing—"

Petró felt that Fritz trusted him enough to give him the straight skinny, so he asked. "If you don't mind telling—"

"Russia's biggest tank—the TU645--was my challenge in life. All I wanted to do was pierce the armor plate on that huge tank with our anti-tank artillery. The plating on that tank was twelve-centimeters thick, yes, twelve centimeters and sloped exactly sixty degrees—" He stopped, as if reliving a mental tussle with the apparent challenge. Then continued, "How do you fire a missile round from two miles away at a tank not visible to the naked eye and have it pierce and destroy that TU645? Any ideas?"

Petró shrugged.

"Yeah, my feelings at the time too. But every summer, I would go with two employees to Camp Wilber in Eastern Oregon, out there past Burns, on the salt flats. That camp's been decommissioned since World War II and still is posted strictly off-limits, even to cattle grazing for a reason I'll get to—"

Petró took another sip of tea. *So this is what the other side was up to, trying to defeat the might of the Soviet military? How did I get here? Talking with the other side in confidence like this. Life is beau-*

tiful, if you live long enough.

"We'd be gone a week. Do nothing but fire round after round. We'd calculate the wind, the direction, set up artillery and then fire away. Once the rounds were finished, we'd hop in the Jeep, drive the coupla miles to the target, see what we did. I'd take pictures, measure the deflection of the armor plate—when we hit—all the usual things a physics PhD is trained to do, analyzing a problem in mechanics."

"What was your target like?" Petró asked.

"Oh, it would have been more fun if we shot at actual TU645s, but, no, just those plates, twelve-centimeters thick, sitting on sand berms. A good simulation of the real thing, of course. Now, what was I saying?" He crunched a piece of ice.

"The first summer I worked on this problem, nothing. My measured deflections weren't worth writing up. Then later that year, I was away from field work, going back to D.C. and getting the scoop on the newest Soviet tank in a briefing and heard we might have to simulate even thicker armor. Going nowhere, I was noodling around with one of Newton's laws, when the answer hit me—"

Petró's eyes went wide. *This is a security breach coming up?*

"It was trivial, once I saw that equation, force equals mass times acceleration. Even the first-year college student gets that in Mechanics 101. Know what I needed, Pete?" Fritz smiled.

"Bigger cannon?"

"Not exactly, but close. I needed heavier rounds. I needed more throw-weight coming in at that TU645. In a word, I needed density."

"And?" Petró knew they'd crossed over into confidence. They only had a few years of life left between them, so any secrets were going to the grave. What they said would be as inaccessible as that

Camp Wilber, out in Eastern Oregon, on the salt flats past Burns.

"I needed something heavier than lead in my rounds. That's what I decided. And God only knows there is enough heavy metal around. I decided on DU, depleted uranium coming out of nuclear reactors. Hanford, across the river," he said, casting his hand northward, "has it by the ton. No supply problem."

"Did that work?"

"Like a charm. If we hit the armor plate, punched it like butter. We took precautions about the rounds, kept them in lead cylinders during transport—the exposure during loading and firing was only seconds—so we felt it was worth the side-cost, if any, if we stopped the TU645."

"And so you retired, the physics hero nobody knew?"

"Yes and no. No recognition. But now everything I told you is an open secret, no longer on the shelf, where it was supposed to stay."

"Why do you say that?"

"Well, fifteen years after I figured this out, some hotheads at the Pentagon must have said, Why not? and used it in the first Iraq War. Now everybody's got DU ammo—"

"Isn't that outlawed, nuclear weapons?" Petró asked.

"Technically no. Sometimes I wonder what I should have done, but the evil genie's out of the bottle."

"Someone else would have—"

"True, I'm sure Defense had other ordnance researchers working on exactly the same problem when I did my work. Still, DU did us more harm than the enemy—"

"What? What's the reason?"

"Gulf War Syndrome, ever hear of that?"

"Oh, yeah, I read about it, years ago in *Pravda*."

"That's my moral question. Those seconds of exposure to radiation for our troops, firing round after round, all day long. Probably worse than we thought. That DU is damn poison from the devil!"

"Like I said, some other guy would've tried it."

"Yep, probably." He crunched another piece of ice." They keep coming up with better, but worse, ways to kill each other off—"

Petró took a sip, wishing the confidence they'd just shared had happened decades before. Would their lives have changed?

63
THREE AVIATORS
(ТРИ АВИАТОРА)

Although the passage of years slowed him physically—Petró was eighty-five—he kept busy. His life was capturing images. But always the traditionalist, he stayed true to his film cameras and forewent the spanking new world of digital wonders.

Thus, many afternoons at his dining table, amid trays for parts and tools, he'd overhaul a camera. He bought enough of the old-timers to stockpile work for years. Mostly Agfas, Rolleis, and other Western makes—but once even a Soviet Zenit showed up—and all acquired at fire-sale prices, On his Oregon trips, Gleb would pick up any newly restored cameras, and soon Petró could expect checks in the mailbox as eBay-savvy Gleb auctioned them off one after another. The rewards were more than enough for Petró's labor to keep him at it.

But he couldn't spend every afternoon hunched over a table, magnifying glasses strapped to his forehead, delicately turning home tiny screws into holes often not much larger, so they seemed, than grains of sand. After a while, his eyes needed a rest, needed to focus on something farther away, and his back had to straighten. He needed a walk.

At such times, Petró was ready for the sort of lone outing, away from the chatter, the scurrying of others at Rentner Place, that would ease him into a meditative mood conducive to taking photographs.

So one day, picking up the Fedka, checking for an extra roll of film, he went out to the carport, got into his old Toyota, then drove off.

Where was he going? He'd been intrigued, for some time, by the historical park across the Columbia River in Washington, where Fort Vancouver sprang to life. The old buildings had promise for photographs.

He headed there, driving up the Interstate, traversing the Columbia River over the 205 Bridge for the eastern reaches of Vancouver, a city long eclipsed in size by its younger, upstart Oregon neighbor to the south.

Petró checked the gas gauge, saw he was okay. He had driven to Vancouver only a few times. But once, when he ran low on gas, he found out there were no gas station attendants to pump gas. Self-service only. Finally, another customer helped him. He'd yet to learn that skill.

A few turns on surface streets and Petró arrived at the eastern entrance to the Fort Vancouver National Historic Site. Far more than reconstructed log buildings from the original settlement, Fort Vancouver outgrew its roots as a trading depot for the Hudson Bay Company and became a United States Army base, once even commanded by General Ulysses S. Grant. Through the years, the Army base that was Fort Vancouver built more barracks, more officers' quarters, and when the Air Corps emerged as a military force, Pearson Field. Still serving civilian aviation, it was right across the road from where the Toyota rolled to a stop.

Petró slipped the strap of the Fedka around his neck and crossed the road, where a yellow school bus, empty, kept a lonely vigil.

ARMY AIR CORPS PEARSON FIELD: The bold letters crowned an old-style wooden flight hangar. An aviation windsock fluttered on a smaller building beyond; and tucked in the near side of the hangar, Pearson Field Air Museum.

Petró wanted a picture of the vintage hangar and walked past the bus and down the curved sidewalk by a few picnic tables planted on a compact sward. He paused at what he thought he had to walk around to get a clear shot of the hangar.

A monument with a bronze plaque loomed in his path. He stepped up closer. What he read transfixed him. Of all the things in the world a plaque could commemorate, this had to be for him.

As the plaque read, on June 20, 1937, a Russian plane, an ANT-25 was making the world's first transpolar flight, Moscow to Oakland, California, when a sudden drop in oil pressure forced an unscheduled landing at Pearson Field, where Petró Kondratovych Kravets now stood, Soviet Fedka in hand.

Petró took a deep breath, not sure what to make of this. He never heard such a story. In 1937, he was ten years old, and they lived in Celo outside Kharkov, and did such news reach them?

The back of his neck grew warm. Coincidence? Or possibly a sign of what it meant to be a Russian who arrived and stood on American soil.

He took another deep breath; he unsnapped his Fedka's front leather flap. He knew without thinking the light in the shade called for $f4.5$, and that's where he set the aperture. He took several pictures, sure he should send them to Gleb as soon as possible and then talk with him on the phone about how proud he felt seeing this.

And amazed. Next to the plaque, a photograph of the plane. Carried more than two thousand gallons of fuel and had a hundred twelve-foot wingspan and, if memory served him right, a bit bigger, oh, eight feet more in wingspan than that U-2 spy plane shot down in 1960. Petró smiled: He'd seen that wreckage.

But this Russian Ant-25 was welcomed in America. It landed on the airstrip in front of Petró because the plane's single engine lost oil pressure.

And what did the Americans think about this heroic flight?

They loved the Russians. The aviators toured the United States and, finally, were guests of President Franklin Delano Roosevelt at the White House.

A tear began to track Petró's cheek. *The days were happy then with America and Russia.*

He walked around the monument that held the bronze plaque, cast in a Russian foundry, showing the ANT-25 in flight. On the other side, the sunlit side of the monument, two more plaques, also gifts from Russia. The first one in the Cyrillic characters of Petró's native language and to its right, one with an English translation.

He read the Russian words quickly, a summary in weathered bronze of the flight of the heroic aviators: Chkalov, Baidukov, Belykov. The two bronze plaques said the same thing.

Petró stood there puzzled. Looked from the Russian to the English, then back. Back and forth. Something caught his eye.

He stood closer, lifted his fingers to the plaque with Cyrillic characters. Yes, the one on the right in English was unblemished, simply weathered. But the one in front of him in Russian had vandal marks. Someone took a hammer to it. Or the butt of a hatchet. Yes, blows to dent the plaque. He rubbed his index finger across the gouged bronze characters, the six words.

He studied the damaged plaque coldly, objectively, as if a photographic print he'd taken out of the darkroom into the natural light.

Six blows from the vandal. Did the vandal choose what to strike? Striking at the Russian words for "heroic," "North Pole" might be random. But—Petró bit his lip—gouging "Moscow," "Pravda," and "Izvestia"? Especially the last two. Someone who lived in Russia would surely know the names in Cyrillic characters of those Russian newspapers.

Was the vandal a Russian émigré like him? A Russian émigré consumed with loathing for the Motherland. Or simply a Russian-hating American?

Russian or American: Both were to blame for the fear set loose in the Cold War.

More tears streamed down his cheeks, standing there alone on an afternoon, when nobody else—unless they would be one or more of the school children who might come out of the air museum—would see him staring uncomprehending at the defaced plaque.

Russian or American—the vandal didn't matter. Too much hatred for so long between the two countries. Yet, on this American soil on which he stood, a monument to one of the most heroic moments in world flight by three brave Russian aviators who conquered the North Pole and were welcomed in America. An occasion for friendship. A friendship that only now in Petró's twilight years returned.

"So many years lost to hate," he muttered, sure nobody would hear his words or see the blur of what his tears took out of focus. He closed the leather camera case because he didn't have the heart to take pictures for Gleb of this mutilated plaque. Maybe some other day, but not this one.

He would leave. Take pictures elsewhere.

He slowly turned to the embracing afternoon sun: photographer's light, full of shadows, and walked toward the log buildings of the original Fort Vancouver a few minutes away. That old fort in Hudson Bay days had friendly neighbors up north he'd like. Way up north, up in the Russian colony of Alaska.

Once we got along. Now, we get along. But for too much of my years, we didn't.

And so in America for his remaining days, Petró Kondratovych Kravets knew the welcome given the three aviators.

Petró walked on, Fedka in hand. In the west, the sun dappled undulant hills.

КОНЕЦ

ABOUT THE AUTHOR

Charlie Dickinson was inspired to write *Losing Laika* partly out of love for a Soviet FED-1 rangefinder camera with which he pursues his hobby of black-and-white photography. The camera was built in 1937 at a work commune in Kharkov, Ukraine SSR, by teenage orphans. The question of what would happen to one of those workers who helped assemble Dickinson's camera was worth a book.

Another motivation for Dickinson was working with U-2 pilot Francis Gary Powers at Radio KGIL in the Los Angeles area after the latter returned to civilian life. Their conversation gave an appreciation of Mr. Powers' passion for flying, essential to how the first chapter fictionally portrays the aviator after his plane crash.

Dickinson lives and writes in Portland, Oregon, and maintains a blog at *cosmicplodding.net*.

ACKNOWLEDGEMENTS

The author gratefully acknowledges *Cigale Literary Magazine* (cigalelit.com) and *Hackwriters* in the UK (hackwriters.com) where excerpts of this work first appeared.

Cover art scanned from the author's Soviet-era poster printed on canvas. Image is copyright-free and in the public domain.

Excerpts from the songs "That's All Right" and "Rockin' Robin" are gratefully acknowledged. Both songs are in the public domain.

Excerpts from the song "The Motherland Hears" ("Родина слышит") are gratefully acknowledged. Written in 1951 with music by Dmitri Shostakovich and lyrics by Yevgeniy Domatovsky, the song became copyright-free in 2021.